"This unique book blends the enduring wisdom of the past with the fresh thinking of today in order to provide a remarkably intriguing look into the future of tomorrow's business world."—**Dr. Stephen R. Covey,** author, *Seven Habits of Highly Effective People*

"An excellent and comprehensive document on knowledge and learning, addressing a broad spectrum of issues and strategies. All this, and in a style that is easy to read!"—**Gordon Petrash**, Global Director, Intellectual Asset & Capital Management, The Dow Chemical Company

"Verna Allee moves us quickly beyond the simplistic discussions of knowledge management into the broad, exciting, and energizing vista of organizational intelligence. She gently and yet persistently lifts us out of the box canyons of dead-end thinking about data and information, making knowledge and wisdom come alive for the business organizations of the 21st century."—**Dr. Charles M. Savage**, author, *Fifth Generation Management, Revised Edition*

"As we enter the Knowledge Era what are the implications for the practice of management? Verna Allee offers timely insights and perspectives on this critical question. The book is an intriguing, thoroughly researched, practical guide that illuminates new territory."—**Jeff Clanon**, Executive Director, MIT Center for Organizational Learning

"Verna Allee shows the way to understand, capture, and apply learning and knowledge to create exciting and dynamic organizations. A must read for all organizational leaders who want to bring order to the chaos."—**Jay C. Wilber**, Executive Director, Quality Network, General Motors Corporation, author, *United We Stand*

"Any leader intent on leveraging knowledge in a competitive organization will benefit from this thoughtful and practical book. *The Knowledge Evolution* provides a synthesis of research and practice, offering valuable new insights for effective management of the knowledge-based organization."—**Stuart S. Winby**, Director, Strategic Alignment Services, Hewlett-Packard Company

"*The Knowledge Evolution* deftly explains why and how a well-grounded theory of knowledge must precede organizational action. In fact, we may not be able to succeed without such wisdom."—**Jean P. Moore**, Practice Leader, Workforce Effectiveness, GTE

D0974687

"In a clear voice, with an exceptional ability to synthesize, Verna Allee shows how your organization can use knowledge to reach a whole new level of performance. The strength of her insights will call you to create a vibrant organization through the purposeful alignment of culture, technology, knowledge, and learning—an organization where each and every one of us could aspire to work."—**Hubert Saint-Onge**, V.P., People, Knowledge, and Strategies, The Mutual Group

"Verna Allee has done a masterful job in writing *The Knowledge Evolution*. Any leader in modern day enterprise will find this book invaluable!"—**John E. Renesch**, editor/publisher, *The New Leaders*

"The understanding of our knowledge assets and how to gain competitive advantage is key to competitive success in the 21st century. Verna Allee's new book charts the course for understanding knowledge and turning it into a competitive weapon."—**Bill Baker**, Benchmarking/Best Practice Sharing, Texas Instruments Inc.

"*The Knowledge Evolution* makes the strategic connection between the knowledge economy and learning. The evolution is traced thoughtfully, the language is clarified, connections are made with integral sources of current activity, and the path forward is compelling."—**Debra M. Amidon**, author, *Innovation Strategy for the Knowledge Economy: The Ken Awakening*

"Verna Allee has provided knowledge-seeking managers with a means to navigate their organizations beyond the level of pure thought-leadership through a learning approach that translates the knowledge worker concept into best practice."—**Gregory H. Watson**, Managing Partner, Business Systems Solutions, Inc., author, *Strategic Benchmarking*

"Verna Allee has taken a comprehensive look at the various facets of knowledge management. A delightful reading for both practitioners and new entrants in the field of knowledge management."—**Bipin Junnarkar**, Director, Knowledge Management, Monsanto Company

"Our individual knowledge is like an ever changing kaleidoscope through time. *The Knowledge Evolution* provides us with a powerful framework through which to observe and enhance the patterns of knowledge, learning, and action in our organizations."—**Charles A. Armstrong**, President, S.A. Armstrong Ltd.

"Verna Allee has concisely summarized the key facets for the comprehensive understanding of this evolving field."—**Robert C. Camp**, Ph.D., PE, author, *Business Process Benchmarking*

The Knowledge Evolution

The Knowledge Evolution

Expanding Organizational Intelligence

Verna Allee

Butterworth-Heinemann

Boston   Oxford   Johannesburg   Melbourne   New Delhi   Singapore

Copyright © 1997 by Verna Allee.

Butterworth–Heinemann.

 A member of the Reed Elsevier group.

All rights reserved.

No part of this publication may be reproduced, stored in a retrieval system, or transmitted in any form or by any means, electronic, mechanical, photocopying, recording, or otherwise, without the prior written permission of the publisher.

Recognizing the importance of preserving what has been written, Butterworth–Heinemann prints its books on acid-free paper whenever possible.

 Butterworth–Heinemann supports the efforts of American Forests and the Global ReLeaf program in its campaign for the betterment of trees, forests, and our environment.

Library of Congress Cataloging-in-Publication Data
Allee, Verna, 1949–
    The knowledge evolution : expanding organizational intelligence / Verna Allee.
       p.   cm.
   Includes bibliographical references and index.
   ISBN 0-7506-9842-X (pbk.)
   1. Organizational learning. I. Title.
HD58.82.A37   1997
658.4'038—dc21   96-48561
                                           CIP

British Library Cataloguing-in-Publication Data
A catalogue record for this book is available from the British Library.

The publisher offers special discounts on bulk orders of this book.
For information, please contact:
Manager of Special Sales
Butterworth–Heinemann
313 Washington Street
Newton, MA 02158–1626
Tel: 617-928-2500
Fax: 617-928-2620

For information on all Focal Press publications available, contact our World Wide Web home pag at: http://www.bh.com/bb

10 9 8 7 6 5 4 3 2 1

Printed in the United States of America

Dedication
For Hal Johnston with love and appreciation

Contents

Preface

The great political leader Winston Churchill once said, "The empires of the future are empires of the mind." As the truth of this sinks in, a whole new area of practice is emerging in business management, centering on concepts such as the learning organization, knowledge management, and collaborative intelligence.

Knowledge questions are new for most leadership teams. We are in the early, formative stages of our understanding, where we are enjoying a creative soup of ideas, experimental business practices, theories, concepts, frameworks, questions, and insights. In this emerging field, this book offers a framework for guiding our conversations about knowledge. The book itself, as a fragment of the knowledge universe, reflects the questions and perspectives that are surfacing.

Who This Book is For

This book is targeted to leadership teams who have responsibility for developing, implementing, and supporting strategies for enhancing organizational knowledge. It will provide valuable insights for executives and line managers seeking ways to create more adaptive and responsive organizations and maximize knowledge value. Information technology providers and facility designers will find it helpful for understanding technology requirements, information system support, communication needs, and work unit design for knowledge-based enterprises. In the human resources field it will serve as a guidebook to understanding learning and knowledge requirements for individuals and work groups.

Most managers I know are more interested in action than theory. With that in mind, throughout the book you will find stories of how companies are addressing issues around knowledge and are putting their insights into practice. This book is also intended to foster good conceptual thinking in the area of knowledge management. We will not achieve mastery in any area without developing good conceptual frameworks that inform our actions.

In modern business there is a prevailing focus on action and immediate results, which often leaves little time for reflecting on our work or reaching shared understanding. This oversight leads to inefficiencies, costly waste, repetitive mistakes, and dangerously self-destructive strategies. The approach to knowledge described in this book provides a foundation for building critical self-reflection into daily work.

How I Have Approached This Work

When people propose new concepts, their usual approach is to note all the previous work in the field, point out apparent inadequacies, then suggest a "new" theory or solution that supposedly works better. (They then staunchly defend their position to the end.) Too often such efforts are not made in the spirit of advancing the field or supporting inquiry. More often they are efforts to carve out a niche in thought leadership. This is particularly true in the western scientific tradition where we tend to see things in terms of right or wrong, true or untrue, and have idealized heroic leadership and individual achievement.

Yet, new understanding emerges through a *social* process of collective sense-making. This process is communal, organic, and wonderfully self-organizing. In a provocative essay in *The Lives of a Cell*, Lewis Thomas[1] draws a delightful analogy for the development of scientific knowledge. He describes the scientific process as an intellectual anthill where each scientist drops their small grain of thinking onto the great pile of thoughts developed by all the other scientists.

In the same way we all build on the collective mind of our culture and society, extracting meaning from our common human experience and knowledge. We must regard even our understanding of knowledge itself as a social activity, an exercise in collaborative intelligence. As a species we have accumulated an enormous body of insights about knowledge, collected over many centuries of recorded thought.

Where I have examined the work of others in this field, it is in the spirit of embracing the best thinking and building on work that has gone before. This book attempts to integrate concepts and relationships that have been described across a variety of disciplines pertaining to knowledge in organizations. My purpose is to build on our common wisdom and reach a new synthesis.

I also humbly acknowledge the monumental work of the great philosophers and the modern thinkers who have addressed many of these same questions. Limitations of space will not allow an in-depth analysis of their contributions, although those who are interested will find I have left ample road markers pointing the way to other work.

A Systems View

I am a systems thinker at heart. As I observe the wondrous interwoven fabric of the world I am intrigued with relationships and patterns. I am far less interested in tearing apart theories and viewpoints than I am in surfacing common elements from various perspectives. I am fascinated by our collaborative social *process* of building the anthill of knowledge. The emerging structure of our own knowledge intrigues me.

Inquiry into organizational knowledge is "messy." Systems thinker Russell Ackoff uses the term "mess" to mean that every human problem is inextricably connected to every other human problem. In other words, a "mess" refers to a system of interacting problems.[2] The question of knowledge in organizations is messy because it is connected to every other question of organizational life: group psychology, individual and social cognitive processes, communication, economic forces, politics, technology, organizational culture and learning, management philosophy and structure. There is no convenient way to isolate "knowledge" as a discrete phenomenon. So this book will touch on many issues and topics that are interrelated with processes of knowledge building.

In my research and inquiry, I am less concerned with what I personally think about knowledge than I am with seeking to understand how *we* understand knowledge—together. How does knowledge behave as an emergent phenomenon of human systems? The paradoxical result of this effort, of course, is that my exploration has led to some insights that are uniquely my own. So now it is my turn to drop my grain of thinking onto the intellectual anthill of knowledge, hoping it will serve as a stepping stone for yet another round of knowledge creation.

Posing the Knowledge Question

As enthusiasm builds for creating and managing knowledge we must ask a very important question: *If managing knowledge is the solution, what is the question?* Just exactly what are we trying to "solve" when we attempt to manage, create, or build knowledge? Different knowledge solutions are attempts to "solve" different knowledge problems or seize a particular opportunity.

We frame a situation according to our underlying assumptions and ideas about what is important. Every question implies an answer. We must continually ask ourselves, "What is the real question behind our questions?" Some of our knowledge questions are about very different aspects of organizational life. Some of our questions reflect our fears, while others reflect our hopes.

My own inquiry into knowledge revolves around these questions:

1. *What's the question? What are we really trying to accomplish with our pursuit of the knowledge question?* We will no doubt find that people are defining a number of different knowledge "questions." Do these problems and opportunities self-organize into a pattern of key questions? How do different perspectives have an impact on the actions people take?

2. *What are the common patterns of thought that underlie our understanding of knowledge, action, learning, and complexity?* As we look at the

pattern of our thinking about knowledge, our questions should include, "What is the pattern of our understanding, the pattern that connects? What are the knowledge principles that appear to guide us in making sense of this apparently chaotic world of shifting markets, finicky customers, and technological breakthroughs?" In looking at these patterns we must ask, "What is missing from this picture? What do we have yet to understand?" In the spirit of these questions, my own reading and conversations have ranged far indeed, encompassing many of the social and behavioral sciences, engaging managers and those who consult with organizations.

3. *What does the pattern of our understanding tell us about our behavior?* In other words, what is the relationship between our thinking and our actions? Certain themes, issues, dilemmas, and questions surface over and over again in our pursuit of knowledge and our attempts to adapt to change. In addressing this question, I have made observations from over two decades of experience in American business as a corporate manager, as an entrepreneur, and as a consultant to Fortune 500 companies, small businesses, associations, and government organizations.

4. Finally, I have sought to understand, *How can we best use our knowledge capacity to reflect on our actions, deepen our understanding, and shift our patterns of thinking? How can we do this in a way that leads to more creative, healthy, effective, and sustainable responses to our environment?* In my search for effective action, I have engaged in numerous conversations with corporate managers, consultants, and specialists. I have also researched company practices through an extensive literature search. In this book, I have synthesized theory and action into a set of emerging practices that are helping people and their organizations realize their goals.

How This Book is Organized

The chapters of this book are organized in a logical sequence, but they do not have to be read in order. Those interested in core knowledge competencies or knowledge capital will be especially interested in Chapter 2. This chapter looks at how knowledge competencies combine with performance capabilities to create adaptive enterprises.

Chapter 3 introduces some of the fundamental concepts in the knowledge arena. Here you will find definitions of terms and an exploration of key concepts and relationships. This chapter explores how knowledge can be understood both as a product of certain actions and as key processes. A knowledge product might be a tangible document such as a report. Knowledge processes are those such as knowledge creation, gathering, sharing, and renewing. You will also find a few navigational aids for knowledge exploration, as well as a theory of time, knowledge, and action.

Chapters 4 and 5 introduce an archetypal framework that links knowledge, learning, and performance in organizations. Chapter 4 describes the basic concepts, while Chapter 5 gives some specific examples of how the framework can be used to enhance performance in a variety of ways.

Chapter 6 explores how organizational structures are changing as knowledge creation and sharing accelerate. We will explore some basic principles for understanding the self-organizing capacity of knowledge and how organizational design supports it.

Chapters 7 through 13 will be a detailed exploration of seven distinct knowledge and performance domains, based on the framework in Chapter 4. These seven chapters suggest key processes and practices for enhancing knowledge capacity. They include assessment questions that will help you analyze your own business practices in knowledge management.

The remaining chapters offer a number of innovative practices and processes that are being implemented in companies. These stories provide concrete examples of how these ideas are being put into practice, and will hopefully provoke further experimentation and development. The appendixes include a comparative analysis of theorists and a sample question set for building knowledge.

The Question Behind the Questions

When asked about the creative spark for his remarkable body of work, the great psychologist Carl Jung said, "The meaning of my life is that life has addressed a question to me." I too, am in pursuit of a life question that calls me to my work. For me that life question is "What is wisdom and how do we find it?" What I have gleaned about knowledge did not surface solely from pursuit of knowledge, it has emerged from my questions about wisdom.

It is my hope that as we celebrate the arrival of the Knowledge Era, we will also look ahead and consider where our knowledge is taking us. As we forge ahead with questions about knowledge, I hope we will have the courage to ask our wisdom questions too.

ACKNOWLEDGMENTS

I wish to acknowledge all those who have shared their knowledge, experience, and encouragement in bringing this work together. In the course of any creative process there are pivotal conversations, insights, and connections that propel the work forward. I would like to acknowledge several people who provided those moments: Charles Hampden-Turner, Juanita Brown, Bill and Rita Cleary, Jeff Clanon, Steve Piersanti, Karen Speerstra, and Michael Ray.

Over the course of this work many moments of insight, inspiration, laughter, and support have been enjoyed with colleagues, friends, and customers, including: John Adams, Kathryn Alexander, Americ Azevedo, Jim Bandrowski, Kim Barnes, Pascal Baudry, Margaret Barbee, Ralph Catalenello, Roy Chang, Paul Costa, Marian Culver, Dan Darden, Eruna Derbyshire, Marilyn Shoeman Dow, Serin Eggling, Turk Enustun, Anna Ewins, Lisa Faithorn, Christian Forthomme, Sharon Franquemont, Frank Friedlander, Peggy Holman, Djann Hoffmann, Paul Horan, Donna Hotopp, Dennis Jaffe, Prasad Kaipa, Ruth King, Carolyn Kosich, Greta Lydecker, Tom Leal, Michael Lindfield, Joel and Michelle Levy, Jim MacLean, Barbara Norton-Kopp, Judy O'Neil, Mac Patrick, George Por, Al Pozos, Derek Ransley, John Redding, John Renesh, Kathleen Robinson, Howard Rudd, Bill Schmidt, Marc Schuler, Bev Scott, Claudia Siegel, Jim Staker, Mark Sullivan, Crystal Surrenda, Bill Veltrop, Autumn Wagner, Andy Walker, Mary Ann Whitney, David Wick, Donnie Williams, Ruth Williams, Bob Wiebe, Mary Kaye Wright, and Danielle You.

First order of gratitude goes to my sister, Fran Kelly, who did an amazing job of capturing the essence of my abstract ideas with her graphics. The steadfast support of my sister Kathi Allee today, as always, is deeply appreciated, as well as that of Pati Hannan. I am also indebted to my father, Lew, whose avid curiosity about almost everything fired my lifelong passion for learning. My mother, Jane, taught me to wonder, to feel the mystery, and to know the power of words. I have drawn courage and strength from the unwavering faith of Hal Johnston who has played many roles in my life, yet is always my friend.

PART I

UNDERSTANDING KNOWLEDGE

CHAPTER 1

Introduction:
The Knowledge Era

Nestled in the rolling, wooded hills of Northern California lies a densely packed industrial and residential area known the world over as Silicon Valley. Despite the idyllic setting, this valley never sleeps. At all hours of the day and night, programmers, designers, and entrepreneurs stare at the cathode ray tubes crowning their computers. They often work around the clock to prepare for product releases and develop new technologies in a frantic race to the marketplace. They wage a heroic battle, not only against their competitors, but even against their own bodies. Caught in the creative frenzy, people catnap under their desks or grab odd moments of relaxation in the hallways. Coffee is king.

Here in the heart of the computer and telecommunications industry, people are literally living by their wits. Success belongs to those who can think, learn, solve problems, and take effective action faster and better than anyone else. Ideas leap from company to company in an open synergistic economy where hundreds of innovative companies jostle for space. Sandwiched between two great universities and relatively free from defense industry-type secrecy, the valley is a creative stewpot of knowledge and ideas building one upon the other.

Silicon Valley typifies the new world of work in the Knowledge Era. You find the same energy along other technological corridors in Massachusetts, New York, Colorado, and the Carolinas. Even in the manufacturing belts of the Midwest and Northeast new knowledge is rapidly proliferating, thanks to communication and computer technologies.

This new world of instant information and global communication technology has overturned our thinking and overthrown the old social and economic order. All around us we see enterprises and organizations transforming themselves, sometimes virtually overnight. We are plunged headlong in a scramble to keep up, to learn, to adapt, to change. We feel that if we can learn fast enough and acquire the knowledge we need, we will succeed.

Moving to Hyperspace at Warp Speed

At some point in the Star Trek™ space adventures, a brave band of universe explorers hits the accelerator. Suddenly, their spacecraft propels them all into hyperspace at warp speed. While they are accelerating the crew faces tremendous G-force pressures. The physical stress is almost unbearable. The entire universe rushes by at dizzying speed. Yet, once they actually reach this fictional hyperspace, still at full warp speed, everything seems normal again.

As we look around our workplaces it seems as if we are all collectively moving into hyperspace at warp speed. Changes come at us so fast we can hardly assimilate them. The whole world is instantly accessible through our laptop computers. We can talk to someone on the other side of the globe while walking our dog. Many of us spend whole days gazing into cyberspace, navigating a virtual world. We connect only through telephones and terminals. Our sense of time and space is being altered in the process. We wonder if things will ever feel "normal" again.

Knowledge, too, is expanding at warp speed. Whole new fields such as genetic engineering have brought us routine procedures in health care that would have appeared miraculous a couple of decades ago. I still vividly remember the astonishment of the nation the first time doctors successfully reattached a severed arm in the 1950s. Today heart, lung, and kidney transplants are becoming commonplace, and gene therapy has moved from being a pipe dream to a reality.

Our work changes constantly. Computer processing is replacing whole groups of workers who used to shuffle paper documents. Contingent and seasonal workers are growing in numbers. Today, Manpower Inc. is the largest employer in the United States, providing temporary and contract workers across the whole spectrum of industry. People employed as "knowledge workers" float from project to project, as free agents. They bring know-how and technical knowledge into an organization, then move on to their next assignment. Often their expertise lies in areas that have only developed in the last few years. Job security is becoming a thing of the past. Today, security lies in what you know how to do, what you can learn to do, and how well you can access knowledge through collaboration with others.

Business leader Rosabeth Moss Kantor compares the work of management today to the croquet game in *Alice in Wonderland*.[1] Nothing in this strange game remains stable for long. Just as Alice has the shot lined up, the croquet mallet (tools and technology) changes into a flamingo that turns and looks in another direction. Of course, the ball Alice is trying to hit is actually a hedgehog with a mind of its own—strongly paralleling the human factor in business.

Clock Worlds and Space-Time

Futurists suggest that profound change results when the underlying science or mythology changes. George Land and Beth Jarman calls these "breakpoints," or moments when profound shifts of mind and thinking lead to dramatically different behaviors.[2] We have been experiencing just such a shift, and the G-forces are tremendous. That shift is the shift from the Newtonian worldview to a quantum worldview. The sciences of quantum physics and chaos have re-ordered our understanding of how things work.

In a warp-speed, hyper-space world these new concepts are often more relevant to our actual experience. Yet, we work in enterprises designed for the linear clockwork world of Sir Isaac Newton and economist Adam Smith. Much of the stress we feel comes from trying to reconcile our emerging understanding of how things work with a world we created according to very different assumptions and principles.

This shift of thinking is simply too powerful to be ignored.[3] Even though people may not speak the language of quantum physics in the workplace (although a growing number do), we see evidence of this mindshift everywhere (Table 1.1). Each of these ways of thinking emerges from a different science. This results in different ways of managing and organizing.

TABLE 1.1   Traditional Thinking, New Thinking.

Assumption	Traditional Thinking	New Thinking
Scientific Foundation	Newtonian physics	Quantum physics
Time Is	Monochronic (One thing at a time)	Polychronic (Many things at once)
We Understand By	Dissecting into parts	Seeing in terms of the whole
Information Is	Ultimately knowable	Infinite and unbounded
Growth Is	Linear, managed	Organic, chaotic
Managing Means	Control, predictability	Insight and participation
Workers Are	Specialized, segmented	Multi-faceted, always learning
Motivation Is From	External forces and influence	Intrinsic creativity
Knowledge Is	Individual	Collective
Organization Is	By design	Emergent
Life Thrives On	Competition	Cooperation
Change Is	Something to worry about	All there is

Both ways of thinking are valuable. As we expand our understanding, old knowledge does not become obsolete or irrelevant. We integrate old understanding with new so that both are transformed. Newtonian science is still valid science. It is quite useful in certain domains. However, it is not much help when it comes to understanding complex systems. In a world of cyberspace, warp speed, global economics, and molecular biology we need *all* the sciences.

The Emerging Knowledge Economy

The Information Age is already nudging the boundaries of traditional thinking. It has propelled us to a quantum leap in complexity. Old ways of managing information simply can't keep up. With so much available to us, choosing what information to gather, share, and process can be overwhelming. As a result, people are becoming concerned with the quality of their choices around information. Intent on sorting out what is useful and relevant, people are beginning to grapple with the relationship between information and knowledge.

The management thinker Peter Drucker has sparked much interest in the knowledge economy. Over two decades ago he coined the phrase "knowledge workers"[4] to decribe managers who know how to allocate knowledge to productive use.

Drucker's fascinating historical exploration of the social purpose of knowledge suggests three distinct phases.[5] The first phase, he notes, was the pursuit of knowledge for the sake of knowledge, enlightenment, and wisdom prior to the industrial revolution. The second phase began about 1700 A.D. with the invention of technology. In this stage, knowledge came to mean organized, systematic, and *purposeful* knowledge, what we can think of as *applied knowledge*. Then, around 1881, Frederick Winslow Taylor's scientific approach to organizing work ushered in the third stage: the critical beginning of knowledge applied to knowledge itself (Table 1.2).

> *Knowledge is now being applied to knowledge. This is the third and perhaps the ultimate step in the transformation of knowledge. Supplying knowledge to find out how existing knowledge can best be applied to produce results is, in effect, what we mean by management.*[6]

TABLE 1.2   Three Phases of Knowledge Transformation.

Phase 1 the Age of Enlightenment	Knowledge for the sake of enlightenment and wisdom
Phase 2 the Industrial Era	Applied knowledge
Phase 3 the Knowledge Era	Knowledge about knowledge

I regard The Knowledge Evolution as a more recent development than does Drucker. Applying knowledge to knowledge in business only really begins when we reflect on the learning and knowledge component of the work itself. The importance of learning and knowledge only became clear to us later, when we began exploring organizations as social phenomena.

The person that led the way in this regard was not Taylor, but Kurt Lewin. Lewin's more psychological approach to the world of work began having an impact in the 1930s. He explored psychic tensions, job satisfaction, motivation, leadership, and participation. He also introduced methods of action research and experimentation that decidedly moved the focus of management experiments from solutions to learning. This important shift from mechanistic engineering to social-psychological concepts was much more self-reflective than Taylor's way of working—and very important. For the inevitable result of self-reflection, in a social and psychological sense, is the application of knowledge to knowledge itself.[7]

Even though the early stirrings of the Knowledge Era were in the thirties, real momentum began building in the 1970s, with the work of Chris Argyris and Donald Schon.[8] They noticed that there are major gaps between the way people say they do things and what actually happens. There is a "disconnect" between people's *espoused* theory of why they do something and their *actual* theory-in-action. They suggested that managers must deepen their self-reflection to include their own thought processes. Now, at last, we were seeing the application of knowledge to our own knowledge and thinking. This breakthrough has led directly to much of the recent work in organizational learning, influencing how we understand the creation of knowledge.

Information and Knowledge as Products

A remarkable phenomenon of the knowledge economy is that information has emerged as a product in its own right. Information that surfaces as a by-product of the core business is important to the success of the enterprise. Today, the cost of the information technology in the average car is greater than the cost of the steel. Information technology, including connectivity on the "information highway," is soaking up more capital than any other investment.[9]

From airlines to farms to utility service companies, every business relies on a tightly interwoven electronic society that speeds data and information to the desktop. When the terminals are down, businesses grind to a standstill. Every industry is a knowledge industry. Everyone is in the information business. Almost everyone is now a "knowledge worker."

Each evening as we shut down our terminals and head for the freeway (or the kitchen, as more and more of us work at home), billions of bits of data are streaming through telephone wires. Central terminals are processing countless transactions at stores, supermarkets, and banks all over the country and communicating it to global networks of suppliers, managers, and customers.

Even an evening of relaxation is loaded with added knowledge-value. My kitchen coffee pot, microwave, and refrigerator are packed with electronic knowledge that allows me to customize their functions. I may select a pay-per-view movie or order merchandise through the shopping channel or Internet. When I pay my bills, I probably do it at my computer terminal through on-line banking. I may even use an on-line reservation service to make travel arrangements—right down to buying the tickets and reserving a rental car. This is the knowledge economy.

The Quest for Knowledge

Against this backdrop we are seeing the resurgence of an ancient quest: The quest for knowledge. We are stretched to the limits in our ability to integrate, synthesize, incorporate, and adapt. Technology breakthroughs in genetic engineering have even brought the capability to create new life forms. Our day-to-day decisions have never before carried such profound responsibilities.

The ability to learn is becoming the new "core competency" for all of us participating in this quest. We find that the greater our capacity for learning and building knowledge, the greater our likelihood of enjoying continuing success. This is now not only true for individuals, it is also a basic principle for successful enterprise. Valery Kanavsky of Hewlett-Packard insists, "The fundamental building material of a modern corporation is knowledge."[10]

> The only thing that gives an organization a competitive edge—the only thing that is sustainable—is what it knows, how it uses what it knows, and how fast it can know something new!
>
> Laurence Prusak[11]

Tom Peters puts it succinctly: "Brains are in; heavy lifting is out. Thence the development of knowledge is close to job one for corporations."[12]

What is happening here? Is this interest in knowledge an isolated phenomena or more widespread? Recently, Arthur Andersen & Co. and the American Productivity and Quality Center decided to find out. Together they undertook a benchmarking study on knowledge management. Over 70 companies participated in the first round and Arthur Andersen plans continual updating. The Knowledge Management Assessment Tool (KMAT) that they used for the study focuses on knowledge strategy and practices in four key areas: leadership, technology, culture, and measurements.

Although 79 percent of the managers responding agreed that managing organizational knowledge is central to the organization's strategy, 59 percent felt they were doing this either poorly or not at all. Further, while 88 percent felt a climate of openness and trust is important for knowledge sharing, 32 percent of the respondents indicated they did not have such a climate at their companies. In many companies there is a perceived lack of commitment to knowledge management on the part of top leadership.[13]

Clearly, knowledge is highly valued. The question is, what are we going to do about it?

Knowledge Management

One response to the growing value is to create something like a Chief Knowledge Officer. Companies like Skandia Inc. and Dow Chemical are beginning to seek accountability for managing intellectual assets. Consulting groups, such as McKinsey & Co., Arthur Andersen, Coopers and Lybrand, Gemini Consulting Group, and KPMG Peat Marwick, have been paying attention to managing internal knowledge for some time. Now Chevron, Hughes Space & Communication, Hewlett-Packard, Buckman Labs, Dow Chemical, Steelcase, Coca-Cola, The World Bank, Lincoln Life, and others are pursuing knowledge strategies as well.

The "question" of knowledge management, however, is posed in different ways. Some management questions stem from traditional thinking. They have to do with questions of ownership, control, and value. Such questions focus around collecting and organizing codified knowledge. There is an emphasis on measurement and planning.

Other people view knowledge more organically and are interested in how it flows and self-organizes. They usually approach knowledge more experimentally. They seek patterns, trying to understand how knowledge grows and multiplies. How does new knowledge emerge? On the flip side of that is concern with what happens when people leave the company. Does their accumulated knowledge and wisdom leave as well? How can the expertise of one or two people expand into knowledge that is held by the whole organization?

Questions also sometimes focus around expertise and competencies. In order to maintain personal expertise, people are forced into narrow specializations at the very time we need synthesis and holistic thinking. How can the knowledge resource of an enterprise be configured for both present and future success? These are a few of the questions and opportunities that knowledge managers are tackling.

Knowledge and Power

The present focus on knowledge emphasizes knowledge acquisition. This perspective is deeply rooted in the capitalistic concept of "ownership." In the capitalist viewpoint more is better. Whoever controls knowledge best will enjoy the most economic gain and therefore the most power.

There is a powerful dynamic relationship between knowledge and power. The great social thinker Michel Foucault concluded that "It is not possible for power to be exercised without knowledge. It is impossible for knowledge not to engender power."[14] Since knowledge and power are so interrelated, a shift in the control of knowledge results in a social and economic powershift as well.[15]

This new knowledge economy has deep implications for the power of the worker. It is bringing a shift in ownership of the means of production, from the corporation to the individual.[16] For in a knowledge society, *workers* own the means of production and have the power to take their knowledge with them.

Therein lies one of the great paradoxes of the knowledge economy. As the possessor of knowledge I can sell it, trade it, or give it away, and yet I still have it. I can turn around a day later and sell it, trade it, or give it away again. In order to continue this process I must continually renew, replenish, expand, and create yet more knowledge. For knowledge today is also perishable. With the explosion of knowledge creation in every profession, knowledge has a limited shelf life and can quickly become obsolete. Knowledge is always changing.

Renewing knowledge is the key to competitive advantage. At Skandia the intellectual capital approach led by Leif Edvinsson includes knowledge renewal and development as major components of the value metrics system.[17] Renewal includes more than creating new knowledge, it also means letting go of old knowledge. It requires continuous inquiry and self-reflection on knowledge and learning process itself. In organizations, new knowledge is created not by individuals, but by teams and groups of people sharing their knowledge and expertise throughout the enterprise.

All this adds up to a radical overhaul of the old knowledge equation. The old equation prior to the Information Age was *knowledge* = *power—so hoard it.* Managers and workers gained power by having information and acting on that information for their personal benefit. The rapid expansion of technological knowledge makes this old equation obsolete. No one can successfully hoard knowledge anymore. In fact, if they do, there is an ironclad guarantee that the knowledge they are hoarding will become obsolete and useless in hours, days, weeks, or at most a few months. Furthermore, trying to lock up knowledge stifles the life-giving flow of information that allows a system to self-organize and renew itself.

Today, the new knowledge equation is *knowledge* = *power—so share it and it will multiply.* That is the economic reality of the new knowledge society.

Knowledge About Knowledge

If we want to share knowledge so it can multiply, then we need to understand it a bit better than we do now. In the popular business literature we find terms such as *information management, knowledge building, knowledge transfer, and organizational learning.* People use these terms in different ways. What do we really mean by these terms and what practical outcomes are we seeking? What is the elusive holy grail of organizational wisdom and creativity that we are trying to recover when we direct our attention to managing information, building knowledge, and fostering organizational learning?

Despite the explosion of knowledge and an increasing interest in knowledge management, we know relatively little about the process of organizational knowledge creation. We are only now beginning to expand our attention beyond individual learning processes to *collaborative* learning and knowledge building. This is very new in Western culture. Most of our cognitive sciences focus on *individual* learners. We have paid little attention to how groups of learners acquire and build knowledge *together*.

Yet, we cannot understand collaborative phenomena by examining an individual. We have come to understand a little about our collective experience through studies of culture, political systems, family dynamics, group dynamics, and organizational behavior. But we have barely scratched the surface of how a group actually learns together or builds collaborative knowledge. Intriguing work in this area includes examining the way "communities of practice" build and share expertise together.

The Learning Organization

Since the publication of Peter Senge's thoughtful and provocative book on systems thinking, *The Fifth Discipline*,[18] in the early 1990s there has been a groundswell of interest, research, and practice in developing learning organizations. Building on the earlier work of Chris Argyris and Donald Schon,[19] Senge's thinking is of seminal importance in the area of building group knowledge. He suggests five disciplines or practices that foster organizational learning: *personal mastery, systems thinking, team learning, shared vision,* and *surfacing mental models.* These concepts are important cornerstones for understanding knowledge building and defining some of the cognitive processes that support change and learning.

Since publication of *The Fifth Discipline*, people are making significant contributions in the learning organization arena. Although the body of knowledge is expanding rapidly, we still have much to learn. The field is less than a decade old in management conversation. Although we have explored social dynamics and work processes in organizations since the advent of Taylor's scientific management and Lewin's field theory, organizational *cognitive* dynamics is still fairly new territory.

Collaborative Creativity

We know even less about collaborative creativity and intuition. For example, most studies of intuition in business explore *individual* experiences of intuition. Westin Agor's groundbreaking studies of intuition in business focus primarily on the intuitive skills of managers and executives as individuals.[20] While his findings do have application to group situations, research on collaborative intuition or organizational intuition as a unique phenomenon in and of itself, is virtually non-existent.

One active researcher in this arena, Sharon Franquemont,[21] has been working with groups organized around creative endeavors, social activism, and personal development. She has been examining the emergence of shared insights, symbolic representations, and creative solutions as groups work together. However, business applications of intuitive processes at the group level have yet to be fully explored. We still know little of intuitive processes for group problem-solving and decision-making in a business and organizational setting.

Knowledge Creation

Recently, a number of writers and practitioners have begun to address the question of knowledge creation in organizations. Premier among these efforts is the work of Ikujiro Nonaka and Hirotaki Takeuchi, who describe the dynamics of project team formation, based on studies of Japanese companies.[22] There is also a growing body of stories surfacing from many countries that are implementing knowledge practices and efforts as well.[23]

FIGURE 1.1   Emerging Questions of Knowledge.

These areas of inquiry are all important in our exploration of knowledge. In addition, living systems theory also offers many insights into the self-organizing properties of knowledge.

Questions of Knowledge

This book explores critical issues and questions that have emerged around organizational knowledge. Here are some of the primary areas that the following chapters will explore.

1. *Defining Terms* First there is the challenge of trying to develop common definitions for terms frequently used in discussions of knowledge. A sampling of these terms includes: *knowledge* itself, *information, data, knowledge transfer, tacit and explicit knowledge, knowledge management, knowledge sharing, organizational learning, team learning, meaning, organizational intelligence,* and *collaborative intelligence.* How are these terms related?

2. *The Nature of Knowledge* There are some fundamental questions to examine around the nature of knowledge. Is knowledge a thing or a process? Or is it both? How can we orient ourselves in this knowledge universe?

3. *Orders of Knowledge* Other questions deal with the various shades or colorings of knowledge. Are there different orders of knowledge in organizations? If there are, what are those differences, and why are they important? How do different orders of knowledge relate to business processes and functions? What distinctions between individual and collective knowledge are important for us to understand?

4. *Role of Knowledge* What role does knowledge play in our organizations? In a world of constant change, how does knowledge serve us? As we become humbled in our attempts to control a complex world, what is it we most need to understand about knowledge itself?

5. *Dynamic Relationships* What is the relationship between data, information, knowledge, and wisdom? How is knowledge creation linked to performance? What is the relationship between learning and knowledge? Are there factors of time and space in knowledge building? If so, what are they, and how will our appreciation of these factors help us expand our capacity for adaptation and action?

6. *Best Practices* What processes support knowledge acquisition, creation, and application? How *do* we share knowledge so that it will multiply? How are companies implementing practices for creating and

sharing insights and learning? What are the key drivers for implementing new approaches?

7. *Supporting Structures and Technologies* What types of organizational structures support knowledge sharing? Are there enabling technologies for knowledge building? What are the critical success factors for culture, values, and behaviors?

8. *Developing Knowledge Strategies* What approaches really advance knowledge? If we are serious about building knowledge, then who has responsibility? What are the roles of leaders, managers, and line workers?

9. *Measurement* Further, how do we know our efforts are making a difference? What results can we identify and measure, if any? What performance improvements can we anticipate?

"Fuzzy" Knowledge

"Knowledge" is not particularly inspiring for managers. For one thing, it feels "soft," abstract, and academic. But we are beginning to realize that "soft" issues are critical for understanding human and organizational performance.

When the first wave of highly rational reengineering failed to bring the desired results, we saw the light bulbs go on in reengineering circles. "Oh, it's the people, stupid." All those "soft" people issues were stalling and sabotaging even the best of restructuring efforts.[24] Even with new technologies, Tom Peters reminds us that "The use of technology is 5 percent bits and bytes (a spiffy e-mail system that spans continents), and 95 percent psychology and sociology (an organization that dotes on sharing information rather than hoarding it)."[25]

The softer and fuzzier aspects of our work are challenging for those who have been raised in the western business tradition. Our usual focus is on *doing*. We aren't used to reflecting on our actions in any rigorous kind of way. We went along successfully for decades without disciplined thinking about our work. Why start now? This whole area of knowledge seems very abstract and theoretical. Can we just cut to the chase and DO something?

Yet, the great game of business is much more than a skill-based game, although most management practices tend to treat it as such. Business is also a vehicle of creative expression for our own minds. It provides a field of experimentation where we can turn our minds and knowledge to intriguing challenges. We focus our creative energies on enhancing performance, developing new products and services, meeting the marketplace, and contributing to the health and well-being of society.

New ideas are the life-blood of an enterprise. Without understanding how knowledge works, we have no idea how to truly support creativity and innovation. If we would master knowledge, we must think deeply about how we know what we know. We must understand how we shape our knowledge into new ideas, and how we translate knowledge into action. The knowledge question is becoming more and more compelling.

Evolution, Revolution, and the Question of Ultimate Good

Regardless of our opinions about it, knowledge happens. Systems inevitably move toward greater complexity and expansion, constantly seeking new connections. Knowledge wants to happen and will happen. We are part of this natural process. We are not somehow making "it" happen. We *participate*. In that participation we become co-creators with our environment. We both influence what is happening and are impacted by it. There is a larger knowledge unfolding that is much greater than we can know or understand.

Advances in information and communication technologies have brought us both hope and illusion. The hope is that we will be able to accumulate masses of knowledge, control the flow of information, and access answers as quickly as we formulate questions. The illusion is that very hope itself. As Henry Mintzberg points out, "Formal systems, mechanical or otherwise, have offered no improved means of dealing with the information overload of human brains; indeed they have often made matters worse."[26]

Technologically we may be able to process more and more bits of data at ever increasing speed. Eventually, however, we will realize that all the knowledge in the world will not solve our social, economic, and ecological dilemmas.

I foresee the time when our frantic pursuit of knowledge will exhaust our personal and social capacity to acquire and manipulate data and information. We will become mired in our misguided efforts to control. Information overload and knowledge exhaustion will bring us at last to a place of letting go and finding a simpler way to manage complexity. Some of those simpler ways are already starting to emerge.

As the Knowledge Evolution matures, we will begin to appreciate that even knowledge does not make us secure. Real security lies in our ability to discern and live by eternal principles that sustain and nurture life, health, and well-being. Values, ethics, and principles are the true DNA of our organizational enterprises. Only the freedom to openly exchange information with each other and our environment allows us to adapt, respond, and co-evolve with our environment.

The expansion of knowledge is an expression of our global community seeking pathways for self-organization. Knowledge carries the information that a system requires for renewal. It is natural, it is inevitable, and it is healthy. Life seeks connection and community. The explosion in knowledge is an expression of that life-affirming impulse.

I do not believe that the benefits of the knowledge explosion will *all* be good, even in the short term. In the early stages, the intense competition for knowledge, and the shifting economies that result, will extract a heavy personal and economic toll. Many people will be displaced in the scramble to reconfigure their expertise, and companies will struggle to keep a competitive edge.

However, I believe in the power of the knowledge journey to lead us ultimately to wisdom. It is worthwhile to pay attention to the journey and appreciate the wonder of ourselves as knowledge creators. I also believe that the Knowledge Era is not the ultimate revolution, but a way station on a much greater journey. Our intense pursuit of knowledge in this particular time of technological expansion and global interdependence is a necessary stage in this larger evolutionary process.

From Knowledge to Wisdom

> *Where is the Life we have lost in living?*
> *Where is the wisdom we have lost in knowledge?*
> *Where is the knowledge we have lost in information?*
> T.S. Eliot, Choruses from "The Rock," 1934

Like T.S. Eliot, I too am concerned about the wisdom we may lose in our search for knowledge. Learning and knowledge-building are purposeful activities. If we would understand knowledge we also must understand purpose. Knowledge *for what?* Learning *for what?* The "for what" is our *purpose*, our intention, the "why bother" of accumulating knowledge. Where, exactly, do we hope our knowledge will take us?

If we would understand how we build knowledge, then we must understand our own purposes. We must be able to reflect deeply on what we are about. We may say we want to acquire knowledge for competitive advantage. What if the knowledge we acquire leads us to question and redefine the very concept of competitive advantage? (As it sometimes does.) Where are we then? Where do we go next? Can we reorganize our knowledge to support a different purpose?

As we grow in knowledge we also learn to question what we believe about the future. We learn to examine our values and assumptions about what we should do. Such self-reflection is driven not by self-doubt or uncertainty, but by deep respect for our responsibilities. It arises in caring stewardship of our society and our planet, as well as our businesses.

Such self-questioning is the wisdom aspect of knowledge. Wisdom is often ignored in discussions of organizational knowledge. Yet, any framework of knowledge that does not include wisdom requires us to operate blind. Without wisdom there is no vision. Without vision we are lost in a sea of knowledge and information with no north star to guide us on our way.

The questions explored in this book are going to go very deep. The puzzle of how we build knowledge is directly linked to questions of cognition, self-organization, intelligence, consciousness, beliefs, and values. My hope is that this exploration will help all of us reframe our knowledge questions. We must go deep to the core of what has meaning for us personally, for those we work with, and for the organizations and enterprises we create.

The future belongs to those who are willing to ask tough questions and dare to dream of a better world. It is my hope that we will not settle for information, that we will not settle even for mere knowledge. Let us dare to do more than gain knowledge. Together, let us seek real organizational wisdom and find ways to make truly wise choices.

CHAPTER 2

Knowledge Competencies for Adaptive Enterprises

Knowledge is the "shape shifter," the mythological creature that can take many forms. It is always changing. Knowledge evolves as our purposes change in creative response to our environment. It reconfigures and expands as we exercise our will and intent to influence and shape that environment in various ways. The knowledge resource is far more organic than mechanical. Knowledge depends on a variety of factors for its shape and movement, such as the way people work together, the questions we ask, and the way information moves.

Important new orientations take place when we view an organization from the perspective of knowledge. The old way of thinking about companies as bundles of resources that produce products and services leaves knowledge out of the equation. In the old perspective, people are regarded as interchangeable components of production. A knowledge-based orientation, however, views people very differently. The worker or knowledge "owner" becomes a relevant unit of analysis. Further, these "units" or people are not really interchangeable since each individual has a unique configuration of knowledge.

The challenge in knowledge-based management is trying to understand how a company, business unit, or work team functions as a collaborative intelligence or collective field of knowledge. The web of knowledge that weaves through an organization supports not only the existing tasks, but also includes emergent knowledge, talents, and skills that represent generative learning for the organization.

Core Competencies for Flexible Response

In the Newtonian thinking that typifies the Information Age, knowledge questions have to do with amassing and cataloging knowledge. As we move towards a new orientation in thinking we begin to address new questions. We become curious about the dynamics and process of "knowledging." We probe more deeply into how knowledge serves us.

For many people the knowledge "question" is responsiveness to the environment. From this perspective the knowledge opportunity is one of quickly acquiring, adapting, or renewing expertise. The goal is to reconfigure knowledge in order to quickly bring new products to market or enhance competitive advantage.

One structured way of organizing an enterprise around knowledge is to develop a core competencies strategy. A competencies strategy is more forward-looking than a narrow focus on managing existing knowledge assets. Such an approach allows people to think in terms of acquiring future knowledge as well as enhancing current knowledge utilization.

The term "core competency" came to public awareness in C.K. Prahalad and Gary Hamel's landmark article in the *Harvard Business Review* in 1990, *The Core Competence of the Corporation.*[1] Prahalad and Hamel define a core competence as a unique bundle of skills and technologies that enables a company to provide particular benefits to customers. They described the competencies strategy of NEC, who identified interrelated streams of technological and market evolution: distributed processing, more complex components, development of complex digital systems and the convergence of computing, communication, and components business. The clarity of their focus helped NEC develop strategic alliances to build the competencies they would need.

Core competencies are those unique characteristics that enable a company to generate innovative products continually and to extend market capability. Examples are Sony's miniaturization expertise, Federal Express's logistics management, Electronic Data System's (EDS) systems integration, or Merck's expertise in drug-discovery and development. A core competency is one that is absolutely fundamental to the success of the enterprise and that gives the firm a unique presence in the marketplace.

The end products and services of a company might be based on one or several core competencies. Eastman Kodak has built its worldwide reputation and dominance in color imaging on a core platform of color negative film. The core competency in the chemistry and structure of color film supports end products for amateur photography, professional photography, and the motion picture industry. Although the end products are different, they build off the same core competency platform.

Competencies or Capabilities?

In order to identify a core competence, Prahalad and Hamel suggest the three "tests" of core competence:[2]

1. It must make a disproportionate contribution to customer-perceived value.

2. It must be competitively unique.
3. It forms the basis for entry into new product markets.

Companies undertake the development of core competencies as a way of shaping long-term capability for future competitive advantage. This process often leads to a profound redefining of the business. It results in rethinking the underlying values and assumptions, identifying new lines of business, and defining critical skill sets that will be important in both the near and distant future. Thus, core-competencies development impacts virtually every aspect of the business and its culture. This often results in transformational change as the enterprise reshapes itself for its future.

Many people use the terms *competency* and *capability* interchangeably. I believe this causes needless confusion. *Core knowledge competencies* and *core performance capabilities* are two distinct, yet critically interrelated aspects of organizational identity.

Core Performance Capabilities

Core performance capabilities are those processes and functions that enable a company to deliver high-quality products and services with speed, efficiency, and high customer service. Core performance capabilities are generic to the success of many enterprises. These may be exceptionally efficient core business processes, such as introducing new products to the market place. Or they might be enabling technologies, such as information technologies that capture detailed information about the customer. Examples of performance capabilities are:

- an ability to bring new products to market quickly (Hewlett-Packard)
- the capacity to quickly modify products or customize services (Rubber-maid)
- the ability to integrate information technologies, such as electronic data scanning, into operations (Procter & Gamble)
- logistics management (Wal-Mart)
- ability to reengineer core business processes (Motorola)
- attracting and recruiting quality employees (Levi-Strauss)
- sharing learning, insights, and best practices (Texas Instruments)

Core Knowledge Competencies

Core knowledge competencies, on the other hand, are those domains of expertise, knowledge, and technical knowledge that are unique to a particular type of business. They form the *content* or *subject matter* of the enterprise. Examples of core knowledge competencies would be:

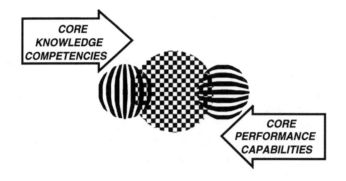

FIGURE 2.1 Organizational Identity. Competencies and capabilities combine to create a unique organizational identity.

- technological knowledge of abrasives and adhesives (3M)
- pictorial imaging technology (Eastman Kodak)
- extraction of petro chemical products from crude oil (Chevron)
- gene splicing (Genentech)
- designing molds for rolling steel (Chapparell Steel)
- development of software code (Microsoft)
- accounting practices (Arthur Andersen)

George Stalk, writing in *Planning Review,* takes a similar view of competencies and capabilities. He defines core competencies as "combinations of individual technologies and production skills that provide a justification for expanding product lines. Capabilities are the mechanisms by which core competencies are made into realities. The two are very complementary."[3]

Every company has a unique organizational identity composed of many elements (Figure 2.1). One way of distinguishing an organization is by the way it combines core knowledge competencies and core performance capabilities. Successful companies develop strengths in both directions. A particular configuration of competencies and capabilities is difficult to duplicate, since they always evolve in the historical context of a unique company culture.

Flexible Response

As a company continuously adapts and changes, core knowledge competencies and core performance capabilities are combined and recombined into new configurations. In this way, the core of skills, technology expertise, and knowledge develops over time with the flexibility and adaptability needed to respond to rapidly changing conditions.

Further, it is important that these reconfigurations incorporate a type of "genetic diversity." Prahalad and Hamel remind us that success often leads to inbreeding, where pools of knowledge and ways of thinking that were successful in the past become institutionalized. Without incorporating new thinking, a company loses its genetic diversity.[4] Equally dangerous is not understanding a core competency and inadvertently outsourcing it, selling it off, or under-investing in its development and upkeep.

The ability to reconfigure competencies and capabilities quickly and efficiently is critical for flexible and rapid response to changes in markets, resources, and the business environment. James Brian Quinn, author of *The Intelligent Enterprise,* says "Looking beyond mere product lines to a strategy built around core intellectual or service competencies provides both a rigorously maintainable strategic focus and long-term flexibility.[5]

Comparing Competencies and Capabilities

Comparing your own company's competencies and capabilities with those of your competitors brings valuable insights into exactly how companies can gain sustainable advantage. In Figure 2.2, three companies are compared. Company 1 is low in both its knowledge and performance capability. Company 2 has very high technological knowledge, but low capability. This means it may be inefficient in bringing goods and services to the marketplace, or might have difficulty maintaining quality and consistency. Thus, Company 2 is held back by relatively low performance capability. Company 3, however, ranks high in both knowledge

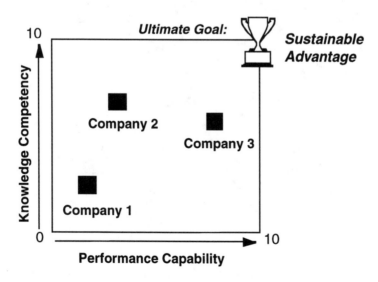

FIGURE 2.2 Competencies and Capabilities.

and performance capability. It ranks slightly lower than Company 2 in knowledge, but has greater performance capability to deliver goods and services.

It is important to remember in any comparative analysis that *none* of the companies currently in your industry (including yours) may be even close to where the industry is heading in the future. It is always important to identify emerging trends and expectations and define the ultimate goal.

Purpose as the Attractor for Knowledge

Let's use the analogy of an atom to think about how competencies develop. We can think of the guiding principles or vision of an organization as forming the core or *nucleus* of the organization. Core competencies are the ever-dynamic, ever-changing collections of electrons that orbit the nucleus. In an enterprise, the nucleus of purpose and values serves as the *attractor* for pulling certain types of competencies into its orbit (Figure 2.3).

A company's identity at any given moment in time is derived from its unique combination of competencies and capabilities. An adaptable organization continually reconfigures these electrons of competencies and capabilities to support and advance the organizing values, purpose, and strategy of the organization. Recombining these elements allows a flexible response to changes in markets and the business environment (Figure 2.3).

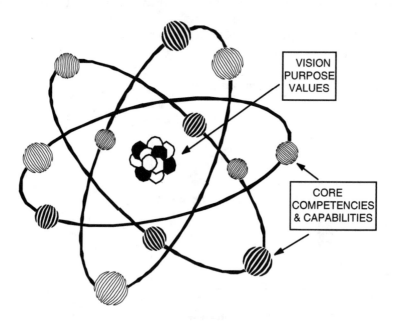

FIGURE 2.3 The Adaptable Organization. The nucleus of the organization is its purpose, values, and vision. The orbiting electrons represent core competencies and core capabilities that serve the purpose and values of the organization.

A Competencies Matrix

A company's unique mix of capabilities and competencies can be described using a matrix method. The matrix identifies the frequency with which a particular competency or capability appears as a critical success factor in every segment of the business. Drawing from the work of Paul Shoemaker,[6] Table 2.1 is an example of how such a competencies matrix could be constructed.

In the example, Competency A is critical to four of the five lines of business, while Competency C is only critical in one area. The table can be as simple or elaborate as needed. This analysis helps in setting priorities and making investment decisions regarding resources, training, recruiting, and technology support.

TABLE 2.1 Core Competencies Matrix. A core competencies matrix helps guide decision making.

Competency or Capability	Line of Business 1	Line of Business 2	Line of Business 3	Line of Business 4	Line of Business 5
A	X	X	X		X
B	X		X		X
C		X			

Enabling or Supporting Competencies

Competencies can be further distinguished by whether they are "core" competencies or "enabling" competencies. Core knowledge or technology competencies are those that are strategic in nature—meaning that they themselves bring competitive advantage. An enabling or supplemental technology or competency is also required for success, but it is less critical to control the competency internally. The enabling competency supports world-class leadership in the core competency or capability itself.

For example, identified core knowledge or technology competencies for Eastman Kodak in their Imaging Sector are:

- silver halide imaging materials
- precision-thin film coatings and finishing
- optomechatronics
- imaging electronics
- imaging science

A strategic competency within silver halide imaging materials is the technology by which such materials are made sensitive to various ranges of the spectrum. Less strategic, but still important, is an enabling technology that supports that competency, the ability to measure small amounts of dye on silver halide grains.[7]

Self-Organization and Competencies

Companies organized around core competencies are noticeably different from traditionally organized companies. Core competencies must be leveraged across business units to promote efficiency and realize a high return from research and development. Thus, these companies are much more focused on cross-functional efficiencies and the integration of business units. Kodak took this tack by developing a detailed flow chart describing how competencies would be managed and utilized. Then, Kodak established six cross-functional multi-level teams, involving more than 300 people, to create a development strategy for each competency.

These companies can also achieve a greater degree of self-organization. With a competencies focus, people have a clearly understood and communicated foundation for making business decisions at any level of the organization. People are generally more empowered to meet customer needs. They organize themselves and their work groups to provide rapid response and quality service. To expand personal competencies, people often are cross-trained or embrace "job enrichment" approaches that challenge their skills across a wider range of responsibilities.

Competency-based organizations look past their end products and services to understand the underlying know-how and skills that give them the ability to out-perform their competition. Such companies also tend to have a long-term perspective on strategy, since competencies take time to nurture and develop. They focus their investment and portfolio strategies more on strengthening competencies over time than on short-sighted immediate financial gain.

All Knowledge is Not Alike

Knowledge wears many faces. When people tell me they would like to build a knowledge-based organization, be a knowledge manager, or attract knowledge workers, I always wonder, "What type of knowledge?" Knowledge has many shapes. We cannot begin to master knowledge until we begin to recognize the many different guises that knowledge wears in our organizations.

People mean very different things when they use the word, "knowledge." This makes defining knowledge difficult, as we will see in the next chapter. For now, let's just say that people generally mean "that which is known," when they say *knowledge*. The word "known" assumes experience or information that can be readily accessed by others.

In other words, *knowledge is experience or information that can be communicated and shared.* This communal aspect of knowledging is a critical factor when we explore the processes of knowledge creation.

As we begin to explore knowledge competencies, we find that any area of expertise has several different knowledge components within it. Both knowledge competencies and performance capabilities are comprised of multiple layers of knowledge. In *Wellsprings of Knowledge,* Dorothy Leonard-Barton groups these into four interdependent dimensions: Employee Knowledge and Skill, Physical Technical Systems, Managerial Systems, and Values and Norms.[8] Other people are beginning to distinguish different types and levels of knowledge as well.

Knowledge as Expertise

Such knowledge distinctions are valuable enough to carry a bit farther. We can begin to surface the different knowledge domains by thinking about professional expertise. For example, take the professional knowledge competency of journalism, focusing on the expert writing skill required for developing articles for newspapers or magazines.

If I were a professional journalist, I would have a broad range of *technical knowledge* of how things work in my own field and related fields such as publishing, printing, and other media. This practical knowledge is my everyday *expertise* for getting things produced and published. More specifically I would have practical, step-by-step *skills* for doing my specific job and for using any specialized equipment or software. In addition, I would have quite a collection of *data* about the field, including miscellaneous facts, statistics, and odd bits of information.

I would also have more abstract and theoretical knowledge. The *ethics* of the field of journalism would be one component. Certainly I would know some of the basic organizing *principles* and *values* that determine professional standards in the field. I would know the key *theorists* and thought leaders. I would also have *professional knowledge* of my field, such as who are the significant writers or publishing entities, and who is distinguished in the field.

While these domains of knowledge are all interrelated—and all equally important for a fully-qualified professional, they are also distinctly different. They range from simple data or know-*what,* through more skill-based applications of know-*how,* to more abstract reasoning levels of know-*why* (Figure 2.4).[9]

As we think about all the different types of knowledge, we can begin to see that a lot of learning takes place in order to build a knowledge competency. Most professionals go through a formal education process to learn the theoretical underpinnings of their chosen field. More applied knowledge is gained through the work itself by actually doing a variety of tasks. We continue to build professional knowledge when undertaking new projects, networking,

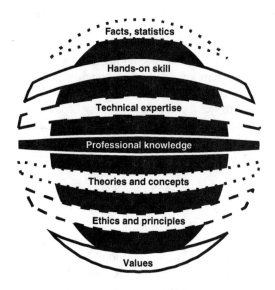

FIGURE 2.4 Knowledge Domains.

making professional "moves" to other industries or business units, reading books and journals, and attending professional conferences.

Core Competencies at Chase Manhattan

These multiple layers of knowledge are beginning to be addressed in the new competencies model at Chase Manhattan Bank. As Stephen Martin describes this approach, Chase is reorganizing people around competencies that serve the customer rather than traditional jobs.[10]

Chase Manhattan is a major player in global financial markets. As Chase became increasingly international in focus, the old market boundaries began to blur and new alliances increased competition. In response, Chase developed a clear, customer-focused strategy and identified corporate core competencies in each segment of the market, describing what skills and traits individuals would need to deliver the business strategy.

To support the organizational core competencies, Human Resources began to define the "supply side" of that equation by matching up what individuals had to offer against what customers demanded. Competencies became the new organizing focus, with the distribution of those competencies relying on detailed analysis rather than old job categories. Competency definitions became the foundation for recruiting, performance standards, and career development. Acknowledging the various levels of expertise, Chase developed a seven-point scale ranging from "minimal knowledge," through "recognizable ability," up to "advisory."

Linking individual competencies to organizational core competencies supports the strategic needs of the corporation. It also allows people and teams to "self-organize" as they match their personal competencies against clients and integrate with others into effective teams.

Martin sums up the reasoning behind the change:

> *Organizations involved in fast-moving markets that continue to use jobs as the aligning mechanism against the customer are bound by the laws of physics to have a problem. When the customer moves on, they are faced with the unattractive alternatives of either having to change people's jobs—which usually represents troublesome, unwelcome and painful change for people—or worse, the hassle is considered too big or too soon after the last reorganization and the customer moves on but the people do not.*[11]

The competencies focus at Chase is supported by database and information technology. That, in and of itself, is nothing new. However, the way the information is organized is radically different. The difference lies in the shift from the old thinking of people as interchangeable workers filling static "jobs," to the perspective of regarding each person as a node of knowledge with a unique bundle of competencies.

Knowledge Competencies at CIBC

When he was with the Canadian Imperial Bank of Commerce, Hubert Saint-Onge championed a core competencies approach to developing human capital.[12] The CIBC competency models describe about four dozen key knowledge and skills competencies that people need in order to provide value to the customer. They describe the various talents employees should have: a knowledge of accounting, selling skills, expertise in credit analysis, and so on. The range and depth of learning expected from a branch manager or loan officer is, of course, much greater than that of a customer service representative.

As a result of shifting to the competency model, CIBC basically abolished training and the fuzzy, hard-to-manage costs running about $30 million a year that went with it. Now, each employee relies on their list of competencies to guide them in taking charge of their own learning. They have access to books and software at their Branch learning room, and they learn from their co-workers and take courses as needed. Managers track learning and competencies development to measure progress.

More and more, people are expected to develop a suite of skills, rather than one or two narrow areas of expertise. Xerox, for example, now rates employees in information technologies on their business skills, technical skills, and leadership skills.[13] At J.P. Morgan, there is a focus on breadth of knowledge for employees. The company tries to move managers across specializations and between segments of the organization to broaden their individual knowledge and experience.[14]

Accounting for Knowledge

There is increasing evidence that traditional accounting methods do not capture the full value of the firm. A comparative analysis of book value versus market value of companies acquired in recent mergers, finds the actual dollar amount paid far exceeds the book value of assets, often by millions of dollars.[15] The only way to account for the surplus is in terms of the value of the intellectual assets and service value of the company.[16] Yet, we still operate as if these have no real value. Although managers can easily justify investment in hard assets, they often feel investments in knowledge and intellectual capital are uncertain and easily deferred.

Despite the challenges of measuring and quantifying knowledge capital and intellectual assets, people in business today have finally realized that the core "asset" of any enterprise is its knowledge. People are beginning to appreciate that knowledge is packaged as products and services. The higher the knowledge content, the higher the value of the end product. The more knowledge inputs that go into a product, the more difficult it is to imitate.

Knowledge-Value Added

The value chain of the enterprise is really a knowledge chain. Knowledge, as expertise and know-how, is input into a product or service at every link of the value chain. Valery Kanavsky and Tom Housel have turned this idea into a new way of calculating value. They have devised a business auditing process that unpacks a business process and calculates knowledge value by focusing on changes in units of information. This knowledge-based valuation process has been implemented at Pacific Bell and Hewlett-Packard, among others. Kindred Pederson of Southern California Edison uses yet another method to calculate knowledge-value added in evaluating employee contributions. Such methods of calculation represent real breakthroughs in bringing knowledge into the value equation.[17]

Along with understanding the knowledge chain of specific business processes, it is also important to understand how knowledge clusters add value to products and services. Overlapping areas of expertise create a knowledge cluster. For example, Artificial Intelligence (AI) products are the result of a knowledge cluster created by the overlap of cognitive science knowledge and software development.

Knowledge clusters are fertile breeding grounds for new products and services. They also fuel innovation and contribute knowledge-value added features to existing products. Many of the mergers we see, especially in technology firms, are largely for the purpose of creating knowledge clusters. GM's acquisition of EDS, for example, reflects a move to enhance automotive products and production processes through the use of information technology and systems integration. Combining the two firms was a convenient way to create the required knowledge cluster.

Balancing the Scorecard

With the realization that old performance measures cannot account for intangible assets, we have seen a move towards more balanced measures for company performance. Scandia AFS has implemented new measures for their "Balanced Annual Report on Intellectual Capital." At Skandia the intellectual capital approach led by Leif Edvinsson includes knowledge renewal and development as major components of their value metrics. They look at return on net assets, contracts issued per employee, information technology expense per administrative expense, number of employees versus managers and training per employee. Edvinsson says, "The intellectual capital of the company is the relationship between all of these diverse elements." The bottom line results? In 1995, Skandia grew ten times as much as in the previous five years.[18]

At the Canadian Imperial Bank of Commerce (CIBC), they acknowledge the difficulty of quantifying and measuring intellectual or knowledge capital, which is referred to as "intangible assets." Yet, in the Knowledge Era, CIBC has come to believe that the intangible assets are the real source of strength for the firm to distinguish itself in the market place. CIBC has undertaken the challenge of creating a "balanced scorecard,"[19] of corporate performance measures that includes three elements of intellectual capital:[20]

1. Human Capital—the capabilities of the individual that are needed to provide solutions to customers.
2. Customer capital—depth (penetration), width (coverage), attachment (loyalty), and profitability of the customers.
3. Structural capital—the capabilities of the organization to meet market needs.

Hubert Saint-Onge helped shape the approach to learning and leadership development at CIBC. He sees the core challenge of intellectual asset management as making the unarticulated or tacit knowledge of the organization explicit, so that it can be shared and continually renewed. "It is important," he says, "to understand how knowledge is formed and how people and organizations learn to use knowledge wisely."[21] At CIBC they use group sharing methods and alignment strategies to support that intent.

Exciting new performance models such as these are bringing about a powerful shift of thinking about the real assets of the firm. Leif Edvinsson and Michael Malone outline some of these new methods of calculating value in *Intellectual Capital: Realizing Your Company's Value by Finding Its Hidden Brainpower.*[22] Karl-Erik Sveiby too has developed a framework for understanding the hidden intellectual assets of the enterprise.[23] The SEC (Securities and Exchange Commission) is also exploring these issues. In April of 1996, the SEC sponsored a special symposium on financial accounting and the reporting of intangible assets under the leadership of M. H. Wallman. Previously invisible knowledge assets are becoming more and more visible on the corporate balance sheet.

With new ways of calculating knowledge value, questions of how to leverage and manage that value begin to arise. The knowledge "opportunity" is often formulated in terms of increasing the knowledge assets of the enterprise. This perspective assumes knowledge is the "core product" of the business, and the questions focus on how do we own it, control it, build it, and maximize its value? In short, how do we "manage" the knowledge assets of the enterprise?

Who Owns It?

Let's take a closer look at the question of ownership. Imagine, if you will, how different the sporting world would be if athletes and coaches owned the rights to their particular moves. Remember when Dick Fosbury changed the whole approach to high jumping by going over the bar shoulders first instead of feet first in the 1968 Olympic Games? What if that famous Fosbury "flop," or Kareem Abdul Jabar's highflying "sky hook" in basketball, were locked up with a patent or a copyright? What if no one could use that particular move without paying a royalty or a licensing fee?

Far-fetched? Maybe not. Intellectual property attorneys are attempting to show that, under current patent, trademark, and copyright laws, athletes could be entitled to ownership of their original and signature "moves."[24] Kareem Abdul Jabar actually has two trademarks pending, on the words "sky hook" and on the image of himself performing the shot.

What if the attorneys make their case? We could see sports innovations, such as Chris Evert's two-handed back hand tennis style, Olga Corbet's backward flip on the parallel bars, or unusual basketball jump shots, tied up with copyrights. After all, certain ballet choreography is copyrighted, why not copyright ice dancing or gymnastic sequences?

Most people feel this notion of "owning" athletic innovation is ridiculous. After all, in the heat of a game or competition you are going to catch the ball any which way you can, so to speak. Who is going to stop and think about whether they want to pay someone a royalty as they are diving for a pop fly? Even trying to codify an athletic move is a problem. No two people execute the same move exactly the same way. Where do we draw the line between my knowledge and yours?

Intellectual Property

These examples illustrate just how murky the waters of intellectual property rights can be. Sticky legal issues bring to the forefront all the paradoxes and frustrations of the information age and the ownership of knowledge. Nothing can stifle creativity and innovation faster than ownership squabbles. Knowledge is so seamless and interwoven it is increasingly difficult to draw boundaries around any segment. Yet, without protection for investments, innovation is stifled at the other end of the spectrum as well.

Intellectual property and "intellectual assets" have become hot topics. When the locus of control of knowledge begins shifting away from companies and toward individuals, critical questions of owning and controlling knowledge begin to emerge.

As workers control more and more knowledge, they also seek ownership and participation in the financial return on that knowledge. Universities that previously used to make research findings public are now seeking patent ownership themselves. High-level scientists, researchers, and inventors are beginning to negotiate co-ownership of patents or royalties as part of their compensation and benefits packages. Journals and magazines are now required to collect royalty and copying fees, so that they can return a royalty to authors of articles. Authors who used to assign their copyrights to journals without a second thought are now carefully weighing their options.

The open information highway of the Internet has also brought intellectual property issues to awareness. People are often surprised to find how little control they have of their work. After the first enthusiastic wave of Internet publishing, the second wave is unfolding with a more cautious approach. People are reluctant to have their web page designs, text, and other creative elements appropriated by other users.

Codified Knowledge

There is no question of the value to businesses of being able to own certain types of knowledge. Brand names are key to corporate identity, and it would be chaotic if there were 30 different companies named Microsoft or McDonald's. Patents also encourage research by assuring return on investment for costly development of formulas and inventions. In terms of lasting value, a patent is generally good for about 17 years, a copyright will last 75 years, and a trademark is good forever (supposedly).

Yet, the range of knowledge, processes, products, formulas, images, and words that can be protected is limited. It would be a prohibitively costly and time-consuming effort to submit every single internal document, e-mail, memo, or doodle for copyright protection. Such protection can also be surprisingly limited. Copyrights, for example, protect only the form of the information, not the ideas themselves. Generally speaking, anyone can imitate, use, or circulate an idea. But people cannot copy a published form of that idea verbatim, without seeking permission or paying a copyright fee.

Managing Intellectual Assets

In order to navigate these murky waters and stake out ownership of knowledge, new positions are beginning to crop up. For example, Dow Chemical has a Director of Intellectual Asset Management. When Gordon Petrash slipped into that slot he found that roughly half of Dow patents were unused, unattended, and had no business unit overseeing their development. Some of these patents sitting on the sidelines, costing hundreds of thousands in upkeep, were potentially worth billions of dollars.

To reverse this situation, Petrash developed a six-step process for managing intellectual assets:[25]

1. Strategy: define the role of knowledge in your business.
2. Competitive assessment: understand your competitor's strategies and knowledge assets.
3. Classify your portfolio: know what you have, what you use, where it belongs.
4. Evaluate: know what your knowledge assets are worth and how to maximize value.
5. Invest: identify gaps and holes to plug.
6. Assemble your knowledge portfolio: repeat the process infinitum.

Not only does the classification and identification process help Dow understand and measure its current knowledge assets, it also helps shape the way they conduct their business. The process helps Dow to plan research and write patents in ways that make it more difficult for their competition to maneuver around them.

This renewed appreciation of intellectual assets at Dow is propelling them to consider an Intellectual Capital Supplement to their traditional corporate measures. At Dow they are beginning to apply lessons learned in patents to other areas of "know-how" by identifying value in different knowledge arenas. Other companies are following suit, such as S. A. Armstrong Ltd., which is actively developing and tracking sixty key intellectual capital indicators.

The Larger Knowledge Asset

Patents and other tangibles, however, are only one form of knowledge asset. They are only the tip of the iceberg, so to speak. The real knowledge assets that actually support the patents are much harder to manage and protect. Underlying "codified" intellectual assets, such as patents, copyrights, and trademarks, is a whole iceberg of knowledge that floats around the organization. The iceberg takes the forms of in-house "experts," shared stories, working solutions, webs of external and internal relationships, communities of practice, and experience. This is the real knowledge asset of the organization (Figure 2.5).

Many people include databases and internal information systems in this supporting iceberg of collective knowledge. For example, financial services companies, such as American Express, have customer databases that are constantly updated. They know what their customers are buying, where they buy it, where they are traveling, as well as their financial profile. This allows them to serve not only the card users, but also forge valuable information and knowledge linkages with vendors, such as airlines and retailers.

Specific strings of information, particular diagrams or narrowly defined processes, can indeed be codified and controlled as patented or copyrighted knowledge. However, to catalog, quantify, measure, and control the deeper knowledge that created those intellectual assets poses a much greater challenge—

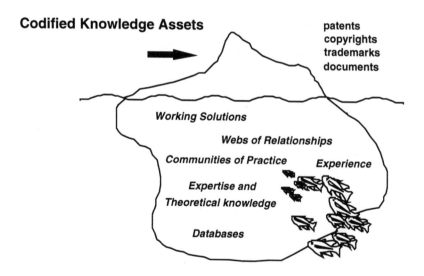

FIGURE 2.5 Knowledge Assets. Codified knowledge that is legally owned is only the tip of the iceberg. The full knowledge asset is much larger.

if it can be done at all. The deeper question of managing knowledge involves this much larger body, the totality of knowledge that resides in the organization supporting the creation of new products and services.

This larger body of organizational knowledge is much less structured. At first glance, it seems like an amorphous, undifferentiated mass. However, people are beginning to attempt to define and manage this less structured knowledge in a variety of ways.

Before devising a core competencies approach, or attempting to calculate knowledge assets, it is important to have a framework that incorporates multiple levels of complexity. Most knowledge frameworks miss this multi-modal aspect by attempting to create categories for knowledge *content*, rather than focusing on the levels of knowledge complexity. Content is always changing, but the underlying structures of knowledge do not. A successful knowledge approach requires a thorough understanding of knowledge itself.

In response to this need, I will introduce a knowledge framework that is proving useful for helping people understand how knowledge and learning support performance objectives. It allows people to understand knowledge development within their expertise. In addition, it helps people relate their own knowledge to that of their colleagues.

CHAPTER 3

The Knowledge Navigators

Albert Einstein once said that we cannot solve our current problems with the same level of thinking that created them. This means that when we cannot resolve a dilemma at one level, we must move to another mode of thinking. In the Knowledge Era this particularly holds true. If our attention is on managing information, we will never move into knowledge. If we focus only on building knowledge, we will never gain real wisdom.

The analogy of navigation is a good one for the Knowledge Era, as they have realized at Skandia. A sea of water, of stars, or of knowledge is not something that we can control or master. However, we can understand such complex phenomena well enough that we may learn to navigate them and unlock their mysteries. Successful navigation requires understanding the relationship between where we are and where we want to be. Then we can use various navigational aids to carry us forward to our goals.

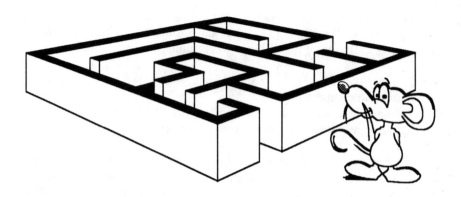

FIGURE 3.1 Do You Feel Lost in the Knowledge Era Without a Map?

Time, Space, and Navigation

In the Age of Exploration (1300-1600 AD) competitive advantage resided with those who had the best ability to navigate the globe. Those countries that ruled the seas—ruled the world. In those days, they found the great challenge in navigation is finding a way to tell time at sea. Unless you know what time it is, you cannot determine longitude. So, you see, in order to master space and thus circumnavigate the globe, you must first find a way to master time. A time measurement allows you to understand the relationship between the point where you are and the point where you want to be. If you understand that relationship, then you can chart a course and find your way home again.[1]

Today we have left the confines of earth and are navigating space, both actual celestial space and cyberspace. The time we must master today is not clock-time but space-time. We have already seen how the traditional time-keepers of corporate performance measures no longer work for understanding knowledge assets. Looking at the stars reminds us also to move away from our usual frame of reference. Then we are far more likely to be able to tell where we really are and see where we need to go.

Now, of course, even the North Star has become obsolete. Our technology has brought us a *Global Positioning System* operated by the Department of Defense. Through a constellation of twenty-four satellites, travelers can get a constant fix on their locations. For the cost of a VCR, you can get a palm-sized device that calculates your exact longitude, latitude, and altitude. It's so accurate, the military had to create two codes, so that civilian users could not use this little gizmo for mischief, such as guiding missiles. Now, we don't even need to look at the stars, we can look in our pocket.

Navigation boils down to a few simple elements: a good map, something like a sextant to tell you where you are, and a timepiece to help you measure your progress. These are good things to remember when trying to navigate:

- In order to know where you are on earth, you must first look at the stars. (Shift your perspective.)
- To chart a course you must know both where you are and what time it is. (Understand the relationship of time and space.)

Time is a critical and much misunderstood aspect of knowledge. Navigation in the Knowledge Era requires understanding the relationship of Time, Knowledge, and Action. We will take a closer look at this toward the end of this chapter. Mastery often comes about in unexpected ways. If we desire to master information and knowledge, then implementing technologies to process and manage data are only part of the picture. Technology alone will not enable us to master knowledge. Our own thought processes hold the key.

In addition, we must use a map that covers the whole territory. If we place our attention on *knowledge* creation, we can find better information solutions. By understanding *wisdom*, we are better able to build real knowledge. *Success in the Information Age will come with mastery of knowledge. Success in the Knowledge Era will come from mastering the domain of wisdom.* A new level of thinking will do more than solve our present dilemmas. It will help lead us into a future much closer to our highest visions of work that is meaningful, lives that are rich in experience, and communities that are healthy, open, creative, and sustainable.

Knowledge Navigation

If we carry the metaphor of navigation a bit farther, here are some of the aids we would need for the Knowledge Era:

Aids in Knowledge Navigation

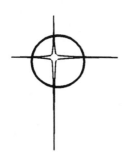

A NORTH STAR: The North star is the organizational wisdom that guides the enterprise to sustainable solutions. Without an organizational North star of purpose and values, knowledge is useless. Such values and intent are usually communicated through a company vision or purpose statement, but not always. Indeed, the informal, unspoken values are often much more important than an overworked mission statement. If knowledge is truly valued, then that appreciation is reflected in the belief system that guides the enterprise.

A COMPASS: The organizational compass consists of guiding principles and strategy. It is values and purpose in practice, that have now become organizing principles for how people work together. Successful strategies for the Knowledge Era are grounded in systems principles and take an integrated, multi-modal approach.

THE CREW: Knowledge is embodied in people. It is impossible to talk about knowledge without addressing the way people work together, learn together, and individually and collectively grow in knowledge. Companies that are serious about knowledge foster an environment and culture that supports continuous learning and sharing.

MAPS & GUIDES: Knowledge-based enterprises deliberately seek good guides, maps, and pathways for building knowledge across multiple performance levels. Processes that support knowledge creation, acquisition, sharing, communication, and organization must be developed, refined, and continuously improved.

SOUND VESSELS: There must be physical vehicles or vessels to support knowledge exploration and experimentation. Vessels include:

- technology support (information systems, databases, communication technologies, Web technologies, and e-mail)
- equipment (groupware, whiteboards, video conferencing equipment, flexible manufacturing systems)
- tools (job aids, knowledge maps, computer-based performance support)
- physical structures (learning centers, libraries, meeting rooms, executive strategy rooms)

FEEDBACK AND MEASUREMENT: There must be ways to assess whether you are "on course." Feedback is like the little ribbon on a sail that guides in filling the sail with wind, or depth gauges that alert you to shallow water. Measurements help you to gauge and manage knowledge assets and support continual improvement.

We will take a closer look at these navigational aids throughout the book, especially in Chapters 14 and 15. Before we move to specific processes or best practices in knowledge management, however, we need to explore the domain of knowledge a bit more. In order to develop guides and processes that support top performance, we will need to explore the underpinnings of knowledge itself.

Where is the Knowledge?

Knowledge is different from information. Not too long ago this was brought home to me in a very personal way. Before moving to a new house I went into the garage to pack up all my books that were stored there. When I opened the cupboards and saw all those volumes, I suddenly felt overwhelmed. Could I have possibly read all these books? These were just the ones I had actually purchased and kept. Not included were the hundreds I had checked out at libraries, paperback novels I had read and recycled to the bookseller, magazines and journals read and discarded, or all the daily newspapers.

I sank to the floor just looking, thinking of all the information and ideas they contained and wondering to myself: Where has all that knowledge gone? Do I really know all those things? Do I truly possess that knowledge? Where is it now? How could all of that be packed into my brain, or is it?

Remember all the books and documents you have read. Feel all the written words you have absorbed in your lifetime. Now think of all the practical skills you have acquired over your lifetime: skills such as walking, speaking, driving a car, separating an egg, playing volleyball, typing, diapering a baby, growing tomatoes. Some teacher or mentor shared their knowledge with you in order for you to learn those things. Where is all that knowledge now? What is this strange universe of personal knowledge? Where is it? What is it? How *do* we build knowledge, create meaning, store and access information?

Our knowledge is embodied in us. Our simplest actions convey the essence of all the information we have digested over our lifespan. We cannot recall all the information contained in the books we have read. We cannot remember the exact words of our teachers. Yet, all those books, all this learning, all this information, has helped us gain knowledge and understanding about various aspects of our world. We don't even know all that we know.

This process of acquiring and integrating information is something we naturally know how to do. We do it all the time. We take in information, process it, sort it, categorize it, store it, and use it to build knowledge and make meaning. Yet, we do not take time to fully understand how this works. We do not apply these natural processes to the way we organize our work or our businesses. We haven't taken time to map the territory.

Mapping the Territory

We are lost in the Knowledge Era without a map. We do not have reliable descriptions of the territory. We use words like *information, knowledge, meaning, understanding,* as if we are all talking about the same thing, but we are not. It is as if we have all set off to visit a foreign country, but someone has played a trick with our guidebooks. The names of the landmarks are jumbled up, the maps appear backwards and someone is playing havoc with the compass.

Where are the maps and guidebooks to help us explore this new world of knowledge and information? Serious thinkers have explored the territory of knowledge, traditionally called epistemology, for several hundred years. We are not the first people to venture into this territory. However, there are many different perspectives out there, and it all seems a bit confusing. How can we make sense of this knowledge domain for the world of business?

First, let's piece together the maps we do have and get a sense of the terrain. Then, we will try to identify the landmarks. Finally, we can explore the pathways together and see if we can surface the patterns of knowledge.

From Etymology (words) to Entomology (bugs)

As we explore this territory of *knowledge* and *information*, it would be useful to be clear on language and understand how some of the words we use came into being. Dictionaries do not help much in making distinctions between information and knowledge.

Here's an example. The dictionary I have defines information as *"knowledge derived from study, experience, or instruction."* Excuse me, but didn't it just say that information is knowledge? It goes on to say that information is *"knowledge of a specific event or situation,"* in other words, "news." OK. I can buy the "news" part, but there is that word *knowledge* again. People use these words interchangeably and it's a bit confusing. How can information be knowledge?

When I look at the definitions for *knowledge,* I find they sound suspiciously like *information.* Are we going around in circles here? Check this out (Table 3.1):

TABLE 3.1 Definitions of Knowledge.[2]

Dictionary Definitions of Knowledge	My Unsolicited Commentary
1. The state or fact of knowing	(Now that's a big help! What's knowing?)
2. Familiarity, awareness, or understanding gained through experience	(See information above)
3. The sum or range of what has been perceived or discovered	(Whew, that's a lot of territory)
4. Learning, erudition: teachers of knowledge	(Oops, another circle, different direction)
5. Specific information about something	(Now, we're back to information again)
6. Carnal knowledge; Obsolete: Sexual intercourse, copulation	(Wouldn't you know, they took the fun out of it)

In the last chapter I suggested that in a general and broad sense *knowledge is experience that can be communicated and shared.* This is a useful way of defining knowledge if we are focusing on organizational intelligence. It reinforces the fact that our experience of the world is shaped in community. We co-create knowledge as a shared social process.

While we're at it, let's try *intelligence.* Hmm, let's see—*intelligence*: the capacity to acquire and apply knowledge. More circles. However, we find a nice connection here in the root of the word. It stems from the Latin *intelligere,* meaning *to choose between.* That gives one a sense that intelligence is what allows us to navigate knowledge.

These words are important. In a fundamental way, our language defines our experience. Whenever we bump up against new experiences we begin creating new words and redefining old ones. Probing into the deeper meaning of words we often use without thinking helps us reframe our shifting reality.

Let's keep looking. Here's the word *inform.* The roots of the word inform lie in the Latin *informare: to give form to, to form an idea.* So the dictionary tells us that *inform* means *to give form or character to: to animate or inspire with a particular quality or character.* This feels about right. We give shape to our experience through language and language shapes our experience. Now it's starting to make a bit more sense. InFORMation: to give form to our experience, the form of language, which can be communicated. The poet, Rumi, puts it another way, "The whole world is form and knowledge is its spirit."

Bugs

This brings us to bugs. Entomology. Let's consider a particular type of bug: the caterpillar. One of the deepest mysteries of the insect world is how a caterpillar transforms into a butterfly. As we know from studies, DNA encodes all the inFORMation of our ultimate form in tiny chemical strands. At our core we are just bundles of information and energy in constant exchange with other bundles of energy and information. What we think of as an object is just a particular configuration of information that generates a form, such as a butterfly.

In order for our caterpillar to undergo its remarkable transformation, a number of factors have to be present. The DNA must carry all the current information, so that the caterpillar will achieve its ultimate form of the butterfly. More importantly, the caterpillar must be in the right environment. There must be adequate food, oxygen, the right temperature, and so forth. There must be a period of gestation, so that the process is not interrupted. Only when everything is there to support it, does the caterpillar become a fully developed butterfly—or moth.

When we realize all the factors that have to be present for any particular form to appear, then we realize that information does not exist in a vacuum. Information always has a *context* of a particular time and culture that shapes its meaning.

Information and knowledge are not the same. Information exists within the larger environment of a collectively held body of *knowledge*. So, information is a subset or building block of knowledge. Any given piece of information might be a subset of many bodies of knowledge.

Deeper Yet

Now, let's burrow down into the root of *knowledge*. This requires poking around in all that Latin stuff in the back of the dictionary. What surfaces from this excavation is the word *gnosis*, which means *knowledge* in ancient Greek. A word that keeps being thrown together with *gnosis* is the word *recognize*. We know what we *recognize*. This means we mentally process our experience, shaping it and giving it mental forms that we can identify. So, we re-*cognize* that experience and bring it into the realm of knowledge.

What is really fascinating about this little word *gnosis* is that over time it has evolved to mean *intuitive apprehension of spiritual truths*. These knowledge questions go deep! It seems the more we probe into what knowledge is, the more we start rubbing up against wisdom. No wonder we might get a little confused.

Just for fun, let's tackle that word *wisdom*. Ah, wisdom. The very meaning of Homo Sapiens is the "wise man," the thinking animal. "Love of wisdom," is also the first and truest meaning of philosophy. Being wise implies that one is capable of sound judgment. Eminent psychologist Robert Sternberg suggests that wisdom is a metacognitive style plus sagacity—knowing that one does not know everything, yet seeking the truth to the extent that it is knowable.[3] In Sanskrit, the word *Veda*, for knowledge, means: *I have seen, I know*, implying a sort of true sight or vision. Our own English definition of wisdom uses phrases such as *an understanding of what is true, right, or lasting.*

Wisdom is the efficiency factor of knowledge management. Wisdom is the talent for penetrating to the very core or essence of things. It is a highly creative and connective way of processing knowledge that distills out essential principles and truths. Wisdom tells us what to pay attention to. Bob Galvin of Motorola recently said one of the mental processing skills we need is "the ability to distinguish the essence of our knowledge. We must be able to factor out what is significant in doing our work."[4] Wisdom is the truth seeker and pattern finder that penetrates to the core of what really matters.

Personal Knowledge

Somehow, in all our excitement around the Information Age, we have overlooked the incredibly deep roots of our personal knowledge. We, as individuals, are not mere repositories of knowledge, and neither are our organizations. Personal knowledge does include certain pieces of information and bits of data. However, my personal universe of knowledge also contains a wealth of experiences and memories that are unique to me. These experiences flavor, filter, and shape what I know and understand.

On a sheer practical level, I have a whole body of knowledge around living in this society, in this era, in this community, in this country, in this family. In addition, at a very deep level I have a recognition of spirit, of mysterious forces and principles that I seek to understand. This thought world *is* my real world.

We do much more than simply accumulate knowledge. As we progress through life or grow in expertise we also develop a flair for integrating, processing, and applying new knowledge. Our knowledge is a constantly shifting configuration of memory, context, patterns, associations, and relationships. It continuously evolves through constant exchange with our environment. In that, knowledge has far more in common with a living breathing organic being than it does with some static artifact that you can conveniently package up and tie a ribbon around.

There is no way we can possibly convey the richness of our personal domain of knowledge to another person. Even this book is but a tiny fragment of my own understanding about how the world works. Not included is the universe of knowledge that allows me to travel the streets of my home town, cook a meal, turn on my computer, play with a child, or catch an airplane (not necessarily in that order).

There is no way I could possibly catalog even my own personal knowledge. What makes us think we can somehow catalog or map all the knowledge that resides in a complex enterprise comprised of hundreds or thousands of people? What on earth do we think we can accomplish by "managing" knowledge?

Tacit and Explicit Knowledge

One of the goals of knowledge management in organizations is to make knowledge more visible. This corresponds to an important distinction between tacit knowledge and explicit knowledge, as described by Michael Polanyi.[5] Tacit knowledge is personal, context-specific knowledge that resides in an individual. Explicit knowledge, on the other hand, is more formal "codified" knowledge conveyed from one person to another in systematic ways. Tacit knowledge relies on experience, hunches, and insights. Explicit knowledge is conveyed through documents, images, and other deliberate communication processes.

Tacit knowledge centers around "mental models" that we carry internally. These mental models are concepts, images, beliefs, viewpoints, value sets, and guiding principles that help people define their world. Tacit knowledge also includes a technical element that includes concrete skills and expertise, the hands-on experience that comes from practice.

Some people see the primary task of knowledge management as that of making tacit knowledge more explicit. Nonaka and Takeuchi, view organizational knowledge creation as an interaction between tacit and explicit knowledge. They see tacit and explicit knowledge working in both directions, in continual flux and movement. This process, which they call *knowledge conversion*, is a social, communal process.

They suggest that as knowledge is socialized and shared, it passes through four different modes of knowledge conversion (Table 3.2). In these four modes, the flow of knowledge moves from tacit to explicit to tacit once again, through the knowledge spiral of knowledge creation.[6]

TABLE 3.2 Four Modes of Knowledge Conversion.[7]

Conversion Process	Knowledge change
1. Socialization	From tacit knowledge to tacit knowledge
2. Externalization	From tacit knowledge to explicit knowledge
3. Combination	From explicit knowledge to explicit knowledge
4. Internalization	From explicit knowledge to tacit knowledge

This idea, describing the movement of knowledge from tacit to explicit, begins to depict knowledge as a fluid and dynamic realm. The physicist, David Bohm, also explored the movement of knowledge as thought and consciousness, using the analogy of particle physics. He alleges that in this flow and flux nothing is permanent, "there can be no absolutely invariant elements of knowledge." Indeed, he suggests, the whole movement of thought, from individual awareness to communication between people, is a continual cycle. This process of knowledge generation goes on indefinitely through time. Thought and knowledge "have to be seen as one unbroken totality of movement, not belonging to any particular person, place, time, or group of people."[8] When we try to affix a thought, concept, or idea to any one person permanently, we ignore the integrity of the knowledge process. This view of seamless knowledge appears to be at odds with modern business concerns with intellectual property and ownership. But is it really?

The Particle and the Wave

Can knowledge be a social process with no clear boundaries and also be something tangible to which we can lay claim? This question complicates the whole issue of knowledge navigation. Is knowledge a "thing," an object, such as a collection of facts and information? Can we treat it as an object? Or is it something else?

Knowledge as an Object

Some people think of knowledge as the sum of everything we have learned. Viewing knowledge as a thing impacts how one would manage it. *Things* are generally owned by somebody, so they are property. *Things* need to be kept or stored someplace out of the rain. They need to be maintained and retired or recycled when they get old and worn. Also, our society tallies the number of things people and businesses own or control as a way of "keeping score" of who is winning the great game of business.

Thinking of knowledge as an object leads people to focus on databases and other storage devices. They are more likely to identify legal "owners" of knowledge components. From this view come terms such as "knowledge transfer," suggesting knowledge can be passed along like a baton in a relay race. The focus is on identifying, organizing, and collecting knowledge—and of course, measuring it.

Knowledge as a Process

Another way of thinking of knowledge is as a *process*. The process perspective brings a very different focus to the domain of knowledge. People who take a process perspective focus more on dynamic aspects of knowledge, such as sharing, creating, adapting, learning, applying, and communicating. They tend to see knowledge as a dynamic soup of constantly shifting, melding, and merging knowledge ingredients. They are less concerned with controlling the flow of knowledge and are more interested in encouraging participation and easing communication.

Michael Polanyi uses the construct *process-of-knowing* to describe the process in which we are engaged, that of acquiring and creating new knowledge. He describes knowledge "as an activity which would be better described as a process of knowing."[9] Charles Savage uses the word *knowledging* to express this perspective. Knowledging is a continual process that flows between individuals and communities. It is the song we sing as an expression of our being, as we co-create ourselves and our world with one another.

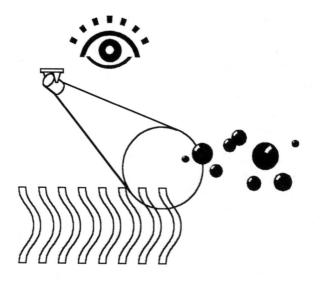

FIGURE 3.3 Wave or Particle? We see different properties depending on what we choose to observe.

Both of these ways of thinking about knowledge are useful for understanding different qualities. The question of whether knowledge is a thing or a process is not unlike the wave-particle paradox in quantum physics. In physics, there are two equally valid experimental processes regarding the properties of light. One set of experiments proves that light is a particle, a photon. Another set of experiments proves that light is a wave, a process.

How can mutually exclusive wave-like and particle-like behaviors both be properties of one and the same light? The answer is that they are not actually the properties of light at all. They are properties of our *interaction* with light. Depending on how we choose to look at it, we can demonstrate *either* property that is useful for us at the moment (Figure 3.3).[10]

It is the same with how we understand knowledge. The properties of knowledge that we choose to focus on depend on how we view its relationship to action, performance, and results. Knowledge has the properties of an object in that we can catalogue, organize, and even measure it to some degree. It also has properties of processes in its continual movement through creation, adaptation, enhancement, and application. Both views are correct from different vantage points.

Knowledge as a Complex System

Yet another way of addressing knowledge relies on an organic metaphor. In this perspective, knowledge is viewed as a creative phenomenon that requires the right environment. In other words, it is a complex, self-organizing system. In the organic view of knowledge, the culture of the organization plays a major role. The organizational environment is the "garden" in which knowledge grows. This viewpoint emphasizes culture, leadership, behaviors, and norms, as well as secondary "enablers," such as supporting technologies and communication flows. This perspective draws on concepts from systems theory and uses terms such as ecology of knowledge.

Knowledge as All of the Above

Devices, processes, and tools for navigating knowledge will have different properties depending on which aspect is being addressed. "Knowledge maps" that categorize and locate nodes of knowledge are useful for managing the *object* qualities of knowledge. (See Chapter 15 for more on "knowledge mapping.") Frameworks that describe *processes* for knowledge creation, or technologies for sharing knowledge, enhance its process qualities. The view of knowledge as a complex system reminds us that we have limited understanding. A healthy dose of humility and respect is important when it comes to something as complex as knowledge.

The Knowledge Management Assessment Tool (KMAT), a survey instrument, developed by Arthur Andersen and the American Productivity & Quality Center, incorporates object, process, and organic aspects of organizational knowledge. This model denotes two dynamic orbits supporting organizational knowledge creation (Figure 3.4). The outer orbit holds the key organizational en-

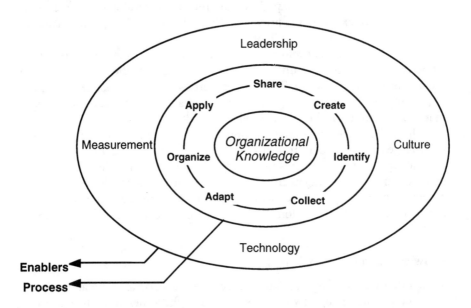

FIGURE 3.4 Organizational Knowledge Management Model (Arthur Andersen and the American Productivity and Quality Center).[11]

ablers that allow knowledge to flourish and grow: *technology, culture, leadership,* and *measurement.*[12]

The inner orbit consists of key processes for knowledge management: adapting, collecting, identifying, creating, sharing, applying, and organizing. These processes depicted in the inner orbit can be categorized according to the object and process views. Identifying, Collecting, and Organizing processes pertain to amassing and managing a body of knowledge. Creating, Sharing, Applying, and Adapting address processes for creating and renewing that knowledge.

Nonaka and Takeuchi also approach knowledge in both its object and process aspects in their knowledge conversion process. The four conversion modes they identify produce four types of knowledge *content:* sympathized, conceptual, operational, and systemic. Thus, the process or "spiral" of knowledge creation results in knowledge objects.[13] In the knowledge spiral *process,* knowledge is amplified as it circulates from individuals through work groups, and finally through the entire organization.

Nonaka and Takeuchi also identify five organizational "enablers," that are more abstract than the Andersen/APQC model, yet are quite relevant for a view of knowledge as system. The enabling conditions they have identified are: intention, autonomy culture, fluctuation, requisite variety, and redundancy. These concepts are drawn from systems thinking and cybernetics. Thus, their exploration of knowledge addresses both object and process aspects. In addition, they have also thought through the cybernetic and systems aspects of knowledge. We will take a closer look at the systems view in Chapter 6.

As general models of knowledge, both of these approaches have value for thinking about important aspects of knowledge creation and management. However, neither of these address the multi-faceted nature of knowledge itself, treating "knowledge" as an undifferentiated mass. Yet, all knowledge is *not* alike. We must probe still more deeply into the knowledge universe.

Time, Knowledge, and Action

There are three key relationships to explore to comprehend the domain of knowledge. These relationships are important to understand, both within each area and among the three areas themselves (Table 3.3). Let's take each set of relationships in order, then we will look at the dynamic relationship among all three.

TABLE 3.3 Three Key Relationships.

How does	*LEARNING*	relate to	*KNOWLEDGE?*
How does	*PERFORMANCE*	relate to	*ACTION?*
How does	*ATTENTION* (*Consciousness*)	relate to	*TIME AND SPACE?*

Knowledge and Learning

Processes for knowledge creation can be simply thought of as "learning." *Learning is defined as gaining knowledge, comprehension, or mastery through experience or study.* Defining the processes of acquiring or creating knowledge as *learning,* allows us to distinguish between knowledge as a process and knowledge as an object. Methods for gaining knowledge can be viewed separately from those used to organize, sort, catalog, and otherwise process an existing body of knowledge.

When we decide to acquire knowledge, we require learning processes to support that effort. Our intention to learn determines the shape of our knowledge. Different intentions around learning result in different bodies of knowledge. In the same way, different types of knowledge require different learning processes. Skill-based knowledge, such as filling out a form, may only require a demonstration and a bit of practice. Theoretical knowledge, however is much more learning intensive. It requires research processes, in-depth study, and critical discussion with experts. Acquiring professional knowledge of business strategy development, for example, involves many learning processes. A good strategist acquires an academic degree in business or a related field, gains experience as a manager, and might undertake an apprenticeship with corporate executives.

Figure 3.5 shows this relationship between knowledge acquisition and the variety of learning processes required. Knowledge Target A requires only minimal learning processes. Knowledge Target B requires more extensive or sophisticated learning processes.

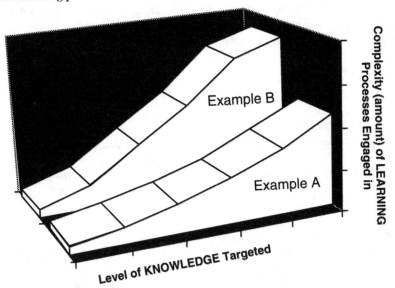

FIGURE 3.5 Knowledge and Learning.

Action and Performance

Another key relationship is that between performance and action. This is a similar relationship to the one described between knowledge and learning. The targeted level or type of performance results in a distinct group of actions or activities that will support the desired performance. The performance goal or desire is the *intentional* aspect, resulting in actual behaviors and actions people take to support that performance goal.

Here's an example. A weekend golfer would not engage in nearly as many activities around the game of golf as a seasoned professional golfer. The professional, having a higher performance goal, would engage in much more practice, study, and supporting technologies, such as video feedback. The simpler performance goal results in fewer visible activities. Increasing performance demands generate more activity. In Figure 3.6, the lower performance goal and supporting activities would be example A, while the more intensive performance focus would be example B.

Time-Space Horizons and Consciousness

Another relationship that is critical in understanding both performance and knowledge is the relationship between our attention and time and space. This is a more abstract relationship, but it is actually quite simple. *The time-space horizon that we experience at any given moment depends on where we place our attention.*

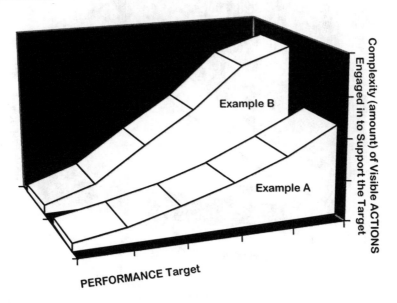

FIGURE 3.6 Action and Performance.

Attention is the *intentional* aspect of consciousness.[14] At the risk of over-simplification we could say, if we are not paying attention, then we are acting unconsciously. So, where our attention is, there also is consciousness. Our sense of space is related to our awareness of time, both on a psychological level and in physical reality, as we have learned from quantum physics.

We know our experience of time and space has a great deal to do with our attention. We have all had the experience where we became absorbed in a project without realizing that many hours have passed. Our attention was totally on the moment. One paradox of time is that the immediate moment opens to the infinite, so when we are completely in the moment we experience time-lessness. When our mind moves off the moment, then we move into a different time sense.

A wide range of time awareness is available to us. We can shift attention instantly by simply thinking of a different time-space dimension. As shown in Figure 3.7, our time horizon can be narrow, as in example A, or very wide, as in B, depending on where we place our attention.

The time horizon is important for understanding both knowledge and performance. The relationship of time to knowledge relates to the flux of knowledge through time. From a longer time perspective, we see the historical development of knowledge and the seamless processes of its manifestation. When our view of knowledge is from a very short time perspective, then knowledge begins to look more solid. We feel we can set boundaries around it and therefore treat it as an object.

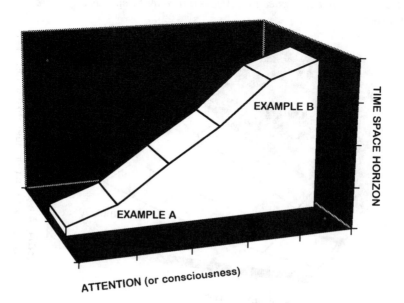

FIGURE 3.7 Attention (Consciousness) and Time-Space.

Time is one of the boundaries we place around knowledge. We will ask for knowledge in terms of this month's budget report, last year's profit and loss, long-term forecasts, press releases going back two years, and so forth. Any researcher knows that time is one of the defining factors for how much "knowledge" they are expected to produce.

The time horizon is also important for our performance focus. Different measures of performance address different *time* views of that performance. A short term inefficiency may actually mean a long-term gain for some types of performance. Slowing down a process for the sake of quality at one point may mean a huge cost or time savings farther down the line. In a short-term perspective, the performance goal or value may be very different from the perspective in the long-term.

From Clock Time to Human Time

Our traditional view of time is as clock-time, where past, present, and future are all separate and distinct from each other. Clock-time is a hard-task mistress. Our relationship to clock-time is adversarial, as we struggle to cram our activities into its narrow confines. However, the clock-time approach negates *human time*, where in actual experience the past, present, and future are all inter-related.[15] Past, present, and future are all right here in the present moment. The present moment is the only place they really exist, for it is only our *awareness* that places something as past, present, or future. In contrast to clock-time, our actual experience of human time is naturally more organic than linear. However, we have conditioned ourselves so strongly by the clock that we seldom experience our natural time rhythms. Even our work spaces insulate us from the rhythm of nature, the seasons, and the turn of the day.

In a social sense, however, we are experiencing a profound shift in our experience of time. As communication technologies collapse all the space on earth into our desktop computers, our perception of time is beginning to move from monochronic (clock time) to polychronic (organic). Monochronic time means paying attention to and doing only one thing at a time. Polychronic time means being involved with and experiencing many things at once.

This shift in our sense of time holds tremendous import for our culture and the way we experience our work. Yet, time is one of the most misunderstood performance factors in the world of business. Once again, like the ancient mariners, we find that to master the Knowledge Era, we must reach a new understanding of time. If we can experience a more organic relationship with time we will discover a more dynamic, evolving relationship with knowledge and action as well.

So, our attention determines much more than just what kind of time or space horizon becomes our focus. Time and space also serve as boundaries for knowledge and determine our performance focus.

The Dynamic Relationship of Time, Action, and Knowledge

Now let's look at the dynamic relationship among all three of these. The diagram in Figure 3.8 depicts these three aspects in continual flow and relationship. Time, knowledge, and action are interdependent. This means that when our experience of one changes, the others change as well.

We might think of this relationship using the analogy of Einstein's special theory of relativity. Einstein's theory demonstrates that aspects of reality appear to vary, depending on the viewpoint (or state of motion) of different observers. This same relativity theory also tells us that space and time are not two separate things, but that together they form space-time. Another expression of this theory is that energy and mass are simply two different forms of mass-energy.[16]

The theory of relativity tells us that motion is always relative to something else. In business, motion relates to how we are performing a particular task. So, when we think about the relationship of time, action, and knowledge in a business sense, we realize that any aspect of performance we address is linked with something else.

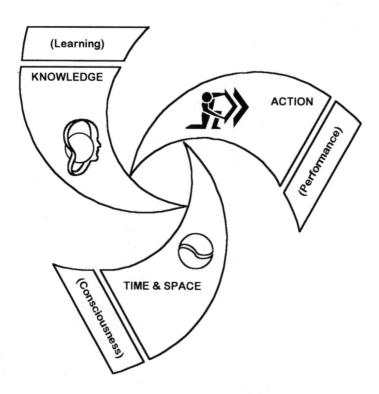

FIGURE 3.8 Time, Knowledge, and Action.

First of all, performance links to some measurement of time. Think *quarterly reports, production schedules, words-per-minute, cycles per second.* We always link performance to time. However, we do this so automatically that we just don't think about it much.

At the same time, performing a task relies on a particular body of knowledge, skill, and expertise. So performance is also relative to the knowledge required for successful completion of the task. What this all adds up to is a *continuum* of time, knowledge, and action, where one cannot exist without reference to the other two. This at least holds true for the actions of living beings capable of learning.

The interrelationship of time, knowledge, and action means when our experience of one changes, the other two change as well. This relationship is why it is so difficult to unravel performance challenges. It is all relative—relative to where we place our attention. Since individuals vary in their values and cognitive comfort zones, we all tend to pay attention to very different performance aspects as well. More importantly, not understanding these relationships leads to unrealistic expectations of how quickly we can master certain tasks.

These differences in attention often appear to put our goals into conflict. However, when we understand this continuum we realize that our various vantage points are not wrong, just different. In those differences lie valuable insights into how we can meet a wide range of performance challenges in our organizations, thus expanding our capabilities.

In the next chapter we will take a closer look at these different vantage points. Each has a very different time perspective, a different knowledge and learning mode, and supports a particular aspect of individual, group, and organizational performance.

Information absorbs the attention of the recipient. Therefore an overabundance of information creates a deficit of attention.

Jeff Hire, Owens Corning Fiberglas

CHAPTER 4

Seeing Patterns of Knowledge, Learning, and Performance

If we are to navigate the Knowledge Era successfully, one of the basic tools we will need is a map of the territory. A good conceptual map is invaluable for helping us deal with complexity. Conceptual maps, usually called *frameworks* or *models*, help us understand organizational performance. We use such maps for everything from strategic planning to work flow analysis and human resource planning.

There are many fields of knowledge that contribute conceptually to our understanding of knowledge and learning in organizations. However, we have the same dilemma as in any field of interest, the information available can be overwhelming. One of the characteristics of the Knowledge Era is that knowledge in any field multiplies so rapidly it is hard to stay abreast of the thinking. Here are just a few arenas that deal with questions of mind, intelligence, learning, and knowledge (Figure 4.1).

My own effort to integrate these fields of thought resonates with larger social struggle to master the Knowledge Era. Many scientific fields are beginning to overlap and combine. We must move more and more toward collaboration, joining forces in new partnerships to build knowledge and reach shared understanding. In our urge to synthesize and integrate, important skills are surfacing that will carry us into the future.

I have learned much from pivotal thinkers in all these fields of expertise, those who have thought deeply about cognition, learning, and complexity. Over time, I began comparing different frameworks and conceptual models from various thinkers. As I explored these different ideas I began to wonder, *"How do we already understand knowledge? What do we do intuitively and naturally to integrate knowledge and deal with complexity? What do different ideas about knowledge and complexity have in common?"*

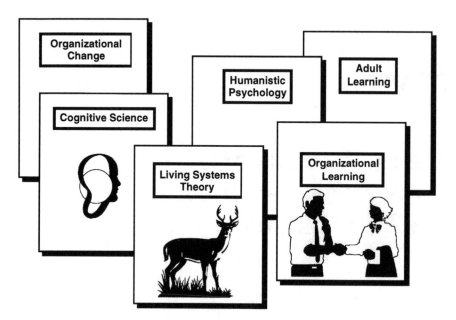

FIGURE 4.1 Fields of Knowledge.

Seeking the Pattern

As I read and learned and experimented, slowly a pattern began to emerge. Different theorists seem to organize their thinking along similar lines. The way someone describes the domain of knowledge in any one of these fields feels very much like the description from another. For example, Erich Jantsch, who writes so eloquently about self-organizing systems, describes several levels of *Managerial Focus* in organizational life.[1] Management theorist, Elliot Jacques articulates similar levels of complexity in his *Stratified Systems* theory.[2] In the psychological field, the *Levels of Consciousness* described by transpersonal psychologist Ken Wilber[3] seem to resonate with Kohlberg's stages of *Moral Development*.[4] (Appendix 1 depicts a comparative analysis of these and other thinkers.)

The more I pondered different systems or models of complexity and cognition, the more it began to seem as if we were all in Plato's cave, pointing to the different shadows on the wall. In Plato's famous allegory of the cave, we mistake the shadows for reality. In the world of knowledge, too, we each think we have the whole picture, but perhaps we only see the shadow of a truer form.

We each operate from our own personal understanding of how we organize knowledge and complexity. Yet, think of how our communication would improve if we could see the common threads more clearly. Is there a way we can all turn to the center and work with the pattern itself? If we could, then we would be able to communicate much more efficiently around information management, knowledge building, and organizational learning.

I began to look, then, for the pattern that connects. In the spirit of the poet Adrienne Rich, I began to dive deep, not for the name of the thing, but for the thing itself. Or as the poet Rumi charges us, "You have pronounced the name: go, seek the thing named. The moon is in the sky, not in the water." (Of course, the moon itself is a reflector also.)

The Knowledge Archetype

When identifying underlying patterns we are attempting to reveal an *archetype*. Archetypes are basic human ways of organizing. They help us understand our experience and find our common humanity. We continually rediscover archetypes over time. Every culture and era seems to discover them anew.

Familiar geometric archetypes are squares, triangles, and circles. Design and architecture incorporate these elements all over the world. They often show up as teaching devices or models as well. Psychological archetypes surface in stories, such as the hero's journey, and in fundamental social structures, such as the relationship between mother and child. These archetypes communicate at fundamental, psychological and cognitive levels. Today, we are beginning to reveal the archetypal patterns of knowledge, learning, mind, and consciousness.

I began to see the possibilities for more effective communication and action—if only we could all turn to the light and work directly from the thing itself, the archetype. So I began to delve more deeply into those shadow structures, looking for the common thread, the pattern, at the core of our understanding.

Gradually the pieces began to fit together. I experimented with different diagrams, seeking to express the emerging pattern by using words that evoke an intuitive understanding of each aspect of knowledge or knowing. My learning community of colleagues and customers here and abroad experimented with me, challenged me, and helped shape the work. We began to explore applications at individual, group, and organizational levels.

The fabric of our knowledge about knowledge is still on the loom, being woven anew with each new discovery and breakthrough. At this point in our knowledging process we are all struggling for a common language, seeking the common threads. The Knowledge Archetype is the warp and woof of that fabric, the basic structure of knowledge and complexity underlying the rich embroidery of all our language, models, and descriptions. Perhaps there is another, deeper structure, or a different pattern, that will yet emerge from our collective conversation.

Knowledge Comfort Zones

Each aspect of knowledge supports particular tasks and operations. Certain knowledge structures are universal building blocks for achieving high performance, regardless of what specific business function is at hand. Neglecting any aspect of knowledge means lower productivity, rework, miscommunication, frustration, or delays.

We all have individual and organizational "comfort zones" where we excel. Our comfort zone is our preference for particular cognitive processes that help us master certain skills. Organizations, too, have different knowledge comfort zones, just as they have different cultures. The challenge for individuals, teams, and organizations is to expand their comfort zone and become effective in all the learning and performance modes.

Learning processes advance knowledge and expand the collaborative intelligence of an organization. Understanding how learning and performance link to the Knowledge Archetype helps people be more responsive to the evolving environment. In order to understand how all this works, however, we must first let go of some old assumptions about both learning and knowledge.

Building Knowledge

Think again of all those books. Most of what you know did not come from books at all. Most learning depends on our experiencing a personal model. For example, you learned to speak by hearing your family members speak. Your body posture probably reflects the person you observed the most as you learned to walk. As you grew up, you practiced thinking by following the thought processes of others around you while they reasoned or thought aloud. I certainly didn't learn to whistle from a book. I studied the way my Dad did it and experimented a lot.

We learn by imitation and practice, and what we imitate does not come from books as much as it comes from other people. When it comes to learning we need to let go of our assumption that most learning comes from formal education and books. Real learning comes from life itself.

Let's look at how we naturally process information and gather knowledge. First, we register some input—a piece of data. Then we go through a series of cognitive steps to situate that new information in our whole realm of understanding. Every step of the way we are making decisions, both conscious and unconscious, about what is relevant and useful, what we can safely ignore or discard, and identifying other information with which it belongs.

We can think of our own personal knowledge as a "web" of knowing where many thoughts, feelings, concepts, ideas, and beliefs weave together. We organize our knowledge by arranging it according to our mental models of how the world works. If this sorting mechanism does not operate efficiently, then we suffer "information overload." We feel the pressure of having too much to absorb and understand in too little time. Or perhaps information feels "hard to find" and somehow difficult to retrieve.

As we build knowledge or develop expertise, we undertake a variety of learning tasks. When we "learn" something, we draw on our deepest and most comprehensive understanding of how everything works to help us find the appropriate response to a piece of information. When we receive a new piece of information, we find the place it fits in our worldview by processing it through our sorting and linking-up processes. Then we stow it away until it is useful to us.

Some information fits nicely into our larger understanding of things and some does not. Many things we simply file away in a mental *Data* "cabinet" as stuff we know, but don't really need right now. We may even have some rather interesting strings of data that have grown too big for the *Data* cabinet. We mentally link these up with other pieces of data until those strings and groupings become *Information*. This natural linking and organizing process makes it easier to find things in memory when we need them.

When we have quite a lot of information about something and can discuss it intelligently, then we have *Knowledge* of that particular subject. If we really understand something we can also discuss it's *Meaning*, the way that it fits into the larger scheme of things and the ways it might be useful in other contexts. If we are self-reflective and have deeply explored the *Meaning* of something, then we may even contemplate the underlying *Philosophy* of the subject. If we are fortunate enough to have *Wisdom*, then we also understand the values and underlying intentions or purposes that are operating.

There is also an additional realm of knowing described in esoteric and spiritual traditions, the level of *Union* or direct experience. In the perennial philosophy of Aldous Huxley,[5] this is an ineffable experience of the ultimate that defies description. (Thus the experience lies beyond the realm of ordinary knowledge, since it cannot be communicated.) This direct experience of union or oneness might be accompanied by a particularly blissful and peaceful feeling state. The feeling state might also be a profound sense of synergy or communion.

Union experiences are often more a gift of grace, rather than the result of a deliberate learning process. However, the *Union* domain is the ultimate integrative and expansive space that allows us to shift our worldview by moving to a different value set. The feeling state of synergy and communion results in a value system that includes the health and vitality of the larger society, the environment, and the planet.

These aspects of knowledge, and the levels of complexity they encompass, are the Knowledge Archtype (Figure 4.2). The concentric circles denote that each level is embedded in a larger context. The perspective of each successive order of complexity is larger and more inclusive than the one before, allowing us to integrate previous orders of knowledge. You might think of this as stepping progressively up the rungs of a ladder. Each step brings us a wider, clearer, more inclusive field of vision.

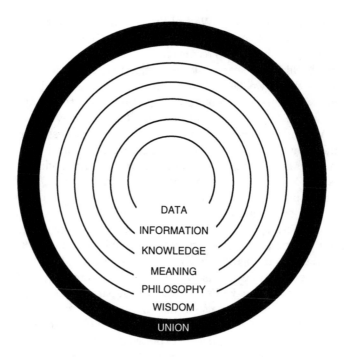

FIGURE 4.2 **The Knowledge Archetype.**

- *Data* floats like so many whitecaps in a larger sea of Information. Data becomes Information through linking and organizing with other data.
- *Information* becomes Knowledge when it is analyzed, linked to other information, and compared to what is already known.
- *Knowledge* operates in the larger social context of Meaning, which encompasses archetypal patterns and forces, as well as our social and cultural biases and interpretations.
- *Meaning,* in turn, is embedded in the larger and more abstract realm of Philosophy, which is the broad territory of assumptions, beliefs, and theories about how things work.
- *Philosophy* and the systemic thinking that typifies this level are embedded in the yet more inclusive Wisdom perspective of values.
- *Wisdom* enfolds our values and purpose. It encompasses the totality of our worldview.
- *Union* is an open, all inclusive, expansive feeling state of oneness enabled by the intellect that allows us to understand and change our values in relation to the ultimate good.

The progression of knowledge, of course, is seldom as neat in real life as it is described here. Sometimes our thought processes do unfold in an orderly fashion. At other times we may experience the quantum leap of a creative breakthrough. For example, we might suddenly switch from focusing on details and minutia to a spontaneous insight involving overall patterns. Remember, too, that knowledging is a collaborative enterprise. We continually forge and temper our knowledge universe in the creative fire that erupts where one mind meets with another. Just as conversations can sometimes skip all over the knowledge map, so also might knowledging happen in discontinuous jumps.

Nature has designed our cognitive process so that we cycle through all these domains of knowing as we process information. The Knowledge Archetype also correlates to theories of brain development, such as those of Paul MacLean.[6] He suggests that as we have evolved as a species, we have developed far beyond the basic instinctual processes of the "reptilian" lower brain. Our middle brain, or "mammalian" brain, processes input at the more emotional level. The outer brain, the neocortex, handles abstract thinking. The neocortex is figuratively our "thinking cap" of abstract reasoning. In the diagram of the Knowledge Archetype (Figure 4.2), you will see the more abstract, complex, and integrative processes depicted at the outer levels, just as the neocortex is the outermost mass of brain tissue.

In this framework, every aspect of knowledge is interdependent on the others in our universe of knowing. It is important to understand this quality of *embeddedness*. For example, the *Wisdom* level of values and purpose interpenetrates and influences each of the other levels, including the level of *Data*. When we accumulate data, it is not readily apparent that values are influencing how we collect data. Yet, our values and assumptions act as "gatekeepers," determining what information we allow in or what we reject and dismiss as not relevant.[7] Our philosophy, meaning our mental models or value-based constructs about how the world works, influences what we observe and how we organize our experience.

At the same time, *Data* serves as a reality check, acting as feedback to validate or challenge the assumptions we hold dear. While our value gatekeepers can indeed hold feedback at arm's length, over time a critical mass of conflicting data can challenge prevailing beliefs. So, our values and *Philosophy* are also influenced by and dependent on data. Each level is interdependent with the others.

An Example

I admire a painting and learn the name of the artist (a piece of *Data*). Later, I learn that the artist is one of a number who painted in a particular style, let's say I learn the artist is one of several French Impressionists. (Now I have some *Information*.) I decide I like this style of painting and begin to learn about other French Impressionists, and some of the particulars about their lives and work. (I now have *Knowledge* of French Impressionists.) Then, I begin to learn about the period in which they worked and how they were making particular kinds of political and artistic statements, particularly relevant to their times and culture. (I am exploring the *Meaning* of their art.)

Continued

(Continued)

I am quite taken with the power of the images and begin to find timeless messages about light, about the way we perceive, and how we experience color and movement. I notice how these artists challenged assumptions about what makes a work of art. (Now we are in *Philosophy*.) At a deep level of experience of their work, I sense a shift in my own perceptions of reality and move to a finer appreciation of the light and movement around me. (Ah, yes, *Wisdom*.)

Note that, in the example, I begin to experience a degree of fluidity in my own perceptions at about the level of *Philosophy*, as I begin to enter more deeply into the interior thought world of the artists. If we think of *Wisdom* as encompassing our entire worldview, then, as we explore more deeply into values, our worldview actually begins to shift as well. The discovery process of gathering information, combined with deep reflection, leads to a profound shift of perspective and a new set of values. Thus, the full learning experience is transformative.

The example also illustrates the embeddedness of each aspect of knowledge. An aesthetic *value (Wisdom)* leads me into learning about the French Impressionists in the first place. My worldview of values, assumptions, and beliefs determines what *Data* and *Information* I pay attention to. At the same time, my experience of French Impressionism is enlivened and enriched by my growing body of *Knowledge*, thus influencing my *values*.

Each mode of knowing and learning presents its own particular cognitive challenges. Thinking processes are very different for each domain. In addition, the types of questions and tasks addressed are also different. Mastery of each learning mode is demonstrated in different types of performance.

If we try to answer a question at the *Meaning* level by bombarding it with simple *Data*, we are doomed to failure. For example, compiling statistics about births is not going to be particularly helpful in deciding whether to have children. Also, learning about economic systems probably would be extraneous if we are trying to reconcile our bank balance.

Knowledge and Learning in Groups and Organizations

The ways we receive, process, and communicate information usually work unconsciously at the individual level. As individuals we master advanced thinking skills through education, self-reflection, and discourse.

An organization (which is composed of many individuals) faces a significantly more difficult task when trying to master knowledge and learning. There is a quantum leap in complexity. The difficulty stems from the sheer numbers of people and groups who need very different kinds of knowledge to support their work. In addition, the communication and learning processes around information and knowledge are much more complex at the group level. Each

The Egg Analogy

FIGURE 4.3 The Egg Analogy.
An organic analogy that comes to mind for this model is an ordinary egg. At the center of the egg are little bits of *Data* in the form of genes. These genes are strung together in coded strands of *Information* called DNA. The entire arrangement, woven into a beautiful double helix, holds all the *Knowledge* of the completed form. The DNA itself is embedded in a chemically-balanced nucleus and nourishing yolk. So, full genetic development depends on context, much in the way our culture and community shape the *Meaning* of our lives. Surrounding the yolk is the white of the egg, representing the integrative yet abstract aspect of *Philosophy*. The shell represents the unifying aspect of our Wisdom worldview that holds the whole thing together. The larger environment surrounding the egg represents the totality of *Union*.

mode of knowledge thrives on different communication modes. Each has its own language for problem solving. Further complications arise in times of stress and when time-frames are short.

Before shifting gears to look at knowledge building at the group level, however, there is an important assumption that we need to explore. That assumption is that there are basic similarities between individual learning and group learning. This assumption hangs on the fact that everything known is known by *somebody*. Organizations are composites of individuals who embody knowledge. This leads some people to assume that group learning is very much like individual learning.

Trying to understand group processes by first looking at individuals is an accepted way to begin an inquiry, but there is a trap in this approach. The trap is that collaborative processes may be very different from individual ones. Frameworks and models that hold true for individuals can fall apart when applied to groups, and vice-versa. A collection of individual intelligences is *not* the same as group intelligence, and at this point in history we do not know a great deal about exactly what those differences are.

As I indicated in Chapter 1, we are still in the early stages of research into collective learning and knowledge building. There is an inherent danger in our attempts to describe the characteristics of organizational knowledge building at this point in time. The best we can do at this point is propose a *theory* that we can test in practice. A theory is really a best guess about how things work. We can expect that the theory will be tested, modified, and changed over time. After all, we no longer believe the earth is flat. (We also no longer believe it is perfectly round.)

We are not operating blind, however. The Knowledge Era has been building momentum for the last fifty years. In that time we have come to understand quite a bit about the society of an organization and the mental processes of managers and workers. One thing we do know is that, at the group level, the socialization process is critical. Individuals continually refine their own understanding by seeking shared understanding with their fellow workers.

Linking Knowledge, Learning, and Performance

If we are to apply this archetype-based theory of knowledge and performance to organizations, then we would expect that advancing learning and knowledge requires *conscious* effort in every knowledge domain. Since the modes are on a continuum of increasing complexity and integration, there are different learning, information processing, and knowledging dynamics for each one. Organizations that are serious about knowledge can attempt to understand these dynamics and consciously map strategies in their everyday tasks and projects to master the necessary learning.

Each aspect of knowledge or knowing has a corresponding *learning* activity that supports it. Learning leads to changes in behavior and performance. Since learning is demonstrated by improved *performance, each learning mode supports a different performance focus.* So, we can now carry the knowledge archetype a step farther. We can link different types of learning to the performance challenges a manager or team might face in the course of their work.

While we are exploring relationships, let us not forget that knowledge and action are also connected with time. In Table 4.1 you will notice that each learning and performance mode also has a different time perspective.

Once we make these linkages between knowledge, time, learning, and performance, we can begin to distinguish some of the important features of the knowledge universe of an organization. It becomes apparent that the underlying

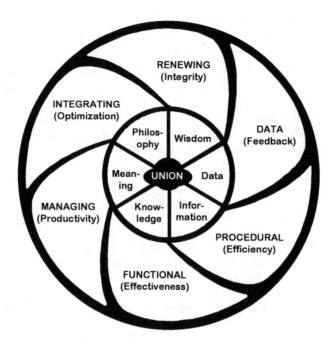

FIGURE 4.4 Learning and Performance Framework

The ultimate goal of those procedures is not of concern in this mode, just their efficiency.

Processes for converting tacit *Procedural* knowledge to explicit shared knowledge are straightforward. *Procedural* knowledge can easily be codified into written sequences, linear schematics, and quantitative measures. Guides and technical manuals communicate written sequences. Linear schematics and flow charts capture each step of a procedure, such as filling out a form or machining a part. Simple conformance measures—such as quantity, length, speed, and temperature—can easily be established and checked for conformance. Learning processes focus around tactile skills, practice, and transfer of information in very tangible forms. Short-term time horizons mean a narrow and very specific performance focus.

At the other end of the spectrum we find that *Renewing* performance is demonstrated by the integrity of the organization in fulfilling its purpose. Processes of knowledge creation involve identifying organizational purpose, developing a vision for the future, articulating the mission of a team or organization, and defining organizing principles. *Renewing* performance measures involve longer time-frames and value judgments. They are difficult to quantify with numbers, so they are much more qualitative.

The process of converting *Renewing* knowledge from tacit to explicit and back again, requires extensive socialization. This is quite different from *Procedural* knowledge, which one or two people can develop, codify, and put into communicable form. *Renewing* learning processes require group dialogue and social learning events such as planning retreats or scenario building.

In the following Chapters we will take a closer look at these relationships for each of the seven aspects. Each mode has its own language and uses different tools for problem solving. We will address some of the specific success factors and best practices that are critical for each mode.

A Note About *Union* Performance

People are often curious about how the *Union* aspect of performance is demonstrated in organizations. Some companies support this performance mode by fostering good citizen alliances with the community, or aligning strategy with deep ecological awareness. Examples of companies that have performance capability at the *Union* level are Ben and Jerry's and The Body Shop. Such companies have strategies of social and environmental responsibility. They act on the belief that their own success as a company depends on the health and success of the larger community and planetary environment.

A few years back Western culture did not highly value this aspect of performance. Today it is becoming increasingly important to demonstrate a larger sense of values and purpose in order to attract quality employees and loyal customers. As we expand our sense of community to include the good of all people and the planet, we have begun to define a new aspect of business performance.

In order to be a high-performing learning organization, work processes must incorporate conscious and deliberate attention to every aspect of knowledge. Unlike linear models that impose a particular order of activity, this framework helps illuminate the natural learning patterns that underlie work processes, human behavior, and organizational systems. Now we will turn our attention to some of the ways this framework is useful for enhancing performance.

CHAPTER 5

Knowledge Archetypes in Action

When we appreciate the multi-model nature of organizational performance and learning, the challenges of knowledge management become more readily apparent. American business culture traditionally has valued only a few of these knowledge domains. We have paid the most attention to the *Data*, *Information*, and *Knowledge* modes, where the procedural and functional work of organizations takes place.

More recently, we have begun to appreciate that company culture and the social context of work has a big impact on productivity. We are paying more attention to how effectively people work together. So we now have some appreciation of the *Meaning* level, where many management challenges deal with culture, context, interpretation of situations, and social dynamics.

At a more strategic level, mission and value statements are basic tools for fostering cohesiveness and alignment. Such purposeful statements reflect the organizational *Wisdom* underlying the creation of the business. More recently yet, we are beginning to appreciate how our underlying *Philosophy* and assumptions, our "mental models," define and influence the organization.

We are beginning to shape a larger, more complex, picture of a viable, responsive, efficient, and well-managed organization. All these modes of learning and knowledge creation contribute to an organization as it grows, evolves, and continually shapes its larger environment.

Supporting Performance

Peak performance requires a clear understanding of processes for creating, sustaining, sharing, and renewing knowledge for each mode. It is easier to determine human resource and learning needs at both individual and group levels by analyzing decision-making processes, knowledge needs, skill requirements, performance measures, and learning processes for each performance aspect. In one case, a manager asked a quality control supervisor to use the data from her division to identify patterns and trends. When she analyzed the request using the framework, she saw that the task involved skills that were two levels removed from where the work group typically focused their work. All their usual tasks required *Procedural* skills. The new work would require *Managing* skills for analyzing patterns and trends. By using the framework, she was able to plan and communicate the developmental requirements for her staff to accomplish the new task.

The real test for any framework, of course, is its robustness. How useful is it across multiple settings? How many different situations does it lend itself to in problem solving? What follows are a few examples of how the Learning and Performance Framework is being used to understand knowledge building, learning, and performance in organizations.

Building Knowledge Products at Chevron

Chevron's information management services group faces a challenge that many internal support services are dealing with in this time of intense competition, shrinking margins, and budget constraints. They have been asked to move from being a cost center to becoming a profit center within Chevron.

At the same time, a number of different things are impacting their unit. For one thing, they had been losing a considerable percentage of their service requests for data and information. People were beginning to access databases and other information providers through their own computers. So the information service providers were realizing competitive pressures for perhaps the first time.

The group also was not managing their contracting processes very well. Customers would make a request, but when the services group responded, they were either providing something other than what the customer really wanted, or they were underestimating the time involved and losing profitability. People in the company often seemed unaware of services, or had unrealistic expectations of what they would receive.

At the same time, CEO Ken Derr had been steadily guiding the company toward a strategic appreciation of knowledge building and becoming a learning organization. If the Information Services group could demonstrate how their services advance these strategic initiatives, then their perceived value inside the company would rise accordingly.

In response to these challenges the group began to carve out a new direction. They began looking for ways they could create strategically aligned information links to their internal customers. To do this, they realized they would need to expand their traditional library and information services to include value-added products and services that support knowledge building.

Early in this process, we worked with the team to explore the underpinnings of a knowledge-based enterprise. As they worked with the Knowledge Archetype they began to see possibilities for adding value with their services. One team member said, "We have been acting as data order-takers, but what our customers need are *knowledge navigators*. People need our help to find their way through all the new information technologies and build the knowledge they need to do their work."

"You're right," said another. "We need to focus on the added value we can bring by doing more sophisticated knowledge integration and analysis."

A key action step in this new direction was developing, publishing, and distributing a service value "portfolio" featuring services supporting knowledge creation at the various levels. As providers of information services, this internal business provides a variety of products and services to business units within Chevron. At the initiative of team leader, Mary Ann Whitney, they used the knowledge framework to create a guide for their information consultants to use when estimating and contracting for services (Table 5.1):

TABLE 5.1 Guide for Knowledge Products.[1]

PERFORMANCE FOCUS	SUPPORTING KNOWLEDGE PRODUCTS
Data	Statistics, financial data
Procedural	Written procedures, standards, specifications, regulations
Functional	Studies identifying best practices, graphs, historical data
Managing	Business plans, budget information, issues and trend analysis
Integrating	Strategic plans, systems maps, knowledge maps, guides to expertise, competitive analysis
Renewing	Values and vision statements, leadership trends
Union	Social, environmental, and international political issues and positions.

Several of the group's new strategic goals grew directly out of this new way of thinking about their role. In addition, they began to identify their own knowledge and performance gaps. They discovered improvement needs around documenting core service work processes, developing contracting and consulting skills, and deepening their expertise in complex analysis. As they began to understand the different levels of knowledge work required for each product they improved their cost estimates and gained more consistency in their deliverables.

As a result:

- The unit's cost recovery trend is upward.
- Customer response and satisfaction have measurably increased.
- They are expanding internal and external partnerships to add value.
- They are achieving recognition for their vital role in knowledge creation.
- They are developing new individual and team competencies for the future.

Managing a Project

As teams become more self-managed, it is important for larger numbers of people to understand the performance challenges within the scope of their projects. The actual tasks of each performance mode could be completed by any team member, according to how the group organizes its work. For example, although managers often have responsibility for *Managing* level tasks, this does not mean only managers have those concerns. The entire team has a stake in the superb performance of the whole. Using the Learning and Performance Framework invites a variety of ways of organizing projects beyond the traditional roles and planning models.

Example

I recently worked with a cross-functional team developing recommendations for increasing diversity. This was a high-visibility pilot project in one business unit that was likely to be implemented across an entire large, multi-division utility company. One important two-day work session with the team required working at every single knowledge area of the framework. No doubt these steps will feel very familiar as I describe part of the process. They are found in most business planning processes.

Renewing

Before we began work, we visited the company *vision* and clarified the *purposes* and *values* of the team.

Managing

We made sure we understood the *scope* of our work and defined the *goals* and *objectives* of the project. We discussed the *constraints, resources,* and *influences* we were dealing with in the organization and its *culture.* We defined the roles of team members and established group norms for working together.

Integrating

We uncovered our *assumptions* and made them explicit, so that people reading the recommendations would understand the thinking behind them. We developed *assumption statements* through *defining terms* and *clarifying language.* These values helped set *criteria* for decision-making. Throughout the work, we checked for *consistency with the underlying assumptions and beliefs.* We also considered how the recommendations would have an impact on other divisions and functions.

Data

We accessed *data* from a Best Practices *survey* of other companies.

Procedural

The survey results had been *compiled, analyzed,* and *organized* as a valuable *information resource* for the team. This resource was further shaped into a step-by-step workbook for thinking through all the relevant issues. The team then analyzed similarities and differences in their own *procedures and practices.*

Managing Again

The group worked with the data and information to identify key *trends* and *best practices.* We discussed differences in company *cultures and norms* that might be important. We considered the implications various actions would have on *management practices* and *cross-functional relationships.* We then determined goals and objectives to gain the highest leverage for change within the *context* of their own company culture and practices.

Functional

Finally, we moved to functional *recommendations,* including recommendations for *tracking results, developing or refining core processes,* and *implementing* the suggestions.

Note that the *order* of the tasks is *variable* according to need. This project was conducted as an iterative process, cycling continuously through all the learning modes. Any project is an opportunity to advance organizational learning. Work processes that cycle through all the learning modes can move quickly and deeply at the same time. This approach covers all the critical performance modes. It also allows deliberate work with assumptions, values, and operating principles where real breakthroughs can happen.

Frequently shifting gears to work in a different learning mode respects people's differences. Hanging out in only one or two modes for too long tends to exhaust team members who are not at home there. Working from the framework assures that all the critical performance modes will be addressed, and helps team members quickly move on to the next task. The sequence of the tasks is not as important as making sure that each knowledge area is covered.

Enhancing Team Performance

The Records Analytical Group of a major oil company was on the line. Their mandate: develop a record retention schedule for the entire company. This was a complex project involving multiple business units across the globe. It was their major project for the year, top priority. Yet, the project just wasn't getting off the ground.

Nothing was happening. Despite encouragement and support to work as a team, people were not pulling together. They were more involved in attending to their day-to-day responsibilities than tackling the team project. Behavior problems were starting to surface: finger pointing, hallway huddles, stalling, and excuses. Although they had recently experienced a training day focusing on personal working styles, they had not realized a breakthrough. They still felt stuck.

At this point, the work group leader suggested we guide the team through a learning day focused on team learning and performance. Part of the work was to help individual team members identify their own learning and performance comfort zones, using the *Learning Links* assessment instrument.[2] The group began to understand some of their different working preferences, gaining valuable insights into communicating with one another, based on the learning modes.

However, the major breakthrough came when we used the Learning and Performance Framework to analyze the project itself. Analysis of the project demonstrated that almost all the project tasks fell solidly in the *Procedural* and *Functional* knowledge areas. Yet, when people identified their own personal comfort zone, almost everyone on the team worked best at the *Integrating* level. We had a whole room full of natural systems thinkers trying to do a *Procedural* level project! No wonder they were stuck.

When the team came to this realization the relief was palpable. "No wonder we are not doing this project. It is two levels away from our comfort zone. We need help!" Everyone was laughing.

One of the company's internal quality consultants was participating in the learning day. The team contracted with him on the spot to give them the support, facilitation, and guidance they needed to bring the project in on time. Over the next several months they continued to focus on understanding their work together using the framework.

People began viewing their work group as a collaborative intelligence rather than a collection of intelligences. By understanding the comfort zones of one another, they redesigned their projects so people could not only work more at their optimal performance mode, but also could expand their skills. Focusing on team learning and knowledge competencies brought a new level of cooperation, appreciation, and mutual support that they had not achieved before. They completed the project on time and achieved company-wide recognition for the work they accomplished together.

Understanding Team Learning

Insight and understanding alone are not always enough to solve team performance problems. Every group of people is unique. Different groups require different solutions. In some cases, people just will not be able to work together successfully. Collaboration requires more than just understanding differences. It

TEAM BUILDING = creating
courteous behaviors, improving
communications, building strong
relationships

TEAM LEARNING = looking
outward to build knowledge
and looking inward to create
alignment -- together

FIGURE 5.1 From Team Building to Team Learning.

requires a variety of social and personal capabilities as well. Developing effective teams requires mastering a whole range of skills and team processes.

Team learning is different from team building. *Team building* focuses on interpersonal behaviors that improve communication and build strong relationships. *Team learning*, on the other hand, is a more inclusive term that includes team building. Team learning involves both looking inward to create alignment and looking outward to build knowledge—together.

Team learning develops as members of a work group learn to consciously reflect on their own learning processes. Team learning is not something that is done *to* or *for* a work group. Team learning is something people must do for themselves. If people do not know how to pay attention to their own group learning processes, then team learning will not move to more advanced levels.

Individual and team learning will happen whether people pay attention to it or not. However, if a group wants to maximize and deepen learning together, then it must be valued, appreciated, and attended to. Team learning is not mechanical, it is organic. Learning unfolds from the purpose and intent of the people involved. Team learning really begins when people ask, "What is it we are all here to do, *and why do we want or need to do it together?*"

Teams that learn together deliberately employ a variety of strategies to support their own learning. These strategies include such activities as:

- Documenting work processes and learning breakthroughs.
- Discussing the way they work together more reflectively than other teams.
- Learning to analyze and problem solve together.
- Visually mapping their thinking.

- Building in time for reflection, debriefings, and dialogue.[3]
- Continuously giving, asking for, and receiving feedback with each other ("360-degree feedback").
- Committing to learning by developing strategies and ground rules for learning behaviors.

Even though we can recognize team learning by observing these activities, there is no simple prescriptive formula for fostering team learning. Coaching and training in learning techniques can introduce learning behaviors. One example of team learning is the US Army's After Action Review process, a structured debriefing designed to help the group reflect and learn together. Similar processes are being introduced into companies for project teams. However, the only real requirement is a desire to learn and grow together. Such a commitment, combined with a willingness to experiment and inquire, will lead a team to its own learning breakthroughs.

The Learning and Performance Framework is but one tool for thinking about learning and performance. There are many other approaches that have value. Different processes and models may be more appropriate at a particular point in a team's progress. The real value in any framework is not that it provides a solution—it doesn't. The value of a framework lies in providing a common language for penetrating deep into the heart of critical questions.

Process Analysis for Increasing Learning and Enhancing Performance

One of the most useful aspects of the Learning and Performance Framework is that *it is not sequential*. Nor is it a hierarchy. Many other frameworks are developed as prescriptive step-by-step processes. Others are developmental hierarchies, suggesting an order of development, or implying that one level is more desirable or "advanced" than another. While the framework does have areas where more complex cognitive processes may be required, every mode is equally important for effective action.

Sometimes it is important to accomplish tasks in a certain order. In other cases, forcing a particular order may be counterproductive to the creative process of the work. The holistic approach of this model reinforces creative processes that evolve organically from *need* rather than an imposed order.

Any time we do a project we are learning and building knowledge. Moving from ordinary "light bulb" learning to the lightning bolt of "aha" learning depends on the design of the work or learning process. Let's look at two projects and map the processes for the larger learning patterns.

A powerful group learning process that often results in breakthrough thinking and innovation is conducting benchmarking studies to identify best practices. I have "mapped" two different processes for benchmarking using the Learning and Performance Framework to identify the type of learning taking place in each activity. The first performance pattern is a fairly typical bench-marking project. It focuses too narrowly on trying to find a "silver bullet" met-ric or performance measure. It overlooks critical questions in other performance modes that would identify management practices and organizational enablers supporting the best practice.

The second is a performance pattern developed using the Learning and Performance Framework. I have not provided detail on all the steps in the process, because what is important here is not how many steps are in a process, but the *learning pattern* for the process. Compare the two patterns.

Note that in the example of a Typical Benchmarking Process (Figure 5.2), the managers' choice of what to benchmark was *not* checked for integration with company strategy. This benchmarking approach did not include uncover-ing assumptions or conceptual models around the process. Nor did the team an-alyze existing performance measures. They gathered the study data without an integrative strategy, so the benchmark questions probably did not include use-ful context or system-level questions.

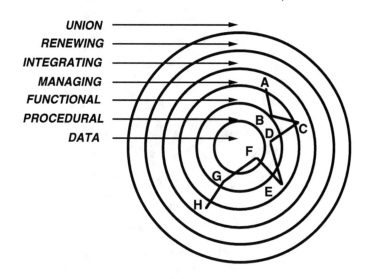

FIGURE 5.2 Typical Benchmarking Process.

Steps in the process

A. Managers decide what process to benchmark (*Managing*).
B. Analyze the process with flow charts and other quality tools (*Functional*).
C. Ask other Managers who they know at other companies (*Managing*).
D. Gather internal data regarding measurements (*Procedural*).
E. Invite other companies to benchmark (*Managing*).
F. Gather process data from other companies (*Data*).
G. Develop a comparative table of measurements (*Procedural*).
H. Set new goals for the process (*Managing*).

Observe the pattern. There was only *one* learning cycle in the process, and *two* important learning modes were skipped completely. Significantly, they are the two domains that people must explore for real breakthroughs in thinking. Without conscious work at the *Integrating* and *Renewing* levels, there cannot be the all important shift of mind where real change happens. Now compare the pattern to the next one (Figure 5.3).

This second benchmarking process has been consciously designed to evoke a transformational learning experience. Throughout all phases of a full study, *all* the levels are cycled through, not just once but several times. Each cycle includes conscious and deliberate thinking around the purpose of the work and the underlying conceptual frameworks and assumptions.

Even if such a learning process does not lead to radical changes, decisions will be solid, whatever courses of action or inaction are chosen. Choices result

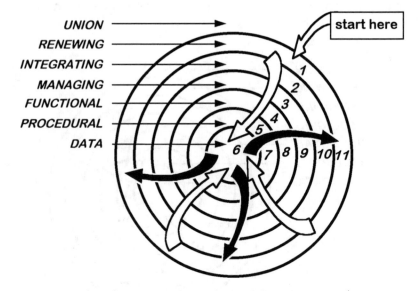

FIGURE 5.3 Benchmarking Process Design for Breakthrough Learning.[4]
Partial sequence of steps
1. Develop a purpose statement *(Renewing)*.
2. Discover the existing conceptual model of the team *(Integrating)*.
3. Create a criteria for effective best practices *(Managing)*.
4. Develop a research strategy *(Functional)*.
5. Conduct the study *(Procedural)*.
6. Collect the data *(Data)*.
7. Organize and display the data *(Procedural)*.
8. Compare to existing practices *(Functional)*.
9. Analyze the data to create a sample set of best practices and enablers *(Managing)*.
10. Revisit and challenge assumptions and conceptual maps *(Integrating)*.
11. Revisit purpose statement for desired outcomes of project *(Renewing)*.

from grounded and deliberate work around all the critical questions for performance. If breakthrough learning does occur, from this learning process virtually every aspect of work will change. Consider the following third example of a successful benchmarking study.

A large telecommunications company, faced with the challenges of deregulation and downsizing, undertook a benchmarking learning project. The purpose was to compare their measurement process for customer service satisfaction with other best-in-class companies. The team members elected to conduct the study and interviews themselves to deepen their learning experience. The project took nine months and included interviews or site visits with nine companies. The team came together with an open attitude, committed to making changes. Upon completion of the project, the team leader identified learning outcomes in every performance area. This systemic learning and change indicates that the learning experience was truly transformational. It also yielded a $5 million R.O.L. (Return On Learning) from a $70,000 study. Here are a few of the key outcomes realized through the learning process (Table 5.2):

TABLE 5.2 Learning Outcomes.

Performance Focus	Outcomes of Benchmarking Learning Process
Data	Found gaping holes in information on customers
	Able to demonstrate the need for certain types of data and details
Procedural	Kept some measures at business unit level
	Replaced some measures with new quality measures
	Developed new internal practices, such as answering phones by the second ring
Functional	New policies were created
	Staffing for the work group was reduced by several people
	Realized a 30% budget reduction
	Outsource expenses were reduced 60%
Managing	Created a whole new role for the department
	Redefined themselves as agents of change
	Funded initiatives for gathering new information
Integrating	Let go of old beliefs around performance and measurement
	Believe they are now operating from a new paradigm
Renewing	Created a completely new vision for their team
	See a new purpose as "catalyst that illuminates the void"

While the earlier two examples focused on individual and team learning, this example demonstrates a much wider impact. This involved the redesign and renewal of an entire functional unit. Implementing a complete change of direction such as this requires being able to address organization-wide issues. Benchmarking, at its best, is a renewal process that helps us discover more elegant ways of doing things and make wise choices.

Organizational Level Performance

Knowledge and learning provide very different lenses for understanding organizational performance. Yet, they are lenses that are perfectly compatible with many other ways of viewing people and work. A comprehensive strategic planning method includes processes that support learning and knowledge building for every performance focus.

As an example, AT&T's Global Business Communication Systems (GBCS) uses a pyramid model as a communication device that has the following elements in descending order:

> Vision
>> Mission
>>> Values
>>>> Objectives
>>>>> Strategic Plan
>>>>>> Tactical Business Plan
>>>>>> People

In their pyramid model, GBCS also shows supporting structures of

- Management Systems
- Business Processes

As this indicates, even though the language might be different, the Knowledge Archetype is solidly at work. The natural levels of complexity range from abstractions of vision, purpose, and values, to more tangible levels of strategic and business planning, to the straightforward operational modes of business processes.

Each of the Performance modes of the Framework is critical for organizational performance. High Performance across all levels results in an enterprise that is healthy, viable, self-organizing, and self-renewing. In Table 5.3 you can see the Low Performance Results for each element. This is the result when the mode is neglected.

TABLE 5.3 Low Performance Results.

PERFORMANCE FOCUS	ORGANIZATION RESULT IF LOW PERFORMING
Data	Ungrounded
Procedural	Inefficiencies and waste
Functional	Ineffectual work processes
Managing	Low productivity, conflict, and frustration
Integrating	Reactive and crisis-focused, sub-optimization
Renewing	Uninspired, lacking clear direction
Union	Self-serving, non-sustaining

Malcolm Baldrige Assessment

One organizational performance approach that has gained popularity in recent years is the Malcolm Baldrige Award Criteria. The Baldrige Award was developed by the U.S. Department of Commerce National Institute of Standards and Technology. Receiving the Award carries great prestige. It is traditionally presented by the President of the United States.

The Baldrige Award Criteria has consequently provided an important common language and framework for communicating about organizational performance. From Motorola to the U.S. Air Force, people in companies and organizations everywhere use the criteria assessment process to gauge excellence.

At first glance, the Baldrige Criteria does not appear to have an explicit learning and knowledge focus. Yet, when we analyze the Baldrige Criteria we find that, indeed, every single aspect of knowledge, learning, and performance is covered (Table 5.4). When we burrow down to the types of learning and performance supporting each criterion, the archetype emerges once again.

TABLE 5.4 The Knoweldge Archetype and The Malcolm Baldrige Award Criteria.[5]

Performance Focus (Allee)	Overall Baldrige Performance Categories	Specific Baldrige Award Criteria
DATA (Data)	3. Customer and Market Focus	3.1a Customer and Market Knowledge (see Integrating)
PROCEDURAL (Information)	4. Information and Analysis	3.2a Accessibility and Complaint Management 4.1a Selection and Use of Information and Data 4.3a Analysis of Data
FUNCTIONAL (Knowledge)	5. Human Resource Development and Management 6. Process Management	3.2b Customer Satisfaction Determination (process) 5.1a Work and Job Design 5.1b Compensation and Recognition 5.2a Employee Education, Training, and Development 5.3b Employee Support Services 6.1a Product and Service Design Processes 6.1b Production/Delivery Processes 6.2a Management of Support Processes
MANAGING (Meaning)	7. Business Results	2.1b Strategy Deployment 2.2a Strategy and Action Plans 2.2b Human Resource Plans

Continued

TABLE 5.4 *(Continued)*

Performance Focus (Allee)	Overall Baldrige Performance Categories	Specific Baldrige Award Criteria
MANAGING (Meaning)	7. Business Results	2.2c Performance Projection 4.2a Selection/Use of Comparative Information & Data 5.3a Work Environment 5.3c Employee Satisfaction 6.3a Management of Supplier and Partnering Process 7.3a Human Resource Results 7.4a Supplier and Partner Results
INTEGRATING (Philosophy)	2. Strategic Planning	2.1a Strategy Development 3.1a Customer and Market Knowledge (Scanning) 4.3b Review of Company Performance 7.1a Customer Satisfaction Results 7.2a Financial and Market Results 7.5a Company Specific Results 1.1a Leadership System
RENEWING (Wisdom)	1. Leadership	1.2b Community Involvement
UNION (Union)		1.2a Societal Responsibilities

It is understandable that most of the Baldrige Criteria group around the *Managing* and *Functional* levels. These have traditionally been more valued in American business. As operational levels, they are also very rich in detail. As our experience grows in systems thinking, we can expect to see additional performance criteria addressing that category.

It is also interesting to note how in the Baldrige model categories 3 and 4, which focus on data and feedback, work across multiple levels of performance. Metrics and measures by themselves are simply data. That data must be analyzed and applied to become knowledge. It is also important to understand that feedback and measurements are very different for *Procedural* level performance than for, say, *Integrating* or *Renewing* performance.

Performance Measures

We are beginning to realize that traditional, financial-based performance measures do not cover the full complexity of an enterprise. Measures are important. They are feedback that indicate how well a system is performing. They tell us how our experiments are doing. But without a balanced scorecard for measuring performance, we can easily focus in the wrong direction. A truly balanced scorecard addresses performance in all the key dimensions of performance. The Learning and Performance framework is an excellent device for thinking through strategic measures for performance.

These examples demonstrate how the Learning and Performance Framework can be used for assessing and improving performance in multiple ways. They show how we can begin to apply knowledge to knowledge itself. The framework provides a common task language that helps people understand the analytical tools and skills needed for working effectively, responding quickly, and moving creatively into the future.

In the next chapter we will look at how all these pieces come together in organizing for knowledge. Then we will look at each knowledge aspect in turn, exploring more deeply the underlying learning modes and the specific types of performance that result.

CHAPTER 6

Knowledge, Learning, and Organizations

Knowledge is always changing. In an organization, knowledge changes around products, services, processes, technology, structures, roles, and relationships. No sooner do we think we have identified a pattern of knowledge than a new one seems to appear. So, if this basic component of organizational intelligence is always changing, how do we organize to support it?

From an old, mechanistic perspective in thinking, we would try to design the optimum knowledge "machine." I'm not sure what that might look like. I have a mental picture of something like a giant fan that sucks in raw data at one end and blows out neat little knowledge packages at the other. However, knowledge at large is too complex and fluid to be designed, processed, and managed in such a fashion. Mechanistic thinking won't work.

From a new perspective in thinking, we would approach things a little differently. When we put on our system viewers, knowledge appears as a complex system. From this vantage point, we find some hard realities (or actually fuzzy realities) to face about knowledge.[1]

Tenets of Organizational Knowledge

1. *Knowledge is "messy."* In organizations, every aspect of knowledge is connected to everything else. You cannot neatly isolate the "knowledge" component of anything. Organizational knowledge relates to culture, structures, technology, and the unique configuration of individuals that make up the organization. Knowledge also sits in the larger social context of a national and global "knowledge environment." So, any attempt to identify knowledge factors faces an inherent messiness. In the knowledge universe, you cannot pay attention to just one thing. No matter how you try to isolate knowledge, you find something else clinging to it.

2. *Knowledge is self-organizing.* Every day knowledge is created, sustained, killed off, and renewed in an organization. Knowledge has a life of its own; it is a self-organizing entity. The "self" that knowledge organizes around is organizational or group identity and purpose.

3. *Knowledge seeks community.* Knowledge wants to happen, just as life wants to happen, and both want to happen as community. Nothing illustrates this principle more than the explosive growth of the Internet. Communities of knowledge are so powerful that they now involve people in conversation with each other all over the globe.

4. *Knowledge travels on language.* Language is the verbal blueprint of our experience. Without a word or a language to describe our experience, we cannot communicate what we know. Every mode of knowledge travels on a different language. Language initiates us into a particular world of experience. For example, traditional management uses the language of statistical control, inspection, and balance sheets. One is not "initiated" into management ranks without learning this language. Expanding organizational knowledge means we must expand the languages we use to describe our work experience.

5. *The more you try to pin knowledge down, the more it slips away.* It is tempting to try to tie up knowledge as codified knowledge, documents, patents, intellectual property, libraries, and databases. Yet, too much rigidity and formality lead to the unwanted side effect of stifling creativity and new knowledge development. This principle brings to mind the tragedy of King Midas, whose daughter turned to solid gold at his touch. He then "owned" a golden statue, but lost the living, breathing vibrancy of the daughter he loved.

6. *Looser is probably better.* Highly adaptable systems look sloppy, but the survival rate of diverse, decentralized systems is higher. This means we can waste resources and energy trying to control knowledge processes too tightly.

7. *There is no final solution in knowledge management.* The patterns of knowledge are always changing. The best approach or solution for the moment is one that keeps things moving along while keeping options open. Flexibility in approach and in thinking is a must. There are always different approaches to try. In fact, the on-going conversation about knowledge is much more important than coming up with the right answer.

8. *Knowledge does not grow forever—something eventually dies or is lost.* A number of people in knowledge management hold an unexamined belief that knowledge continuously grows. Yet, think how exhausting it would be to have endless growth. *Constant growth does not hold true in nature, and it does not hold true for knowledge.* There is a big difference between *advancing* knowledge and simply building knowledge. Unlearning and letting go of old ways of thinking, even retiring whole blocks of knowledge and expertise, contributes to the vitality and evolution of knowledge.

9. *No one is really in charge.* At the core, knowledge is a social process. Only people *together* make knowledge happen. No one individual makes knowl-

edge happen. What this means is that no one person can take responsibility for collective knowledge. Knowledge managers cannot really manage knowledge itself. However, they can and do help devise and support processes for acquiring, creating, sharing, and applying knowledge. A knowledge manager can also attend to strategies for removing barriers and creating a knowledge-sharing culture.

10. *You cannot impose rules and systems.* If knowledge is truly self-organizing, then the most important way you can advance it is to remove the barriers to self-organization. Knowledge will take care of itself in the right supporting environment. It is a waste of effort to create guidelines, rules, or technology systems that no one cares about or supports. It is more valuable to see what is working well and devise ways to support and enhance the natural processes.

11. *There is no silver bullet.* There is no one magical leverage point or best practice to advance knowledge and expand organizational intelligence. Knowledge must be supported at multiple levels and in a variety of ways if it is truly valued. Genuine solutions require a systems approach, careful thought, reflection, experimentation, and constant adjustment.

12. *How you define the knowledge "question" determines what and how you try to manage.* As we have already seen, the knowledge question can present itself in many ways. If an organization is concerned with ownership, then energy focuses on acquiring codified knowledge that can be protected with copyrights and patents. If people are concerned with knowledge sharing, then they emphasize communication flow and documentation. Concern with key knowledge competencies for the future leads to seeking more effective ways to create, adapt, and apply knowledge. Attending to *all* of these areas would reflect an extremely high value for knowledge and requires a great deal of commitment.

Given all that, there are still a number of ways that we can advance knowledge. It is possible to identify processes, structures, and organizational enablers that support the creating, sustaining, sharing, and renewing of knowledge.

The Learning Cycle

One of the most obvious cornerstones of knowledge building is understanding how people learn. We spend our whole lives learning. Learning is the process of integrating information and applying it to our changing needs. Learning consists of gaining new information and increasing understanding in order to do things better.

Learning, whether individual or group, occurs in cycles. The learning cycle has received a great deal of attention from cognitive psychology and advocates of learning organizations and several variations have been suggested. The learning cycle is basically a cybernetic model that regards learning as a process involving a series of experiments. Some of the best known work is that of David

Kolb.[2] E. Edward Deming also popularized a variation as the Plan-Do-Study-Act cycle. Other perspectives include John Redding and Ralph Catalanello who emphasize the importance of continual and deliberate learning cycles in organizations.[3] Most learning cycles fall into four phases generically described in Figure 6.1.

Learning cycles apply to individuals as well as groups. It is possible to go through learning cycles without reflecting or testing our ideas with another. However, something magical and synergistic begins to happen when we engage in learning with each other. Things begin to sizzle between two individuals as they build off the learning, knowledge, experience, questions, and aspirations of one another in a generative and co-creative manner.

When we expand our learning frame of reference to include teams or an organization, then the socialization or sharing factor at each stage becomes critical. For example, the knowledge creating spiral of Nonaka and Takeuchi emphasizes socialization processes that support knowledge creation and application.[4]

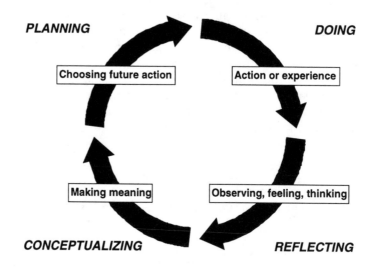

FIGURE 6.1 The Learning Cycle.

- *Doing* refers to an action, experience, or event. In collaborative learning, this is usually, but not always, a coordinated action that gives the group a common reference point.
- *Reflecting* means making observations about the event. Reflection is a key focus of activities such as the After Action Reviews of the military and other types of debriefs.
- *Conceptualizing* is the process of interpreting events and creating mental models or concepts to explain them.
- *Planning* is the phase where behavior is adjusted by making plans for future events or experiments. Then the whole cycle repeats as the learner initiates yet another *Action.*

Nevis, DiBella, and Gould suggest another variation on the organizational learning cycle that links learning more explicitly to knowledge.[5] They describe three stages of learning that progress through:

1. knowledge acquisition—development or creation of skills, insights, and relationships;
2. knowledge sharing or disseminating what has been learned;
3. knowledge utilization—integrating knowledge so it is broadly available and can be generalized to new situations.

These researchers also discovered that learning does not always occur in the linear fashion implied by a stage model. It can take place in informal, often unintended ways. Knowledge and skill acquisition take place through socialization and utilization. They emphasize that, "True knowledge is more than information, it includes the meaning or interpretation of the information."

Transformational Learning

Additionally, not all learning experiences are alike. Some are deeply transformational. *Transformational learning is a process of discovery and deep reflection that leads to profound shifts of direction, behaviors, values, beliefs, and operating assumptions.* Transformational learning is learning that causes a reordering of our worldview across the entire spectrum of knowledge and action. It leads to changes that are sweeping and systemic.

We can think of learning as a continuum from the ordinary "light bulb" variety to the profound reframing of a core understanding. Transformational learning is more like a powerful lightning bolt—learning that can unleash extraordinary power for changing our lives (Figure 6.2).

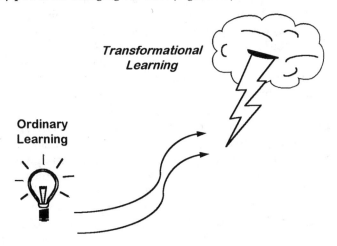

FIGURE 6.2 Transformational Learning.

On the personal level, a transformational learning experience might be triggered by a shock or jolt, perhaps a sudden change. The jolt could be a joyful event, such as a new baby. Sometimes people are prompted by such experiences to examine their lifestyle, their daily habits, their professional choices, their attitudes, virtually every aspect of their lives. If the experience is truly transformational, they may find, over a period of weeks or months, that they have shifted to a very different way of life. They will have a new foundation of different assumptions and beliefs that manifest as profound external changes.

A business example of transformational learning would be the experience at Canon when they found they were losing market share in the photography business. Through a deep learning process focused on defining and building core competencies, they shifted from thinking of themselves as a *photography* company to thinking of themselves as an *imaging* company. This led Canon into a completely new line of products where they quickly became a market leader in personal copiers.

Transformational learning becomes possible when a company develops the capacity to challenge and change its own assumptions and beliefs. Shifting underlying assumptions and beliefs can release tremendous new energy. For example, this type of self-questioning might lead a company to move from a narrow focus on customer satisfaction to a creative and renewing focus on customer delight. Customer satisfaction is functional in scope, limited to meeting needs. The idea of customer delight expands the concept to the realm of values and opens up many more innovative responses to the customer. As another example, Honda used the stretch metaphor of "Tallboy" to develop an innovative new car design for Japan.

The shift to the more expansive and creative realms of knowledge and learning is critical for long-term success. Without it, an organization will eventually lose its vitality by continuing to rely on structures and operating principles based on the successes of the past. Michael Marquardt and Angus Reynolds have traced the learning progression of companies that are moving into a global environment. The ones that are most successful in a global marketplace aggressively pursue a strategy of openness and learning.[6] As an organizational system begins to reflect upon itself, it becomes truly open to *both* its internal and external environments. Only then can it creatively and appropriately respond to a changing world (Figure 6.3).

Double-loop learning is advanced learning that involves varying degrees of self-reflection. Even though self-reflective learning occurs in the *Procedural* and *Functional* modes, the focus is on effective action rather than "the right" action. Once self-reflection begins to involve one's own basic assumptions and values, considering the context in which actions take place, then the quality of learning changes. Only these deeper levels of self-reflection allow dramatic shifts in one's worldview, values, and purpose. When basic assumptions change, then that deep shift is reflected in change at every other mode of action as well.

The degree of openness in the internal environment is an indicator of how much learning takes place. People need to be able to express their views through

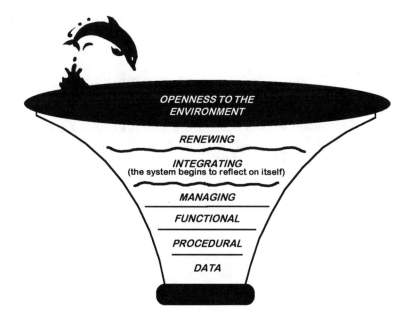

FIGURE 6.3 Openness to Transformational Learning.
     Figure 6.3 depicts a cross-section of the Knowledge Archetype from
     Chapter 4 (Figure 4.2). The wavy lines between modes depict the transfor-
     mative shift that occurs as a system (an individual or an organization)
     begins to reflect upon its own existence. Self-reflective challenging of one's
     assumptions and beliefs allows a greater openness and responsiveness to
     the environment, thus making it possible to change form or identity.

open discussion. Much of the learning in organizations results from daily, often
unplanned interactions among people. If people cannot comfortably and safely
challenge each other's thinking and assumptions, then transformational learning cannot happen.

  A dramatic example of such openness is at Electricite de France (EDF),
where abnormalities or deviations are reported throughout their entire system
of fifty-seven nuclear power plants. They follow up with a learning-focused inquiry, then disseminate the learning throughout the company. Consider how
much learning can take place if people view mistakes as opportunities for learning and knowledge building.[7] However, it takes an open, inquiring, non-threat-
ening internal environment for this to happen.

  We can find other evidence that people are beginning to appreciate the
value of openness in their internal environment. For example, some companies
like IBM are deliberately expanding their modes of knowing by valuing diversity. They are building an internal web of knowledge that includes a rich, dy-

namic mix of cultures, philosophies, and values. This is a deliberate strategy for understanding the diverse marketplace. They are expanding the creative possibilities of their *inner* environment in order to be more responsive to the *external* environment.

At Chevron, the process of becoming more open involves both external awareness and internal openness. External openness began with competitive intelligence and industry benchmarking. Over the last eight years or so, they have expanded that scanning process to examine world class best practices, as well as emerging trends and technologies. Internal openness has been fostered through new communication links, and by coaching and training in new behaviors. The concept of feedback has been central to this process. As an example of how much the culture has evolved, a group of employees recently gave behavioral feedback to CEO Ken Derr. They voluntarily held a videoconference to analyze how his actions reinforce the vision and values of Chevron. His positive response to their feedback, and the way the story has circulated, continues the momentum for a culture of learning and inquiry.

The Dynamics of Learning

With this expanded view of the learning cycle, a simple two-dimensional circle does not quite capture the dynamics of the process. I like to think of the learning cycle using a torus analogy with the Learning and Performance Framework. The *torus* or donut shape is one of the basic shapes of the universe. We see it in tornadoes, whirlpools, the structure of magnetic fields, and elsewhere throughout nature. Duane Elgin has even suggested that the torus may be the shape of the cosmos.[8]

Using the analogy of the torus we can think of the learning cycle as a continual movement from concrete *Procedural* and *Functional* actions, to the reflective conceptual domains of *Integrating* and *Renewing*, then back again. We cycle from abstract concepts and values, to concrete action and experimentation, to reflection once more. Transformational learning includes every single domain of learning and knowledge. Thus, it involves a continuous and comprehensive learning and knowledge cycle (Figure 6.4).

Learning is an essential quality of living and social systems, so it is intrinsic to organizational life. Learning happens whether we pay attention to it or not. However, if people are seeking greater flexibility and adaptability, then that requires very deep learning. Large-scale change requires reconfiguring the underlying logic of the organization, as well as its more tangible structures and processes. Learning must involve every single mode of knowledge and action for deep change to take place.

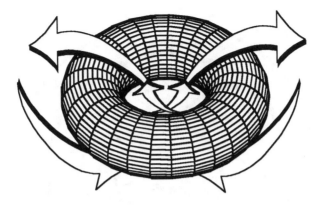

FIGURE 6.4 Transformational Learning Cycle.

The Organization as a Learning, Knowledge-Creating System

Knowledge, learning, and performance are always evolving through continual learning processes (Figure 6.5.) Understanding both the components of knowledge and supporting processes helps us advance our capacity for adaptive change. When faced with changes in our environment, we can develop knowledge strategies to meet the challenge.

The Learning and Performance Framework is one tool for identifying knowledge patterns. As our knowledge about knowledge grows and changes, this framework will eventually yield to other ways of seeing. For the moment, though, it can help us move forward in our understanding. It is also flexible enough to encompass other ways of seeing as well.

When we view organizations as knowledge-creating complex systems, we can begin to see how different technologies support different languages or modes of knowledge. Some of these technologies are hard technologies, such as information systems or Intranets. However, a surprising number are soft technologies, such as collaborative processes.

Each domain, too, requires different processes for learning. Each mode utilizes a unique set of processes and tools for creating, sustaining, sharing, and renewing knowledge. *Procedural* learning is different from *Renewing* learning. Documentation for sustaining knowledge takes a very different form for *Procedural* knowledge than for *Integrating* knowledge. Now let's look at how different organizations process and develop knowledge.

The Changing Organization

The way we organize our work has been changing dramatically. One reason organizations are changing so much may be that the old structures simply created

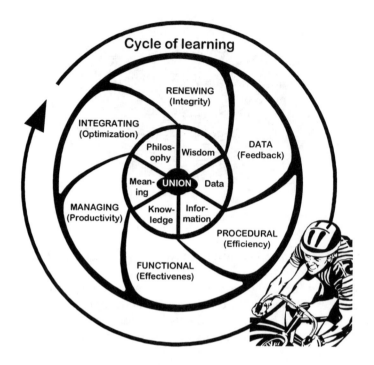

FIGURE 6.5 Knowledge Learning and Performance.

too many barriers to learning. Knowledge and learning want to happen. Yet, in the traditional multi-layered bureaucracy, information and knowledge does not flow freely. There are too many constraints and controls for information to move easily through the organization.

Structures are changing everywhere in response to the need for more flexibility and openness. As long as China had a central economy it was essentially stagnant. Only when Deng Xiaping decentralized the economy and turned control over to the parts did it really take off. Today, China has the fastest growing economy in the world. It has averaged almost 10% growth in each of the last dozen years. Everywhere, the trend toward decentralization is accelerating in companies as well as economies.

Examples of highly decentralized companies are Ansea Brown Boveri, with a headquarters staff of less than 200 people coordinating its world-wide operations. New companies, such as Veriphone, that are not constrained by an old structure, organize by new thinking principles. Veriphone prides itself on being a "virtual organization," relying heavily on communication technologies to link its people.

These trends all mark the evolution of American business structure. Over the course of history, according to Raymond Miles and Charles Snow, four broad forms of organization have emerged.[9] The first of these, *the functional organization*, appeared in the late 19th to early 20th century. *The divisional organization* surfaced just after World War I and flourished throughout the 1950s. The *matrix* put in a brief appearance, then quickly yielded to the *network form* that became apparent in the 1980s. The network is something of a hybrid, seeking to utilize the best of the previous forms, with a focus on dynamic relationships rather than rigid roles.

The functional division structure was usually accompanied by an elaborate bureaucracy. It was typified by a hierarchy, where one gradually worked up through the system through specialization, moving from one standardized job to another. Such companies were organized for coordination from above rather than horizontally. This form of organization is amazingly persistent. Elizabeth and Gifford Pinchot estimate that approximately 90 percent of our organizations follow this structure, at least on formal organizational charts. However, behind every bureaucracy there usually lurks a lively informal structure that is the way the work actually gets done.[10]

Large bureaucracies tend to stifle innovation and impede swiftness to market. Yet, without enough structure to provide stability, there can be so much chaos that the whole thing—economy or enterprise—just disintegrates. Bureaucracies and hierarchies worked superbly well in a slower, more stable economy. Their efficiencies of scale and consistency worked to advantage in dominating the market. Today, however, such bureaucracies lose market share because, like giant ocean liners, they take a long time to turn. Nimbleness is now the order of the day.

From Bureaucracies to Networks

This evolution of structure has worked hand-in-hand with the rise of knowledge as the core resource of the enterprise. The shift from *divisional organization*, to the *matrix*, and then to the *network form* arose from a desire to create companies that utilize knowledge across processes and functions. Matrices and networks are attempts to minimize structure and loosen up barriers between work groups.

One of the leaders in this looser, more open way of approaching the world of work is General Electric. They began paving the way for the "boundaryless" organization in 1989, by introducing the GE workout, a kind of town-hall open meeting. They shook things up even more with a massive leadership training program focusing on prioritization, integration, operationalization, and recalibration—all words that focus on strategy, systems thinking, and constant change. In the process, they have simplified and streamlined the whole company. They reduced twenty-nine pay grades to five (incidentally laying off thousands of people). A 360-degree appraisal has opened up the internal environment to allow a freer flow of information and feedback.[11]

When Dee W. Hock founded Visa, he was determined to create a different organizational form. Visa owns a globally respected brand name used by 23,000 institutions in 200 countries and territories. Over 355 million people, making more than 7 billion transactions yearly, use Visa's products. Those billions of dollars in purchases represent the single, largest block of consumer purchasing power in the world.

Visa is organized with teams. These teams are interrelated, but are not centrally controlled. The independent teams coordinate their work through flexible and robust communication networks according to a few basic organizing principles. Organizationally, Visa appears to parallel the scientific precepts of complexity and chaos. Member companies own Visa, distributing its power and functions to the maximum degree. Yet it is durable, finding its own stability in the turbulent world of finance.

Hock himself dubs Visa and the Internet, "chaords," seamless blendings of the principles of chaos and order, competition and cooperation. He is presently researching the creation of four or five more such structures in education, government, social services, and commerce.[12]

According to the Pinchots, the post-bureaucratic organization will be structured to support and coordinate self-managing groups and teams. The new architecture lets people connect in multiple directions, both within the company and externally. In order to get at the intelligence that resides within the organization, people must have the freedom to make decisions and choose their own actions. Along with such a shift in structure, leadership shifts from command and control to creating a climate of trust and shared understanding. Companies must focus on creating a supportive culture and enhancing the ability of people to self-organize.[13]

At the extreme end of the network structure is the *virtual organization*. Virtual companies coordinate much of their business through the marketplace. They are meeting grounds for free agents buying and selling goods and services (or knowledge). They leverage the knowledge and skill of outside suppliers with internal experts to create unique market positions. Virtual enterprises may even have virtual products that rely heavily on streams of information and communications technologies. Davidow and Malone, authors of *The Virtual Corporation*, suggest thinking of these virtual enterprises as patterns of information relationships.[14]

The Worker as a Knowledge Node

With shifts in structure come shifts in power, as we saw in Chapter 1. In a bureaucracy, the title you hold determines your power. In the decentralized, "networked," and virtual organizations, power comes with *what* you know and *who* you know. The one underlying trend that all these shifts have in common is that work is moving to where the knowledge is. The worker, as the holder of knowledge, has moved front and center in organizational design.

The knowledge worker now has the political clout to dictate his own working conditions. Knowledgeable people have more and more power to shape the organization and create new forms of work to suit their individual preferences.

Networks of Knowledge

The world of work is a highly creative and interactive social environment. Wherever knowledge connects with knowledge, new combinations spontaneously take place. Ideas spark ideas, which synthesize with each other until more knowledge results. The dance of knowledge is inevitable, it is completely natural, and quite wonderful. It echoes the creative dance of Shiva, the divine being in Hindu mythology, continually dancing the world into form.

One of the metaphors people use to describe the dance of knowledge is *knowledge networking*. "Network" is an abstract concept referring to a set of nodes and their connecting relationships. When I think of the way people bring their knowledge together in ever new combinations, I think of water. Water has a very interesting quality of "wateriness" that cannot be explained by the structure of the hydrogen and oxygen atoms that it is made of. Water happens thanks to flickering clusters of molecules that briefly come together. This bond is loose and easily broken. It lasts just long enough to give water its watery characteristics.

I think of knowledge networks as flickering clusters. People come together in knowledge clusters just long enough to accomplish a particular task. Then they disassemble and move on to other projects and knowledge clusters. Such relationships cannot be "structured" or designed. They emerge as a property of the system in which they operate—and they are constantly in flux.

In *5th Generation Management*, Charles Savage describes such a networking arrangement as one where each knowledge node can communicate directly with every other node, without having to filter through a hierarchical arrangement.[15]

The Strategic Center

Successful web organizations have a strong strategic center that plays a critical role as a creator of value. The strategic center of a network adds value to all its component parts by forging a powerful vision that involves everyone. This center also imparts a clear identity (such as a brand name). In addition, the strategic center provides effective systems support and creates a climate of trust and reciprocity. Successful strategic centers are provided by such companies as Apple, Benetton, Corning, Genetech, McDonald's, McKesson, Nike, Nintendo, Nova-Care, Sun Microsystems, and Toyota.[16]

Despite a strategic core, networks have fuzzy boundaries. The boundaries that define a network are often more psychological than structural, defined by areas of accountability and authority.[17] Other "hidden" boundaries can be political influence or a circle of colleagues and cronies. More visible structural boundaries may be defined by tasks or work processes. Areas of interest or expertise form still other kinds of knowledge units within a network. Yet, in most cases, it is not always clear who is in and who is out. This gives the networks an openness and vagueness that can be unsettling for people who are used to more rigid organizational structures.

Jessica Lipnack and Jeffrey Stamps, in *The Age of the Network*, explore emerging organizational structures that combine teams, hierarchy, bureaucracy, and networks. One of their examples is Eastman Chemical's "pepperoni pizza" organizational chart, depicting self-managed teams and rotating leadership.[18] In their view, The Age of the Network means that connections, relationships, and the flow of information are all now critical success factors for people and companies.

According to Sally Helgesen, author of *The Web of Inclusion*, these new networks do not develop from some preconceived plan, but arise out of learning and experimentation. They are characterized by open communication channels that allow people from very different levels to work together, sharing expertise, knowledge, and resources. They create new networks and redistribute power.[19]

Connective Tissue

What is the connective tissue that holds a network together? Common purpose and value, of course, form the nucleus. The strategic center of the network embodies those purposes and values and holds their integrity. In the more loosely structured knowledge networking environment, people must have a common context and purpose. Integrative processes involving communal and social reflection around purpose, internal logic, and values allow true self-organization.

But there is more. Every successful network also has connective tissue in the form of languages and communication systems that carry information and feedback. In organizational life, connective tissue might be essential threads of standardization. Standards such as ISO 9000 are part of an international language of manufacturing that allow companies to evolve and work in similar ways, regardless of whether they are American, Brazilian, Japanese, or European. Such standards and protocols are helping to weave together a global society and economy. A few simple protocols allowed the Internet to self-organize. The entire planet is self-organizing with the construction of complex systems that use resources efficiently, are resilient after disturbances, and are very adaptive.

The Patterns that Connect

Another type of connective tissue that we see in web relationships is replication of forms and structures. Nature uses repetitive patterns and forms everywhere.

The pattern of electrons in an atom mirrors the movement of stars and planets in the solar system. Another expression of repetitive patterns is fractal geometry. Fractals explain how every tiny branch of a tree holds the same basic structure as the larger branches and of the tree itself. Repetitive patterns are a fundamental structure of organization.[20]

We use repetitive patterns to manage complexity. A room of a building reflects the design of the whole structure, which in turn mirrors certain design principles of the community of buildings around it. Buildings generally have a design integrity with the patterns of the streets and the city they are a part of. This holds true in forest villages and in great cities. Each part mirrors the pattern of the whole.

Design principles are connective tissue for an organization. In our endless creativity, we constantly tinker and experiment with our designs. We are beginning to abandon design principles that result in bureaucracy and artificial hierarchies of function. New design principles that allow flexibility, while maintaining coherence and consistency, are emerging.

Some of the new design principles are grounded in connecting technologies and the way people communicate. Others have to do with work relationships, such as working in teams rather than holding individual responsibility areas. Other design principles have to do with how people organize their work and functional units, such as the design principle of holonomy.

Holonomy

A holon is a whole that is also a part. The word "holon" was coined by Arthur Koestler in 1967, and the expression "holonic organization" is sometimes used to refer to social structures such as communities and organizations. For example, family groups share some organizing characteristics of communities, which share certain organizing characteristics of townships or cities.[21] The Japanese use holonic management concepts in their worldwide initiative on intelligent manufacturing systems.

One way to understand holonic organization is to think of the holographic image that now graces so many credit cards. In holographic photography we have perfected a technique of capturing an image so that even a tiny fragment of the photographic plate holds the entire picture. Each fragment or part reflects the whole.[22]

The holonic organization is basically a metaphor. It is a set of ideas that seem relevant to how organizational structures self-organize. From this holographic or holonic perspective, each part of an organization somehow reflects the whole. Now, let's see if we can extend this holonic metaphor to knowledge. This would mean, for the purpose of understanding knowledge, that an individual knowledge node reflects a similar knowledge structure for the business unit or team. That larger knowledge node, in turn, would reflect similar knowledge characteristics in the organization as a whole.

In order to communicate about knowledge, people need to be able to discuss it in a way that makes sense at the individual, team, and organizational level. It is confusing to have individual knowledge competencies described one way, another "language" for team knowledge competencies, and yet another model of organizational knowledge. Consistency in language aids communication enormously. Seeking basic patterns and structures of knowledge is one way to find that common language.

A knowledge framework, such as the Learning and Performance Framework, when used at multiple levels (Figure 6.6) is a holonic approach. In this case, one would explore how each individual functions in each of the seven domains of knowledge, learning, and performance. In turn, you could look at the team, a business unit, or the entire organization. There are benefits to this approach in that it streamlines communication.

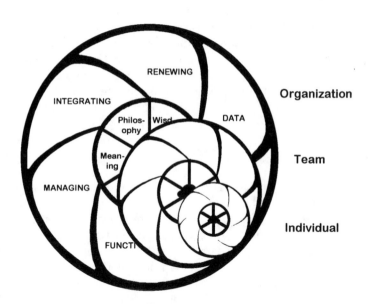

FIGURE 6.6 Individual, Team, and Organizational Knowledge.

Individual: What is the individual's core configuration of skills, training, and expertise? How deep is their knowledge competency in their area of expertise? Do they have performance capability and knowledge of basic work processes for each mode?

Team: Which knowledge domains are critical for this team's success, and how well does the team match those needs? Does the team have the overall knowledge competency they need for addressing the subject area of their task? Do they have multilevel performance capabilities for delivering results on that knowledge?

Organization: Are there structures and processes in place to support building knowledge competencies and enhancing performance capabilities at multiple levels? Is there clear purpose and intention so that people can self-organize? What is the overall knowledge and performance profile of the organization?

The holonic metaphor is a useful way to think about knowledge and knowledge networks. It is far more important to have ongoing inquiry into knowledge and learning than it is to get the whole thing exactly right. Although the language may vary, the direction of the new structural trends is the same. The urge is to create autonomous parts that work together to optimize the whole.

Knowledge as System

Thinking about knowledge questions in this holonic way can be quite useful. The drawback, of course, is that this is only a metaphor. There is always the risk of getting stuck in a metaphor you can't get out of. This holonic view means you might miss some other critical aspects of knowledge that are not readily apparent.

Knowledge is continually in motion. Think again of water. That sticky quality that water molecules have that allows them to come together, also allows them to come apart easily. If we begin to structure knowledge too rigidly, we destroy its fluid quality. Water that is stagnant becomes brackish, stale, and unfit to drink. Water that is frozen is no longer even water. It is ice that has lost many of its water qualities. Only water that is continually moving through the natural recycling process is fresh and life-giving. It can only move, adapt, and change shape when it is liquid—when it flows.

Understanding knowledge as a system means incorporating system principles into organizational design requirements. Nonaka and Takeuchi list five systems principles or enabling conditions for knowledge creation.[23] These organizational enablers are all drawn from cybernetics and systems thinking. Such design principles are connective tissue for holding the integrity of the system. In light of what we have explored here, let's see how these work.

1. *Intention.* Intention is a core component of purpose, vision, and values. These are addressed in the knowledge modes of *Union* and *Renewing* in the Learning and Performance Framework. Successful networks have a strong central core of purpose, values, and intentions.

2. *Autonomy.* Autonomy is the ability of individuals to act independently. If people understand purpose, vision, and values, they have the foundation they need to make decisions. When they also understand their own knowledge, performance specialties, and goals, as well as those of their co-workers and the team, then they can act autonomously. They can self-organize as needed to do the work at hand *and* plan for their future needs.

3. *Fluctuation and creative chaos.* According to Nonaka and Takeuchi, fluctuation, and creative chaos stimulate interaction between the organization and the external environment. This interaction is encouraged by continual dialogue, questioning, and reconsidering existing premises. This particular type of

self-questioning is the core learning process for the *Integrating* knowledge mode. If work processes are designed to incorporate this modality, then people and work groups are stimulated to reflect continually on their deeper mental models around their work.

4. *Redundancy* refers to intentional overlapping of information, knowledge, and business activities. We have known for some time that this systems characteristic is an important one for a healthy enterprise. The challenge is how to put it into practice. It is easier to see overlaps in processes and structures than it is to see overlaps in knowledge. However, a common language for managing knowledge allows tacit knowledge to become explicit, so that it can be better analyzed and understood. The holonic design concept allows for maintaining a creative knowledge balance with an appropriate level of redundancy.

5. *Requisite variety.* This term describes the organization's ability to match its internal diversity to the variety and complexity of the environment in which it operates. Communication enhances variety. Variety is also enhanced by deliberately stretching past one's comfort zones and expanding one's language. A systems approach to knowledge ensures that we do not overlook critical variety in our learning modes, knowledge competencies, and performance capabilities.

Thinking of knowledge as a system is very useful when it comes to devising ways we can support it. The trouble with systems, of course, is that everything is connected to everything else. If we focus too intently on knowledge, we ignore other aspects of complex systems.

The Ecology of Knowledge

Knowledge is the language of information exchange for the system it supports. Continuous renewal of knowledge sustains the continuous renewal of the organization. If knowledge atrophies, so does the organization. If we want to enhance the knowledge-carrying capacity of the enterprise, then we must continually expand the language of our experience.

We must understand the ecology of knowledge, lest our well-intentioned efforts inadvertently damage the ecosystem of our own organizational intelligence. Communication technologies alone are not enough. We must also understand the languages of our communication to be sure we are covering the entire range of our experience.

In order for knowledge to be truly self-organizing, people need more than sharing a common purpose and values. They must understand and value their own knowledge competencies and performance capabilities. They also need to be able to identify the *other* critical knowledge components they are seeking. Ideally, there would be a common language for knowledge itself in the organization. Remember, all knowledge is not alike, nor are learning processes all alike. People need to be able to specify the knowledge they seek and communicate that need in a way that will get a response.

The next few chapters will guide you through an assessment process for understanding organizational performance, knowledge building, and learning. This knowledge assessment will help you identify and support core knowledge and learning competencies or languages.

PART II

BUILDING BLOCKS FOR KNOWLEDGE

Each of the following chapters includes a list of key questions for assessing performance. These questions are important for building knowledge *about* knowledge in your own organization. The question set that weaves throughout Chapters 7 through 13 helps to illuminate generic organizational knowledge competencies. These questions focus on performance capabilities that apply to all industries. A question set for building knowledge in a specific subject area is quite different (an example of such a question set is in Appendix C). The questions also would be somewhat different for understanding individual or team performance capabilities.

As you explore each question, ask yourself, "In regard to this question . . . "

- Where are we now in our organization?
- Where would we like to be?
- How can we close the gap?

CHAPTER 7

Doing the Data Two-Step

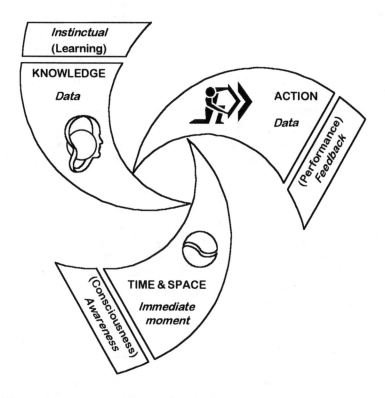

FIGURE 7.1 Relationship of Time, Knowledge, and Action—Data Mode Performance.

TABLE 7.1 Data Mode.

KNOWLEDGE ASPECT *Data* Instinct, awareness, sensing	ACTION FOCUS *Data* Gathering Information
LEARNING DYNAMICS *Instinctual* The data level of learning is at the sensory or input level. Little actual learning takes place.	PERFORMANCE CAPABILITY *Feedback* Receiving input, registering data with reflection.
Examples: • perceiving changes in light • noticing something is happening • sensing heat or cold • instinctive reactions, such as emotional reactions (fear response)	*Business Examples:* • compiling statistics • gathering metrics or measurements • opening and distributing mail

TIME HORIZON: Immediate moment
CONSCIOUSNESS: Awareness

Data mode activity (Table 7.1) involves having the capability to gather *the most essential raw data that the organization needs*. The *Data* mode does not concern itself with processing the data, combining it into clumps of knowledge, or high-level integration with strategy goals and objectives. All that comes later. *Data* activity simply focuses on gathering basic information and having the capacity for registering significant variations.

The domain of consciousness associated with the *Data* mode is simple awareness, consciousness of the environment that allows registering of input or variation. It is the most fundamental sensory mode of consciousness. Little learning takes place. Response and action, while possible, are purely instinctive.

The time horizon of the *Data* mode is confined to this immediate, particular moment. Attention focuses on what is happening right now: taking in events, registering change, noticing variation. Significant data includes emotional responses. Emotions are data; they are feedback. Our senses and feelings alert us to changes, dynamics, and events at a very subtle level. It is important to pay attention to this "softer" type of data as well as "hard" data that may surface as numbers and statistics.

Understanding Data

Data is feedback. We gather data with all our sensory organs: noses, ears, eyes, and nerve receptors in our skin. We receive data from our physical responses to events. We may register fear, distaste, attraction. Everything we use to perceive, scan, and sense brings data to our awareness. Without similar processes for registering data in an organization we do not know what is happening. It is as if our eyes are closed and we are operating blind.

Data is variation that is significant enough for us to notice. If your hand is completely at rest on a table, you don't feel anything you touch. You might have a sense of warm or cold, but the receptors in your skin are sensing variation in temperature. You do not feel the table until you move; something has to change. Then nerve receptors in your fingers register variation and you "feel" the texture of the table.

We instinctively gather data all the time. We unconsciously register a myriad of variations as we walk down a hallway. We also gather data in our organizations, whether we do it consciously or not. As living creatures we are naturally wired for noticing change, movement, and variation. A global company virtually has eyes and ears all over the world, registering a multitude of variations in the environment. There are changes in the economy, in relationships with customers and suppliers, in competition, and in discoveries in related fields.

Gathering Data

Everyone in the organization constantly takes in data. Yet, few companies analyze or understand their data-gathering processes. A few areas get special attention, of course, such as competitive intelligence, customer feedback, or information from financial markets. However, most data seeps in under the doors, slips around through the phone wires, whispers through the hallways, or is picked up like a virus around convention halls and conferences. This kind of data receives very little attention, yet it comprises the bulk of the sensing, scanning, and perceiving activities of the enterprise.

It is important that there be a variety of channels for data gathering. No single form or media is sufficient to capture the complexity of the external environment; it takes a wide variety of data-gathering activities for an organization to be in touch with its environment. Yet, at the same time, there needs to be a reasonable filtering process for incoming information. It becomes costly and counter-productive to process too much data.

With the capabilities of information processing technologies, data gathering has exploded. People can directly access extensive databases right on their desktops. Lexis/Nexis, Dialogue, and other information service providers have put the whole world of knowledge at our fingertips. Publications are proliferating like mad as desktop publishing makes publication ever easier. Through the Internet, people can participate in forums on virtually any topic that interests them.

Variation

Think about all the incoming messages you receive every day. Today we have phones, e-mail, voice mail, newspapers, television, movies, faxes, answering machines, the Internet, ground mail, packages—we have a multitude of incoming messages in all kinds of media bombarding us every day. Internal data, such as e-mail messages and reports, are having a population explosion. How do we make choices about what to pay attention to or not?

What attracts our attention is the unusual, the significant variation. Is the stock market up or down? Are clothing styles beginning to change? Did our competitor introduce a new product or abandon an old one? Is there a new drug to treat cancer? We notice the variations. The purpose of all our sensory apparatus for data is to bring to our awareness the variations that are significant for our survival, success, and well being.

Internal data is just as critical as external data. It is important to continually take the organizational temperature, so to speak. Key indicators of organizational performance must continually be gathered and processed. We must also know what is changing internally.

One of the most powerful contributions of the Total Quality movement is the way it has brought about a deliberate attention to variation within the organization. Donald J. Wheeler calls a deficiency in understanding variation "numerical illiteracy."[1] The consistent and masterful use of quality tools overcomes such a deficiency through emphasis on metrics, measurement, and statistics. This language of variation fine-tunes the sensory apparatus of an organization so that it is more receptive to data and feedback.

Data Addiction

The first level of knowledge management is managing data. The amount of detail that can be sliced into data bits is astonishing. However, just because we *can* gather a certain type of data doesn't mean we *should*. The most important aspect of managing data is knowing when to stop. "More is better," is the prevailing mindset about data and information. As a consequence, all knowledge and information has been treated as an object, reducible to bits of data that can be processed quickly. This objectification reduces all the key knowledge questions to "How many bits of data can move through our pipeline, and how fast can we move them?" Questions of speed, quantity, and access tend to become the focus of knowledge management, not the way the data is organized, its relevance, or its ultimate usefulness.

The result of this mindset of "more" is a classic addiction pattern. Around we go on the information merry-go-round, hoping that if we cycle through or "process" enough information, knowledge will somehow magically emerge. We are not getting what we need most, of course, which is real understanding. In a classic addictive response, we try to fill the void with more knowledge substitute—more information, more bits of data. Whenever we feel frustrated or inadequate, our response is to get more data—now!

In the system dynamics approach of Jay Forrester, popularized by Peter Senge, this creates a classic causal loop archetype of "shifting the burden."[2]

When managers have difficulty making decisions, their anxiety increases. The quick fix for the anxiety appears to be more information, so they request more data. If the request is filled, they receive even more data that they still cannot absorb or really use. The decision gets harder still, anxiety increases, they request more information . . . and on through the cycle of addiction. The unintended side effect is that they place an increasing burden on the information support system, expenditures on hardware and software go up, profits go down, stress and decision pressures increase (Figure 7.2).

Data feeds this addictive cycle with its seemingly endless capacity to replicate into information. In an interview with Bill Moyers, poet Stanley Kunitz observed the infinite capacity of words. "Words are so erotic, they never tire of their coupling. How do they renew themselves? In their inexhaustible desire for combinations and recombinations."[3] Data, as words, statistics, numbers,

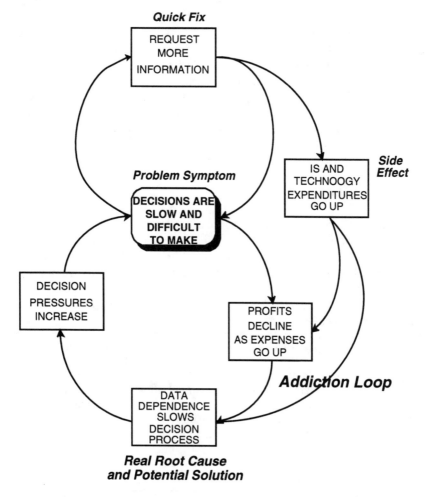

FIGURE 7.2 Data Addiction.

and simple observations, also has an inexhaustible capacity to combine and re-combine into new clusters of information. These bits of data endlessly link and link again into new configurations. Data is the cellular level of an information system. Much as the uncontrolled cell growth of cancer devastates the resources of the body, wild data accumulation saps the resources, budgets, efficiency, and energy of the organization. At what point does data overload cause a breakdown in the immune system of an organization? Data growth without boundaries, without checks and balances, fuels the addictive cycle of more data, more infor-mation technology to process the data, and more complexity that generates yet—more data.

The only way to break this addictive cycle is by moving to a higher level of self-awareness, self-reflection, and creative choice. The real solution for difficult decisions often is not more information, but more *reflection*. The ultimate solu-tion for hard choices is not an *Information* solution, it is a *Wisdom* solution. Clarity around our purpose and values guides us to our best choices.

Only when we become aware of our addictive pattern around information can we begin to reflect on our own dynamics in a more detached way. It then be-comes possible to unravel the logic of the addiction, move to a solution space in another learning mode, and break the pattern.

We must have data-gathering processes that enable us to notice the signif-icant variations that are critical for our success. However, extraneous "noise" beyond that becomes distracting and costly to manage. The art, of course, lies in knowing what is critical and what is "noise."

Data Level Performance

Understanding performance in each knowledge mode requires understanding key processes or dynamics for that particular mode. Processes can be catego-rized as processes for creating, sustaining, sharing, and renewing knowledge (Figure 7.3). These processes are different for each mode and involve many sub-processes (Table 7.2).

TABLE 7.2 Knowledge Dynamics.

CREATING	SUSTAINING	SHARING	RENEWING
generating	identifying	socializing	changing
acquiring	organizing	communicating	improving
combining	storing	distributing	expanding
	collecting	teaching	deepening
	representing	transferring	adapting
	analyzing		
	codifying		
	applying		

FIGURE 7.3 Knowledge Dynamics.

In *Data* mode it is possible to utilize information technology support for most of these processes, particularly for sustaining and sharing data throughout the organization. Let's take a closer look at these processes.

Creating *Data* Knowledge

Behind every piece of data lurks a question. Data generation directly reflects the breadth and depth of questions that people ask. The more feelers individuals have extended to the environment, the more data will result. The more people actively seek feedback and appreciate variation, the more data they require. In order to understand the data creation process for your enterprise, you must first be able to understand the questions that people are asking.

Data questions attempt to identify variations either in the external environment or regarding key internal processes. Externally, data can be acquired in the marketplace through direct purchase or research. The format can then be modified and shaped to respond to the particular questions. Questions regarding internal variation and feedback require internal generation of the data.

There are both tacit and explicit data-creating processes in an organization. Formal data creation is usually "managed" by a responsible group such as information services. However, there is also a powerful informal data-generation process lurking in the shadows. Informal or tacit processes around data knowledge take place in individual offices and workgroups. There people compile and generate data for their personal use. One of the challenges in data acquisition is being able to make this type of internal data visible so it can be shared.

Sustaining *Data* Knowledge

Organizing, storing, and collecting data is becoming easier all the time. Information technologies have advanced enormously in recent years. Storage capacity, collection mechanisms, and data processing capabilities are expanding rapidly. Our mastery of the art and science of organizing, representing, and storing data has become the most powerful accelerator for the Knowledge Economy.

It is important to note, however, that *knowledge management is not the same as data management*. Being able to organize information is a key organizational enabler for knowledge, but it is only one component.

One of the difficulties in sustaining data is that its documented form varies in so many ways. Companies are pursuing designs for data warehouses, where data can be normalized and more easily accessed. The difficulty with standardizing data is that the process ignores variation outside a prescribed norm. When that happens, the result is fewer sensory feelers, not more.

Sharing *Data* Knowledge

Advances in information technology have greatly simplified data sharing. Distributed data bases, electronic reports, and communication technologies have augmented the ability of people to access and share data. Sharing technologies, such as Lotus Notes, Internet, and internal webs, make it possible for people to self-organize around data sharing. Data mining tools and techniques such as those developed by Silicon Graphics help people reach shared understanding of essential data.

The language of the Data mode is the language of variation, often measurable variation in the form of statistics and measurement. Teaching people an appreciation of variation and developing skill in using Total Quality Tools, such as control charts, help foster more awareness of data and its usefulness. Using data effectively is easier when people develop a common language around variation and feedback. If people do not know how to notice variation, then they cannot effectively apply feedback data or understand performance measures.

Renewing *Data* Knowledge

Any viable system must have a way to renew itself. People often continue to compile data long after its usefulness has faded. Organizations are awash with reports no one reads and compilations of data that are no longer relevant. There must be a way to retire old data. Sun Microsystems puts a note at the bottom of its reports that people must call a certain phone number by a particular date or the report will be discontinued. Owens Corning has a strategic goal of becoming paperless in order to reduce this type of waste. Another renewal strategy is to continually revisit the questions that generate the data in the first place through dialogue and self-questioning.

Assessment Questions

So what are the important *Data* level performance questions? If you can answer yes to the following questions, then you are well on your way to high performance at the *Data* level.

1. Does the organization receive a variety of data from the outside through multiple channels?
2. Have you identified the significant external variables for the organization? (for markets, customers, environment)
3. Do you have a way to capture and compile data that will illuminate variables over time? (An example would be revenue figures from year to year for significant competitors, or changes in government regulations.)
4. Do people understand variation and measurement for their own work?
5. Are people supported with resources and training to capture, access, and compile relevant metrics and measures regarding their work?
6. Are there internal feedback mechanisms, such as employee surveys, and focus groups?
7. Are there widely available internal reports of significant variables?
8. Is there a process to "retire" data and measurements that are no longer relevant?
9. Do people have ready access to databases, trade journals, and library resources relevant to their work?
10. Do you have processes and technologies to distribute and access data throughout the organization?

Organizing Data

It should be obvious from these questions that high performance at the *Data* level has only partly to do with databases. Databases are actually misnamed. They are really information bases, because the data is organized. Once data begins to be manipulated, it starts turning into information. Data organized into strings of numbers representing monthly or yearly sales is actually information. Sorting data into categories, such as identifying job candidates with specific degrees or types of work experience, also organizes data into information.

It is almost impossible to remain on a pure *Data* level. Let's take the example of a database supporting the general information needs of a business. The core database problem today is not storing or moving data. Storage is easy. Moving data is easy. What is difficult is storing the data so that it can be extracted in certain patterns, called reports. Patterns give data meaning.

Patterns and data are very tricky things. People expect the data to reveal certain patterns that will help them make decisions. However, in order to manipulate data into patterns, we have to program a certain level of pattern into the data to begin with. Our own mental models, questions, and assumptions determine the patterns we program into the data. Oops, this lands us right back in the space-time continuum of the knowledge universe. There is no such thing as "pure" data. Our values determine what data we notice.

My friend, Americ Azevedo, at the Institute of Science and Technology at Golden Gate University, was demonstrating how to build a database for one of the university students. They had worked together for about three to four hours. All at once, it dawned on the student that he was trying to capture a whole realm of knowledge about the organization, its structure, its purpose, how people work together, the different expertise areas. It suddenly became important to understand how people make decisions, how they communicate about their work, what the specific tasks are, and so on.

"Wow," he said. "I have to KNOW something in order to build a database."

He had discovered that databases are really about extracting, capturing and communicating the knowledge that resides in an organizational system. However, before one can capture and display data that is meaningful, it is necessary to understand the underlying logic of the entire organizational system.

A Little Data Story

One day when I was noodling around knowledge questions with my friend Americ, he told me this story from his early days in the computer world.

Sometime in this early age of information technology I farmed myself out as a Western Girl Temporary employee. I was assigned to do "data entry" for a new automated order processing system for a branch of the State Bar of California. They were just moving from manually typing order forms and packing slips to having them processed by the big mainframe computer. My job was to get the data onto input forms that corresponded to the exact positions of data on IBM punch cards. The punch cards would be processed by a key punch operator.

I noticed that customers filled out order forms with pretty much the same information as I was inputting. However, their address and order information came to us in a manner too undisciplined for keypunch to handle. We had to "translate" the raw data into usable "clean" data that could be entered by the keypunch operators.

Now this seemed a little silly to me—to be basically doing the work a second time. So, I suggested that the order forms be redesigned. Why not have the clients put the data in themselves, in more exact spots, with little guide numbers along the bottom. The keypunch operators could use the guides for corresponding to the IBM card data positions. Then we could eliminate almost all the coding. So that's what we did.

Anyway, the point is, instead of focusing on filling out data forms, my attention naturally wandered over to asking where the data comes from and where is it going! I realize now I was shifting up to the next level of questions. By moving my attention to Procedural *level questions focusing on procedures and understanding conformance to standards, I began to see where a whole lot of work could be eliminated at the level of* Data *input.*

What Americ did in this process was shift to another knowledge and performance mode. He did, indeed, start with a question about *Data*. However, to resolve the issue of redundancy at the *Data* level, he had to move to the next level of questions and address the *Procedural* level of performance.

People often make category errors when they are trying to solve problems. They attempt to apply the logic and problem-solving mode of one level when they need to move to another. We saw this in the data addiction example earlier in this chapter, where throwing a *Data* solution of "more data" at a problem often does not make decisions easier.

We will see as we go along that each mode of knowledge creation produces a particular set of challenges. These often seem to have obvious solutions. However, if we shift to the next level of questions, we might find much more elegant solutions. This is exactly what Einstein meant when he said, "We cannot solve our problems at the same level of thinking that created them."

CHAPTER 8

Gigamonsters and Other Dragons:

Procedural Knowledge

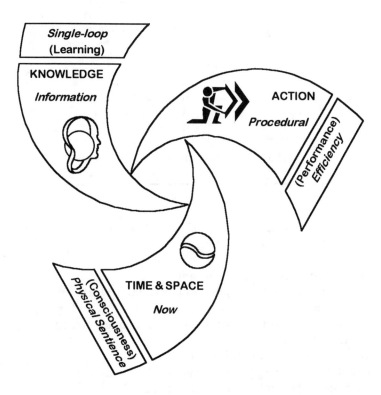

FIGURE 8.1 Relationship of Time, Knowledge, and Action—*Procedural* Mode.

TABLE 8.1 Procedural Mode.

KNOWLEDGE ASPECT *Information* Action without reflection	ACTION FOCUS *Procedural* Doing something the most efficient way
LEARNING DYNAMICS *Single-Loop* Procedural learning entails redirecting a course of action to follow a predetermined course. Learning is mostly trial and error.	**PERFORMANCE CAPABILITY** *Efficiency* Conforming to standards or making simple adjustments to modifications. Focus is on developing and following procedures, such as policies, rules, sequences of steps, and regulations.
Examples: • creating linear linkages of data • sorting and categorizing • serial processing • linear logic • detail focus • noticing inconsistencies • simple experiments	*Business Examples:* • writing procedure manuals • records management • documenting details of processes • developing user guides or specifications • creating classification and filing systems • checking consistency of output • conducting financial audits • implementing regulations • editing documents • performance support systems *Tools:* • Check Lists • Process Capability (Conformance) • Control Charts • Flowcharts

TIME HORIZON: Very short (present—now)
CONSCIOUSNESS: Physical sentience

In this fast moving world, procedural glitches fill our day with little frustrations and sometimes just stop us cold:

- We find ourselves in the wrong line.
- We must learn a set of keystrokes to run our new software.
- Maintenance ordered the wrong part.
- We need to convert our documents to the same format so my computer can talk to your computer.
- We want to adjust the thermostat.
- I need the four-line phone jack instead of the two-line.
- He forgot to get directions to the meeting.
- I need your e-mail address.

- It's time to fill out my expense report and I lost my receipts.
- And the fax just ran out of paper—again!

This is the world of detail we must master to have high performance at the *Procedural* level. *Procedural* knowledge is the backbone of order and consistency. Without it, there would be chaos, with everyone doing their own thing. Conformance to certain standards and procedures ensures that processes run smoothly, machine parts fit together and computers can communicate.

Think of all the procedures and regulations you follow in the course of a single day. We all stop at red lights, yield at crosswalks, form orderly lines in the cafeteria, don't talk loudly in the theater (at least *I* don't), try to keep our checkbooks balanced, and enter the correct sequence of numbers placing a credit card call or using the automated teller.

The usual learning process for refining procedures is trial and error. Learning organization theorists refer to this trial and error method as *single-loop learning*, action without reflection.[1] A common analogy is that single-loop learning is like a thermostat that checks whether it is too hot or cold, then turns the heat on or off accordingly. The key learning focus is conformance to a standard and simple corrective action.

An example of *Procedural* learning, in Western culture, at least, is tying your shoe laces. You probably tried it a few times, gave up in disgust, whined a bit, and then went to look for Mom or Dad. Of course, I only had the patience for one quick demonstration, insisting I could do it myself. Then off I went and practiced by way of good old trial and error until I got it right. (I never mastered *keeping* them tied.)

The time horizon for *Procedural* performance is narrowly confined to the immediate present. It is a wider horizon than the *Data* mode, but still concerned with events immediately at hand. The narrow time horizon means there is a narrow conceptual or "space" horizon as well. Thus, the span of control for a procedure is usually within one person's grasp. A single person can accomplish many of the activities that support *Procedural* performance.

The related mode of consciousness is physical sentience. Beyond the pure awareness of the *Data* mode, physical sentience is an embodied awareness. This is consciousness of ourselves as a physical agent that can act upon the world. We know we can exercise choice in our actions, that our body will act in service to our will.

Procedural Languages

Procedural knowledge rides the language of sequences, categories, and conformance to standards. Knowledge creation relies on linear language and logic. We usually organize large amounts of data by sequence or category. A particular piece of data might fit into a sequence. On the other hand, it might have similarities to other data and fit into a particular category. A category has an identity, a label. Identities kick into motion the processes of self-organization.

We spontaneously create categories all the time. File folders are set up by categories. The little boxes we fill in on a form are categories. Making categories is so easy and natural that we often do not think much about how we create them, we just do it. This is fine if we are just sorting things for ourselves, but in communities such as organizations, it is more efficient to use common categories. Unfortunately, we often do not socialize our categories with other people until we find we have problems communicating or locating information. This results in waste, inefficiency, and rework, as we backtrack trying to make things match. Creating categories is also tricky because language changes and categories become obsolete.

Another important *Procedural* language is the language of conformance to standards and statistical control. Whenever people are developing rules, specifications, and protocols, they are in *Procedural* mode. All these assure smooth function in communication, work processes, and mechanical processes.

Information Technology and *Procedural* Learning

Databases require a special way of thinking. The way we organize "data" into separate tables or categories impacts how reports, forms, and queries are generated. These are all different processes for manipulating the data into representations of information and knowledge. Category mismatches make it difficult to integrate databases.

Database design always reflects our own thinking processes. The way we organize a database directly reflects our own mental models of how things work. The more we rely on information, the more we need to understand the way we conceptualize our world and co-create the meaningful patterns of the data.

Database systems mark different historical moments in the evolution of information technology and also reflect changing ways of thinking. Some of the early principles of database management stemmed from limitations on machine performance. As large amounts of memory become cheaper and processing capacity increases, database systems can more easily reflect the information and knowledge reality of the organization.

We want our computers to think as we think. As our processing demands become more sophisticated, we put increasing pressure on technology to keep pace. My first computer, a little Apple Mac Plus with a tiny black and white screen purchased in 1986, had a "huge" 40MG hard drive. Today, I require a "gigamonster" personal computer with a gigabyte of memory, a back-up tape system, a CD-ROM drive, sound, full-color monitor, and a color printer. Upgrading is epidemic, as we insist on memory-intensive user-friendly interfaces and ever higher quality standards for output.

Evolving technology allows a database developer to reflect more and more on the creation of knowledge and the making of meaning. Databases are gradually becoming a mirror image of the larger mind of the organization. Data, ultimately, is what the developer uses to "test" the system, pumping various data cases through the system to see how well the system performs its various tasks. The tasks themselves, however, are derived from the knowledge needs of the people in the organization.

The problem of course, is that we are not very good map makers of our thought world, and a database relies on our tacit or explicit conceptual maps of organizational procedures and processes. When we describe our world, we tend to break it down into bits and pieces or component parts. We seldom stop and reflect on overall structures, patterns, and relationships. We draw database designs as tables, bins, and boxes from a scientific perspective that values categorizing, dividing, separating, and cataloging. In the richly complex world we find ourselves in, this fragmentation does not always serve us at greater levels of complexity.

However, databases do serve *Procedural* learning very well. They act as repositories for rules, regulations, policies, and procedures that people refer to frequently. These can be organized into self-guided programs that help people access and learn common terminology, subject matter, procedures, and responses. Such programs, or integrated performance support systems, use computer technology to put solutions and information at the fingertips of service workers. The following example demonstrates how technology supports trial and error *Procedural* learning.

Example

Andersen Window has implemented an interactive system that allows retailers and contractors to custom design window configurations for customers. A designer constructs a graphical representation on-screen of the wall where the new window will be installed. A list of options allows the selection of windows with which the designer and customer can experiment.

As people try out different configurations, the system generates a parts list with prices, comparing the different options. The system network automates a wealth of information about Andersen Windows products that is easily updated and distributed via the network throughout the United States.[2] This system supports trial and error learning during the window selection process. Then, through automation, it performs cost calculations, displays specifications, and generates guidelines.

Performance Support

People often refer to computerized performance support systems as *knowledge systems* or *knowledge bases*. These do represent an exciting and powerful evolution in our capacity to create, sustain, share, and renew knowledge. The state of the art and technology in this area, however, focuses mostly on organizing *Procedural* knowledge around one specific subject area.

Advocates of these systems claim they support more complex modes of knowledge, such as helping people understand organizational culture or support strategic decision making. As decision complexity increases, however, traditional databases and information systems become less useful. Highly complex decisions incorporate "hard" knowledge systems, but also utilize many "soft" technologies. We will explore support for these other decision modes more fully in the following chapters.

As far as helping people understand culture or strategy, a performance support system can support *individual* learning in these areas, by providing information about these subjects. However, most performance support systems are not designed as collaborative learning processes. Technology is helpful in imparting information *about* culture, but the actual lived learning experience of an evolving culture is very different. Learning processes around organizational culture can include information resources, but culture involves more *Managing* mode learning. This requires additional types of supporting technology as we will see.

Creating *Procedural* Knowledge

Procedural knowledge and performance is identified with the *Information* class of knowledge, because of the linear logic both employ. Information is linked data. Whenever people organize raw data through linear stringing or categories they are creating *Procedural* knowledge. *Procedural* knowledge is also generated whenever people refine step-by-step processes for standardizing simple, everyday work processes. An example might be a checklist of items needed to complete a mortgage loan.

Either an individual or a group can produce *Procedural* knowledge. One or two people can develop a policy, define conformance standards, or design a simple process. This is in stark contrast to more complex modes, such as the *Integrating* mode, that generate knowledge almost exclusively through group processes. Even at the *Procedural* level, cross-functional teams are valuable to prevent needless redundancy and creeping bureaucracy.

As with every mode of learning and knowledge creation, *Procedural* knowledge procreates spontaneously in any organization. If unexamined, however, these processes can either be too invasive or inadequate for optimal effectiveness. Richard Teerlink, President and CEO of Harley-Davidson, is a big believer in quality, but doesn't think much of policies and procedures. In most cases, he feels they are designed to protect us against the 5 percent who are abusers and abuse the 95 percent who do it right.

People need training and support for documenting and following procedures. Tight procedures ensure consistency and quality for smooth operations.

People also need to know they can test the logic of conformance requirements and provide feedback for improving procedures. They should not, however, need reams of policies for how to conduct themselves in a professional manner. If *Procedural* mode knowledge creation follows this direction, then something is badly out of sync in corporate values and culture.

Guidebooks, directions, policy handbooks, instruction manuals, process documentation, user's guides, filing systems, and skill-based training modules or performance support are all components of *Procedural* knowledge. These identify critical sequences and variations that need to be attended to for high performance and consistent quality. All of these are vehicles for converting tacit knowledge to explicit codified knowledge that can be shared. Developing such products fuels knowledge generation and creation.

Sustaining *Procedural* Knowledge

Information technologies are greatly facilitating our ability to sustain *Procedural* knowledge. Centralized networks allow either one central point or multiple points of input for data. Individual users can input daily results for compilation and distribution across the network. Databases allow sophisticated processing for representing and displaying information in multiple formats. Computer databases, employing object-oriented modeling techniques, encapsulate procedural knowledge with data. This enables continual updating by providing vital linkages to actual work processes.

Given advances in technology, it is relatively easy to capture, collect, and represent *Procedural* knowledge—at least on the technology side. However, on the human side, it is enormously challenging to design classification and indexing systems for retrieval of records and information. There is a whole art and science devoted to this. Many large companies have an internal records consulting group devoted to establishing filing systems and documentation procedures.

People are eager to access *Procedural* knowledge, but are less enthusiastic about contributing to it. Sustaining product databases, user's guides, or procedure manuals, whether they are paperless or hard copy, is an on-going challenge. Someone must be accountable for updating and accuracy. Since information technologies are so critical for support in this mode, a large part of responsibility for sustaining *Procedural* knowledge has resided in the information support services group.

However, the trend in designing information technology support for *Procedural* knowledge is to devise ways that data and information can be centrally organized, yet locally maintained and customized. Strategic data centers view themselves more as keepers of the standards, rather than compilers of data. This approach allows flexibility, while maintaining consistency and integration. Web technology is facilitating this distributed approval.

Sharing *Procedural* Knowledge

Codified *Procedural* knowledge forms a first level User's Manual for the organization. Its form is far less important than the mere fact of its existence. New employees can fast-track learning key procedures, norms, and standards when the organization makes them explicit and communicates them through a variety of media. Some companies have extensive on-line or Intranet resources where people can access needed information through their desk-top computer. Others rely on a corporate library, training programs, or internal "experts" acting as an informal network of mentors to convey knowledge.

The language of the *Procedural* mode is the language of standards, rules, codes, calendars, and step-by-step directions. Information systems are ideal for distributing this type of information throughout an organization. Documentation residing in a central database allows instant distribution of updates without having to physically reprint booklets or insert new pages into dozens of binders. The same holds true for data that is accessed through web sites.

The most used "soft technology" for sharing *Procedural* knowledge is skill-based training. Certain categories of knowledge and skills are so basic they are requirements for almost every member of the firm. Computer-based training has led to great efficiencies in transferring this first level of knowledge. These often take the form of self-directed learning programs that allow a user to work through material at their own pace. Federal Express is widely recognized as a leader in this approach, with a pay-for-knowledge system rewarding workers for completion of training modules.[3]

The practice of Total Quality Management also provides tools for sharing *Procedural* knowledge within work groups. Tools such as flowcharts, checklists, control charts, and Process Capability diagrams help people socialize learning and maximize *Procedural* efficiencies. These provide important visual representations of everyday work processes and variations. Quality tools are invaluable for shaping tacit knowledge of people's work into explicit shared knowledge.

Renewing *Procedural* Knowledge

Procedural knowledge is closely linked to *Functional* knowledge. Much *Procedural* knowledge renewal occurs when major work processes are reengineered. Yet, these linkages are often overlooked.

Procedural knowledge serves an important role in the checks and balances that keep a system working efficiently. Implementing something new always means something old must be dismantled. That dismantling includes interwoven systems of procedures and information that support and feed basic work processes. When people ignore or miss these linkages, they can inadvertently eliminate a high-leverage control point that stabilizes the system.

Knowledge and performance are systemically linked. Whenever there is a dramatic change in one aspect of performance, it has an impact on all other modes. There is a saying in systems thinking that the flutter of a butterfly's wings in China can lead to a thunderstorm in Kansas (or is it the other way around?). Revisions and changes at the *Procedural* level may go largely unnoticed. However, they could also be like small disturbances in a chaotic system, where they cause great instability farther down the line (see example). This is why a systems approach to change is so important.

A *Procedural* Knowledge Breakdown[4]

Not attending to procedures and implementing simple checks contributed to the financial collapse of Baring Securities, bankrupting one of the UK's oldest banks in the process. Irresponsible trading in derivatives on the part of Baring's Singapore manager resulted in a whopping $1.4 billion loss in 1994. When they unraveled the fiasco, astonishing inefficiencies came to light that allowed problems to escalate to catastrophic proportions.

The main difficulty was that each local office maintained its own office infrastructure. They handled their own systems, controls, accounting, settlement, and administration. Leeson, the trader responsible, was in the position of overseeing *both* trading and settlements, so there was no other responsible person to detect rigged reports. Barings did not even *own* a copy of a standard software used to verify margin accounts. Leeson was also able to hide his transgressions by creating an unreported account, which he was allowed to establish supposedly on behalf of a buyer who wished to remain anonymous. Headquarters chose not to examine Leeson's phenomenal success too closely, even though that in itself was a significant variation.

The company also chose not to join the International Swaps and Derivatives Association that would have brought new knowledge about derivatives control into the organization. It was common knowledge in the Singapore financial community that, through Leeson's arbitrage trading, Baring's held an extraordinary position in the Nikkei exchange. However, the only communication and feedback from the Singapore branch to headquarters came through Leeson. The entire financial catastrophe could have been avoided if some simple procedures had been implemented and maintained.

Procedural Performance Questions

Thank goodness there are people who excel at *Procedural* performance—they keep the rest of us on track and coloring inside the lines. They are the people who coach and guide us when we need to learn a very precise series of steps. They help define the most efficient way to accomplish a task. They help ensure quality and consistency. They will even walk us through all those forms, check-lists, audits, procedures, rules, regulations, and policies that keep things from turning into total chaos.

High performing organizations have their *Procedural* house in order. They appreciate that people need support, encouragement, and guidance in order to create and share the information they need in this mode. Here are some of the key questions that are indicators of high performance.

1. Do people get basic skill training in using equipment, software, and work tools?
2. Do people document their work flow and procedures using Total Quality techniques, such as checklists, flow charts, and statistical tools for under-standing variation?
3. For new employees, is there a formal orientation to policies, procedures, and standards?
4. Are there clear, commonly understood guidelines for handling transac-tions with vendors and suppliers?
5. Is there a way people can access consistent answers to frequently asked customer questions?
6. Is there an open, collaborative, ongoing process for creating, updating, and retiring procedures, regulations, policies, and standards?
7. Do filing systems follow a consistent logic across the organization?
8. Are there standards for organizing computer systems at the enterprise, local, and individual level?
9. Are databases and information interfaces organized in a way that is con-sistent with how the organization actually functions?
10. Do people employ methods to ensure the consistency of the key outputs of their work?
11. Are there clearly understood and communicated consequences for failure to conform to standards?
12. Can people quickly and easily access information on equipment, machine specifications, software, tools, policies, and regulations?

Taming Gigamonsters: Beyond Linear Logic

Linear logic is the backbone of computer technology. At the core of all computer codes is a binary number system, 0 and 1. This binary system utilizes a simple "yes—no" type of linear logic. This is why speed is so critical in computing processes. No matter how complex the task, a computer can only process se-quentially. (Even humans have difficulty paying attention to more than one thing at a time. While we may think we are doing several things at once, our at-tention actually switches very rapidly back and forth between them.)

A *Procedural* level "solution" to the limitations of linear processing is more speed. Speed, of course, is limited by the ability of electronic technology to move electrical impulses through circuitry. But, what if we shift to the next level of complexity for a solution? What if we find a way to move beyond binary processing?

Recently, computer scientist Leonard Adleman watched as associates in a research lab worked with strands of DNA. He was intrigued with similarities in the way they cut, spliced, and copied the strands of DNA and the way he manipulates numbers with computers. Then he wondered if DNA could somehow be harnessed to tackle calculations, perhaps more efficiently than man-made machines?

He devised a test using a batch of synthetic DNA molecules to tackle a math problem involving a theoretical travel itinerary and published his results. His success set off a flurry of experiments and speculation in the computer world. You see, DNA uses *four* building blocks, not *two*, as does the binary system of 0 and 1. This four-building-block concept offers exciting possibilities for simultaneous rather than linear processing. The possibility of using actual strands of DNA could yield some solutions a million times faster than electronic computers, because DNA relies on simple chemical reactions, rather than the movement of electrons on circuit chips.

The conventional computer can be likened to a race car that is very fast, but can carry only one passenger. The proposed DNA parallel-processing computer would be more like a fleet of buses; slower, but capable of carrying more passengers at once.[5]

This story illustrates how each mode has limits to problem solving. Sequential processes are a *Procedural* mode solution. Simultaneous processing solutions are associated with the next level of complexity, *Functional* learning. Whenever we reach the limits of thinking at one mode, moving to another mode can help us find solutions.

CHAPTER 9

Building Functional Knowledge

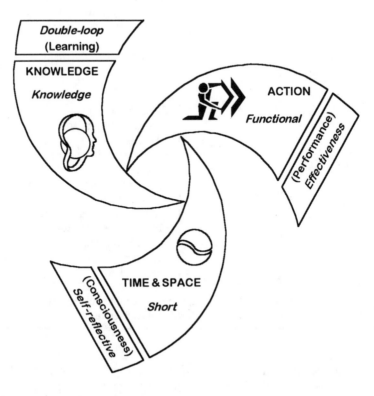

FIGURE 9.1 Relationship of Time, Knowledge and Action—Functional Mode.

TABLE 9.1 Functional Mode.

KNOWLEDGE ASPECT *Knowledge* Self-consciousness, reflection	ACTION FOCUS *Functional* Doing things the most effective way
LEARNING DYNAMICS *Double-Loop* A larger perspective that involves evaluation and modification of the goal or objective, as well as design of the path or procedures used to get there. Learning requires self-conscious reflection.	PERFORMANCE CAPABILITY *Effectiveness* Evaluating and choosing between two or more alternate paths. Goals are effective action and resolution of inconsistencies. Focus is on effective work design and engineering aspects, such as work flow analysis and process redesign.
Examples: • quantitative analysis • comparative analysis • creating meta-categories • cumulative processing • parallel processing	*Business Examples:* • reengineering processes • developing contingency plans • setting priorities • work-flow planning • scheduling production • setting daily and weekly goals • compiling historical data • identifying best practices • financial tracking • computer systems engineering • designing databases and knowledge systems *Tools:* • accounting software • databases • Intranets and groupware • flowchart and work-flow software • project management software • priority matrixes • Activity Network Diagram • PDPC Process Decision Program Chart • comparative matrixes • pie charts • Pareto charts

TIME HORIZON: Short, immediate past, and present
CONSCIOUSNESS: Self-reflective

Performance capability in the *Knowledge* or *Functional* mode means that functions and processes work effectively. The focus is on the design aspects of business operations, work flow, and the knowledge bases required to support them. The goal is to find the best solution, or the "right" way through logical thinking, engineering, and analysis.

People with talent for the *Functional* mode have a passion for the analytical aspects of their work. They enjoy using the quality tools, like to prepare for contingencies, and always attend to backup plans and copies. They push the rest of us to base our decisions on good solid data and information and to consider alternate approaches.

Functional learning marks the beginning of thoughtful reflection on our actions. This is the self-reflective domain of consciousness. Learning organization theorists call such self-reflective learning *double loop learning*. Double loop learning is an ability to reflect on one's actions, choose alternatives, and modify one's behavior. It means we can detect errors, then correct them in ways that involve the modification of the organization's underlying norms, policies, and objectives.

There are varying degrees of self-reflection. As we will see, *Integrating* and *Renewing* mode thinking requires deep self-reflection. Here, at the *Functional* level, there is self-reflection also. However, this self-reflection is *not* the kind of self-inquiry that might shift deeper assumptions. To understand why this is, we must look at the time horizons.

Time-Space Horizon

Functional performance has a larger time horizon than *Procedural*, but is still relatively short. Immediate past and present refer to the very recent past (say, a few months) and the present time (spanning only a few weeks or, at most, a month or two). The focus is still very much in the present, on what is happening now in regard to current activities. Longer planning horizons are not particularly relevant to the immediate concerns of *Functional* performance.

The time horizon also determines the problem-solving scope or "space" requiring attention. This slightly expanded horizon allows room for analyzing and refining an entire work process. It involves a greater span of control that may include many procedures or sub-processes within it. Thus, the expanded horizon also allows for more "depth" of self-reflection, logical thinking, and analysis, but not to the degree that underlying values would change.

At the *Functional* level, basic assumptions about the workplace and business operations are not challenged. There is general agreement about what the immediate objectives and tasks are. Questions at the *Functional* level have more to do with reaching those immediate goals as effectively and efficiently as possible. Therefore, learning and knowledge building focus on the tasks and work functions at hand.

Collaborative Work Processes

Functional learning also moves along the social continuum toward teams and group work. A work process usually involves a number of people, who socialize and discuss the work. While one person may attempt to design an entire process, the most effective work designs evolve collaboratively. As complexity increases, tools become more collaborative.

In this mode, visual diagramming techniques aid communication and compiling of knowledge. Other tools include project management software and databases holding historic data. Total Quality tools are used to design, manage, and control processes. Scheduling tools and software help insure consistency in workflow and production. These provide common ground and language for work groups.

As an example, think of operating a production line in a 24-hour manufacturing facility. There may be two or three complete shift changes in the course of 24 hours. Every shift change involves "knowledging" together. A tremendous amount of knowledge is needed to keep a production line running efficiently. That knowledge resides both in the workers themselves and in documents such as control charts, maintenance schedules, production schedules, process flow diagrams, and status reports. Workers hold tacit knowledge of the operations, while the documents and other materials convey explicit shared knowledge.

As a building block of *Functional* knowledge we would also find *Procedural* documentation of machine operations, policies, procedures, and safety guidelines. *Procedural* level knowledge also supports the smooth function of a production line. The degree of shared documentation indicates *collective* or *collaborative* learning processes, as opposed to individual knowledge building.

Functional Knowledge—Historical Context

The knowledge aspect of the functional mode is—*Knowledge*. The use of the word "knowledge" here is a nod to business and educational traditions. Applied, or functional knowledge, makes up the bulk of the world's shared knowledge. This mode of knowledge is easy to codify and document.

Functional knowledge is also the foundation for the great industrial economy that has carried us into the twenty-first century. Every economy builds on the collective knowledge base that precedes it. At the same time, each emerging economy carries us forward to another mode, demonstrating deep structural shifts in knowledge. *Functional* knowledge began moving to the forefront with the scientific discoveries of the eighteenth century. It was further fueled by the evolution of the great university systems and rising industries, such as steel making, machine tooling, and transportation.

Evolving Ways of Organizing

Functional knowledge relies heavily on traditional ways of organizing and sharing information. We have seen that data serves as a building block in a string of information. Information is a building block in a still larger body of knowledge. When we reach a critical mass of information, we begin to organize it into categories and meta categories, thus creating blocks of knowledge.

Traditionally we organize entire enterprises by grouping related workers together into functions or into job categories. We organize and index large clusters of related information by topic or subject and store them in file cabinets, manuals, and databases. These meta categories have allowed us to organize the large amounts of knowledge supporting a business. They have been very useful.

However, the service and knowledge-based industries emerging in the Knowledge Era are beginning to generate huge quantities of knowledge that do not lend themselves to traditional ways of cataloging and indexing. Neither can they be codified or documented as easily. The work cannot be organized in the old ways, because people perform multiple tasks throughout the day and work across functions.

Individuals have unique configurations of talents that simply do not fit categories. Today we must hyphenate descriptors of all kinds. We have Afro-Americans, bio-chemists, multi-media, performance-technologists, and cyber-librarians. People also don't stay put. They rotate in and out of projects and work groups. They need to access knowledge bases from remote geographic locations and even carry blocks of knowledge with them as they move from one assignment to another. All this mobility means that the way knowledge is created, shared, and renewed is changing dramatically.

Building Knowledge Bases

New ways of organizing knowledge are surfacing as technological capacity increases. We are beginning to hear information systems people and managers refer to building "knowledge bases." The emergence of this term in management literature clearly points to a fine-tuning of our ability to discriminate between information and knowledge. People sometimes define knowledge as "organized information." The question is, *how* is information organized to be knowledge? What invisible line does information step over to become knowledge?

Relationships are key. Data evolves into knowledge when it first begins to combine in strings of data linked by common characteristics. At that point data has become information. When information in turn is combined, recombined and accessed as meaningful clusters of knowledge, then the building of a knowledge base has begun. Discovering relationships *between* clusters of information provides breadth and depth, thus creating knowledge. Knowledge bases are those that begin to weave the web of information into various patterns of relationships.

Knowledge bases are becoming increasingly complex. There is a higher *knowledge complexity* in the content and a greater *technological complexity* as well.[1] These knowledge and technology dimensions combine into various configurations that define a range of simple or complex technologies to support knowledge building. Complex knowledge systems require more development time to prototype and produce. If knowledge must also be distributed, accessed, shared, and changed in multiple locations across the globe, then the technology complexity is quite high as well.

Complexity and Knowledge Bases

Commercially available tools, such as spreadsheet programs, database programs, and applications like Lotus Notes, have made it easier for both large and small companies to create shared knowledge bases. These have greatly facilitated creating and sharing knowledge with a low level of knowledge content complexity, such as *Functional* mode knowledge.

Higher levels of complexity in content represent a greater challenge. Consulting groups are in the forefront of creating knowledge bases for complex knowledge. In their practice they need to share theories, methodologies, and consulting modules that help their people perform projects. They also need to share knowledge about people in the organization and their capabilities. This helps people staff their projects appropriately.

As an example of an effort to capture such knowledge, Arthur Andersen began creating a Global Best Practices database in the early 1990s under the leadership of Robert Hiebeler. The purpose is to capture and share detailed information about successful business processes and management practices. During development, they learned that it is more important to move forward quickly with a prototype than have every design detail pinned down in the traditional software planning cycle. The more people experiment with and use a knowledge base, the quicker it evolves into a more collaborative and usable tool.[2]

Self-Organizing Knowledge

Experiments in creating knowledge bases are widespread in companies and professional groups. A quick browse of the Internet reveals company after company offering on-line knowledge resources, such as Federal Express's package-tracking database. The Internet itself is a global experiment in knowledge creation. Back in 1945, in a world of manual typewriters, visionary Vannevar Bush imagined a computer environment where people could access knowledge through a mesh of associative trails. (He called this system a "memex" since the word computer was not yet in our lexicon.)[3] The world he envisioned has come alive via the Internet and Web technology.

The hypertext markup language (HTML) standard of the Internet is a radical departure from the old way of organizing knowledge. Old-order organizing uses classes and subclasses. For example, when you dial a phone number, the switching process does not sort through every number that exists. It first selects the class designated by the first number, then the subclass defined by the second number, on down to the last. So the sorting process starts at the top and drills down. To move to a new number set, though, you must start at the top all over again.

The familiar HTML interface of the Internet, however, lets people click on a highlighted word and jump to another page, following their own intuitive chain of associations. This means association trails can run in almost any direction. Also, a connection or trail once laid down can be saved, retraced at will, and shared as a road map to guide others to a particular node of information. The ease of creating connective webs is sparking experimentation on an unprecedented scale.

On the Internet, *knowledge rides language*. People connect by seeking key words that represent their interest area. Please note that there was not some database guru or super geek trying to organize all the world's knowledge into categories with fancy interfaces. The Internet is self-organized—spontaneously and explosively. The connective tissue of the Internet is provided by technology protocols and the shared navigational device of HTML language.

Hundreds of companies are developing private, internal Internets, or *Intranets*, as an inexpensive yet powerful alternative for internal communication. AT&T, Levi Strauss, 3M, National Semiconductor, Silicon Graphics, and Next Computer are among them. The new technology is serving as a great equalizer in which the same electronic information can be viewed by any employee, regardless of their PC platform.

Connecting internal knowledge nodes via Intranets is sparking unprecedented collaboration and sharing of expertise. Individuals and work groups can post their own web pages. In one heavily team-based company, the Intranet has become the primary way people communicate their skills and availability for projects. People with a Web page have work. Those without one must rely on traditional channels to make contact. The Intranet is a major step forward in the ability of people within an organization to self-organize.

The building of knowledge is a continual growing, living, breathing process. Our information systems and knowledge bases must be able to evolve as our questions and structures change. They cannot do this if they are organized by functional relationships instead of knowledge relationships. Topics, language, and categories can change almost overnight, rendering databases and filing systems obsolete. Fundamental orders of complexity and knowledge, however, do not change. The organizing principles of knowledge itself last through time.

Creating Functional Knowledge

Sharing and refining *Functional* knowledge, such as engineering schematics and process documentation, is much easier today than it was even ten years ago. With graphics capability, computers, and communication technology, even geographically distributed work groups can share practical knowledge about their work.

Knowledge creation at the *Functional* mode occurs whenever people refine and shape their work processes and operational procedures. Widespread education and use of quality tools for process documentation have increased the ability of people to generate, apply, and renew functional knowledge. There are norms of working and standardized ways people do things in any organization. Whenever people draw schematics, share the best way to do something, or develop charts showing historical data and important variations, they are creating *Functional* knowledge together. Other examples are work-flow documentation, contingency plans, production schedules, and engineering schematics of every kind.

Sustaining Functional Knowledge

It is important to capture and organize knowledge about work processes and best practices. Whenever a new person joins an existing team or functional work group, they need to be able to come up to speed on how things work. Codifying, organizing, and documenting basic operational knowledge is fundamental for workplace effectiveness.

The way knowledge itself is organized is an important consideration for sustaining *Functional* knowledge. Organization of knowledge is a hot topic these days in government agencies. For example, The U.S. Air Force Center for Quality and Management Innovation is developing an infrastructure for sharing best practices. Captain Donnie Williams is one enthusiastic participant in this effort. He explains that the key to their success lies in being able to develop a classification scheme that will work across all databases, including those residing in other government agencies. For example, the recruiting process would use the same code across all the agencies. This departs from subject classification in that it organizes around *work processes*, not topics.

Another government project along these lines is an effort to revamp the Standardized Industrial Classification Codes Manual to reflect process organization, rather than traditional functional models. They are expanding the classification system so that each company can code performance measures by a four-digit code. The performance measures are all the various statistics reported and filed by various agencies. Another similar undertaking is the overhaul of the Classification Manual of job classification and occupational titles.

The problem with any classification or coding scheme is that it is a freeze-frame photo of knowledge at a particular point in time. Yet, knowledge is always moving. The language moves on, knowledge expands, and it no longer fits the old boxes.

The way we organize *existing* knowledge also shapes *future* knowledge. Organization is as important as content. Linkages between items and overall classification schemes determine how new information integrates with old. The structure therefore shapes what people see as relevant or not relevant. It acts as a gatekeeper, allowing some things into the knowledge system and omitting pathways for other types of information. When it comes to organizing knowledge bases, it is good to remember just how slippery knowledge is. Looser is better. You can waste a lot of resources trying to button it down too tightly.

Sharing Functional Knowledge

The language of this mode centers around work processes and operations. It is the language of work design, practical engineering, and work group organization. Virtually any communication channel or media can be used for conveying, socializing, and sharing *Functional* knowledge. However, we have become so enamored with information technologies that we often overlook valuable low-tech methods of knowledge sharing.

Any physical work space carries information and messages. Production areas in plants convey *Functional* knowledge with color-coding, directional and informational signs, and physical layout. Walls of meeting spaces hold flow charts, schematics, production schedules, control charts, and performance records. Drawers hold engineering drawings, and individuals have repositories of knowledge such as files, saved articles, and personal organizing systems.

There is no one best vehicle for sharing Functional knowledge. All of these media can be used and many more besides. The important thing is to train people in the use of analytical tools for understanding work processes and use them often. The key to sharing functional knowledge is to be sure people know the languages of the mode and are rewarded for using them. In addition, self-reflection and knowledge sharing must be supported by removing organizational barriers to communication and fostering a learning culture.

Renewing Functional Knowledge

Renewing Functional Knowledge involves much more than simply maintaining a knowledge base, although that is often a key enabler. Continuous improvement approaches, Total Quality management, and work process reengineering are very effective for renewing *Functional* Knowledge. Renewal also occurs when people question the way they organize that knowledge in the first place, as is happening with the government reclassification projects.

Functional Level Performance Questions

Companies with high level performance in the *Functional* mode realize productivity gains from fine tuning their business processes. They know how to engineer work processes and enhance knowledge sharing for maximum effectiveness. The following questions are critical success indicators.

1. Do people in the organization consistently and regularly use process and work-flow analysis tools?
2. Do people conduct contingency planning and create backup systems?
3. Can financial analysis be conducted on a project by project basis?
4. Are people using project management software, tools, and techniques?
5. Do people have the historical data they need to understand their progress?
6. Do people understand the key performance and productivity measures for their work?
7. Can changes in customer requirements or technology be easily incorporated into designs for products and services?
8. Do people work together as teams to seek improvements and redesign their work as needed?
9. Do people actively seek, gather, and share internal best practices?
10. Do individuals make regular contributions to shared knowledge resources?
11. Are there clear communication processes and channels for work status reports, such as production and meeting schedules?
12. Is there regular, on-going cost/benefit analysis of your technology support systems?
13. Do you experiment with knowledge building technologies, such as groupware and internal web sites?
14. Do you have the capacity to customize and update the design of knowledge and databases?

Solving a Functional Problem

A small company manufacturing highly sophisticated parts for electronics had an operations problem. Their primary manufacturing process required a number of highly sensitive machines running continually over any 24-hour period. However, they were experiencing so much down time of machines needing repair that productivity was slipping. If a machine went down it would take several hours to arrange for service, complete the repairs, and bring the machine back on line.

Through process analysis, problem solving, and improving coordination with repair people, they achieved considerable improvement. The total repair time was reduced to about half of what it was. Still, the improvement team felt they could do more. So, they decided to benchmark best practices in machine repair with other companies. Best practices research discovered a company that had almost no down-time for machine repairs in a similar industry. In short order, the improvement team arranged for a visit with the other company.

When they visited the other operation, they found that the company, with almost zero down-time, did not have a dramatically different repair process, as they had anticipated. They achieved their remarkable record in repairs and maintenance by using self-managed work teams. The team members on each shift not only ran the equipment, but handled repairs on it as well. The improvement team realized that they would not be able to achieve the same results unless they implemented a similar approach.

When they returned from the visit, their improvement efforts had completely changed focus. Now they began to look at self-managed work teams in earnest, exploring ways they could develop a similar team environment. In order to solve the *Functional* level problem in machine operations, they needed to address issues of organizational culture, behavior and norms, roles and relationships. The new level of thinking required to solve their problem came from the *Managing* mode. Once again we find that when we cannot solve a problem at one level, we must shift to a different mode.

CHAPTER 10

The Making of Meaning

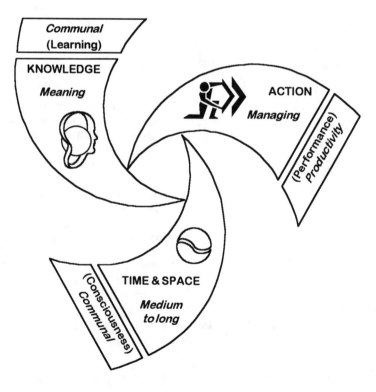

FIGURE 10.1 Relationship of Time, Knowledge and Action—Managing Mode.

TABLE 10.1 Managing Mode.

KNOWLEDGE ASPECT	ACTION FOCUS
Meaning	*Managing*
Understanding context, relationships, and trends	Understanding what promotes or impedes effectiveness

LEARNING DYNAMICS	PERFORMANCE CAPABILITY
Communal Learning	*Productivity*
Learning requires the making of meaning, which involves understanding context, seeing trends, and generating alternative paths to reach a goal. From this perspective it is possible to detect relationships between components, as well as determine roles and relationships between people.	Effective management and allocation of resources and tasks, using conceptual frameworks that analyze and track multiple variables. Encompasses planning tasks and measuring results. Also includes managing roles and relationships, providing leadership and direction for workgroups, and attending to company culture and communication processes.

Examples:
- multi-tracking
- generating and choosing alternatives
- seeing trends in events
- seeing relationships
- creating and interpreting symbolic language and events
- identifying variables

Business Examples:
- attending to the organizational culture
- tracking and interpreting results
- advocating for and allocating resources
- establishing goals and objectives
- managing roles and relationships
- interpreting events
- facilitating communication

Tools:
- performance evaluations
- budget processes, tools, and software
- supervisory, team, and managerial training
- Run Charts and Histograms
- Tree Charts
- PERT Charts
- planning processes
- Cause & Effect Diagrams
- Force Field Analysis
- Gap Analysis
- Group processes
- communication technologies
- Storyboards

TIME HORIZON: Medium to long (historic past, present, very near future)
CONSCIOUSNESS: Communal

Meaning happens in community. The aspect of consciousness associated with this mode is *Communal* consciousness. Context and community are so tightly interwoven we cannot separate them. Moving unspoken tacit knowledge into shared explicit knowledge requires socialization within our work community. While this is true in all learning modes, it is particularly true of *Meaning* or *Managing*. We cannot interpret organizational events as a solo act.

The time horizon of this mode is medium to long, which includes the historic past, the present, and the near future. The problem space boundary has expanded to include looking at multiple interwoven processes, understanding trends or variables, and considering both tangible and abstract influencing factors. As a consequence, the tools of this mode allow for more complex analysis of multiple factors. Solutions also move beyond engineering solutions to include culture and behaviors.

Self-reflection also expands beyond the boundaries of one's own individual actions or those of an immediate workgroup. The "self" that is reflected upon is a larger sense of self that includes one's communal work group and the organization as a whole. This expanded self-reflection makes it possible to reflect on roles, group dynamics, and social relationships.

A workplace is a collective social construct. Through a collective social process, we create culture, roles, norms of behavior, relationships, and physical environments. This society and community that we are part of shapes and influences all our actions. In turn, our repeated actions create norms of behavior, laying down pathways of familiar action in the organization in a similar way that repeated actions create neural pathways in the brain.

Language Carries the Meaning

Conversation leads to shared understanding. Complex systems, such as organizations, utilize internal communication for cohesive action and response. Collaboratively, we define our experience through language, and language shapes what we experience. What we call thinking, in a fundamental sense, is really just "languaging." We literally cannot know something without a word to describe it. Knowledge is theoretically infinite, because we have an infinite capacity to use language and create new words.

Noted systems thinker Bela Banathy got into systems work in the late 1950s. He was designing a curricula for foreign language education at the time. He says, "The most fascinating aspect of systems is revealed to us when we understand what language is all about . . . the ability to express ourselves in language is the most remarkable example of how systems work."[1] There is an intimate relationship between language, experience, and the systems we create. We know things are changing when the language we use begins to change.

There is a Zen teaching koan or riddle: *Whatever you say a thing is—it isn't.* The correlate riddle is, *Whatever you say a thing is—it is.* Both are true. Language symbolically represents our experience and yet, as a symbol, it is not the real thing. Even though language can never fully capture actual experience, a word holds the story of that experience in a way that can be shared with others.

This is why poetry and metaphor are such powerful devices for helping us integrate our experience. Poetry has sometimes been described as the making of meaning. Poetry, as shared expression, moves meaning to a deeper level of integration than the purely personal. It reminds us of the profound implications of being fully human in a complex universe.

> Poetry is news—news of the mind, news of the heart—and in the reading and hearing of it, poet and audience are fused. Strangers converge, but community emerges; the shared experience of being present when poetry is read reveals a particular life to be every life—my life, your life, you, me, us. It doesn't happen on the Internet in cyberspace; the mere transmission from afar of information or knowledge among parties with common interests is of course communication, but what occurs at poetry readings is communion.
>
> Bill Moyers[2]

The poetry or symbolic language of business life lies in our business stories and all our communication devices around our work. Business tools, methods, and processes give us a common language for our experience and work together. For example, the language of accounting and financial reporting provides a way for us to communicate about our experiences of money and profit. Total Quality tools brought a communication breakthrough because they gave us symbols, language, and diagrams to share our experience of work processes. At the *Managing* level our tools move beyond those that tell us *what* is happening. They help us begin to work with questions of *why* something is happening.

The Making of Meaning

Another way of thinking of the *Managing* mode is as "the story." Stories play a vital role in our work lives. In any organization the underlying collective story forms the rich texture of a company culture. We are so immersed in the story that we often do not recognize it for what it is. It helps to know who we are in the story and how our actions help shape the group story.

The story is the context of all our daily activity. All of us are in the middle of the collaborative myth-making of our company, just as we live our own individual story. A hypertext software developer once observed that the universe is not really composed of atoms, it is composed of stories. What we perceive in everything is a story. Think how these elements apply to an organization (Table 10.2).

TABLE 10.2 Context: The Elements of a Story.

Story element	In an organization
Setting	Where and when something takes place
Characters	Who plays what role, job descriptions, reporting relationships
Context	Culture, behavior standards, norms and expectations of the organization. Company history and present situation
Character motivation	Leadership values and identity
The challenge at hand	Goals and objectives
Sequence of events	Multiple tracking of activities, anticipation of variables
Unforeseen events	Unforeseen events
Use of resources	Allocation of resources
Final outcome	Results
What the story teaches us	Collective learning

We indoctrinate people into any culture by telling tales. Southwest Airlines is a great example of a company where the outrageous and humorous stories people tell form the backbone of customer service. President Steve Keller is one of the most colorful CEOs in American business and a superb manager of meaning. He sets the tone of the culture by spinning yarns of company heroes, including himself, as an example of desirable behavior. The constant telling and retelling of tales of outrageous customer service efforts fosters a culture of empowerment and friendliness. The unique culture of Southwest Airlines has helped them gain leadership in their market.

Symbols also help us make meaning of our experience. A corporate logo often carries archetypal symbolic meaning that helps to shape the company culture and identity. Symbols such as pyramids, globes, arrows, squares, blocks of certain colors, and all these in combination provide telling glimpses of an underlying story.

Robert Shank of the Institute for Learning has inquired deeply into the connections between computer logic, artificial intelligence, and adult learning. He says the only way we learn anything is by telling stories.[3] When we meet someone on an airplane, what do we do? We tell stories. I tell you one; you tell me one back.

Any trainer or educator worth their salt knows that people do not learn until they get to do something and then *talk* about it. They need to tell the story of what they just did. The only way we know we have learned anything is when our story changes. What we always notice are *changes* in our own story.

We say something like, *"Wow that was a great conversation."*

"Really, how did it go?"

"Well, I said this . . . and then I said that . . ."

"Hmmmm, what did the other person say?"

"Gee, I don't really remember, exactly, but it was a great conversation!"

What that person is telling us is how their own story is unfolding. What they "learned" during the conversation was a new story, a new language. They know learning took place, because they themselves said something new and insightful—for them.

Stories hold the context people need for making decisions and choosing a course of action. The most advanced corporate multimedia training programs use stories as the core teaching device. The learner works their way through a simulation of an actual situation, such as responding to a call for service. As long as their responses are correct, they simply keep working through the simulation. However, if they make an incorrect response, then a short film clip runs on the computer. What they see next is an actual person from their company telling a *story* of what happened when *they* did that and what kind of mess resulted.

Understanding *Managing* Performance

The *Managing* mode of performance and knowledge building has to do with understanding all the factors that promote or impede effective action and productivity. Those who attend to this mode are really the managers of meaning in our organizations. They hold the "why," helping interpret and explain events. They understand the story or logic behind the budget, behind the performance goal, behind the behaviors. From the context of the organizational story, we evaluate and choose from multiple paths of action and make appropriate choices.

Analysis in the *Managing* mode goes beyond just determining if something is or is not working well. It has to do with understanding all the factors that promote or impede effectiveness. Therefore, people who are attending to *Managing* performance may do any or all of the following:

- interpret events
- organize activity in the context of the corporate strategy
- manage roles and relationships
- help establish goals and objectives
- advocate for and allocate resources
- track and interpret results
- develop plans and budgets
- attend to the organizational culture

The language of this mode includes three important sub-languages. The first is the language of the story or context, similar to historical narrative. The second is a language of operational analysis, using conceptual frameworks and systematic approaches for analyzing and tracking multiple variables. The third language addresses human behavior and the social dynamics of the workplace.

Managing Mode Tools

Just as *Functional* learning is the foundation of the Industrial Era, the *Managing* mode of knowledge supports the service economy. Understanding human behavior and process engineering are *both* vitally important for delivering consistent quality of service. In the Knowledge Era, attracting, supporting, and keeping high-caliber workers is a key success factor. Organizations that understand *Managing* performance know how to attract the right people and provide the analytical tools they need to be productive.

The products of this mode could take the form of operational budgets, goals and tactical targets, implementation plans, complex schedules, and problem solutions. Other products define social behavior, such as organizational charts or reporting relationships, performance evaluations, behavioral ground rules, or accountability matrices. We find analysis tools, such as collaborative problem solving, run charts and histograms, tree charts, cause and effect diagrams, or financial analysis techniques such as determining profit and loss.

This mode requires being able to analyze and work with human dynamics. You cannot "engineer" human behavior in the same way you can engineer a work process or procedure. This requires a different type of knowledge: knowledge of culture, behavior, and human performance.

Managing Mode Talent

People with natural talent in the *Managing* mode find context is very important. They want the whole story. They are excellent at asking questions that will uncover the full situation: past, present, and anticipated. They want to know everything that is happening. People might even accuse them of micromanaging, but they are probably just curious, since they love to know everything that is happening.

When you ask these people a question they may very well respond, "it depends," because they are constantly weighing all the variables and considering multiple alternatives to determine what is appropriate for the situation. They are natural community builders. They facilitate the building of relationships and group cohesiveness. They probably enjoy project management, tracking resources, establishing realistic goals and objectives, and helping people define their roles and responsibilities. They have a quick grasp of planning processes and the tools of this level.

It is important to understand that the *mode* of the work is very different from the *functional role* of who actually does the work. So, when we speak of *Managing*, we are not necessarily talking about the manager role in a work group. The *Managing* level tasks must be accomplished in any work group for effective performance. However, team members could share the responsibilities, as in a self-managing work team, or they could rotate tasks among individuals. It does not mean that only managers attend to these tasks.

Creating *Managing* Knowledge

Managing mode knowledge surfaces in a variety of ways. Tools that support generating new knowledge may require either collaborative or individual approaches. Some statistical tools and analysis can be completed by an individual. For example, one or two people can conduct financial analysis, especially with the aid of some of the more intelligent software that is now available. An individual person can also create a histogram, control chart, or comparative matrix. These are all ways of creating knowledge that helps people make decisions and improve their work.

However, most decision processes and other types of analysis for this mode really require a group. When people begin to explore *why* something is happening, the work becomes much more collaborative. Organizations are complex systems and no one person alone can understand a system. A team or work group, acting as a group intelligence, brings much more knowledge into the process than one person can hold alone. As complexity increases, the work moves along the social continuum toward more collaboration and teamwork.

Knowledge creation in the *Managing* mode is largely by group process. As a rule, teams and work groups generate the knowledge. Whenever people come together to analyze and interpret events, their interpretation is new knowledge. We often do not recognize interpretation and understanding as knowledge. We generally do not view meetings and collaborative problem solving processes as places for knowledge creation. We think of them as places where decisions are made. Yet the logic, reasoning, thinking, analysis, and social contracts that were part of that decision making process *are* knowledge products.

Viewing meetings as knowledging events is a dramatically different perspective and a most important one. Once people value meetings as knowledge generators, then they pay more attention to meeting dynamics. Training large numbers of people in facilitation and meeting effectiveness techniques brings a different quality of participation to the table. People pay attention to *how* they are learning and thinking together, thus enhancing learning. They more deliberately produce knowledge products, such as problem solutions and action plans. They attend to their communication processes and are more open to other people's ideas. They learn to use analysis tools together as a way to enhance communication and understanding. They *know* they are creating knowledge and understand its importance.

Companies that value this learning mode experiment with different ways of coming together. They use groupware technologies and internal on-line chat spaces. They utilize different meeting formats and capture shared understanding graphically. Consultants such as David Sibbet of Graphic Guides, and others from Whole Systems Associates, use graphic facilitation techniques to uncover insights and metaphors that bring knowledge breakthroughs.[4]

Sustaining Managing Knowledge

Managing knowledge is very different from the other modes. Codifying and sustaining it requires a variety of techniques. Here we have shifted from the engineering and schematic language of the *Functional* mode to a much more narrative language that uses symbol, metaphor, and stories.

Internal training and education serve the purpose of sustaining and perpetuating this type of knowledge very well. Some companies only provide skill-based training that supports *Procedural* and *Functional* tasks. Companies that value learning and knowledge creation, however, will be as interested in how people *think* and learn together as they are in how they perform their *tasks*. In these companies, training programs help make explicit the tacitly held knowledge of culture and context. Such programs reveal and communicate the underlying logic for decisions and behavioral norms.

For example, companies that care about service deliberately indoctrinate people into a particular culture. The Disney Company, Southwest Airlines, and Andersen Consulting do this exceptionally well. They spend weeks training, mentoring, and coaching new people in understanding the company culture and norms of behavior. In places where culture is not attended to in a deliberate way, people still soak it up anyway. Without explicit education into the culture, however, people have to pick it up tacitly. If they misunderstand cues and signals, they can make inappropriate choices and miscommunicate.

It is equally important to provide training for the thinking skills needed in this mode. Managing knowledge involves more abstract reasoning and analysis. People do not automatically know how to take a disciplined approach to thinking and problem solving. Training in Quality Tools, financial analysis, root cause analysis, project management, budget processes, performance management, team communication, work styles, or thinking styles gives people the common language they need to generate and share knowledge.

There is an important caution around sustaining *Managing* knowledge. It is easy to go overboard in trying to capture and document this type of knowledge. A creative balance must be achieved. Stories are alive and continually changing. Think of the water analogy again. If you try to lock up this knowledge into institutionalized behaviors or centrally archived documentation, you only slow down its movement. The story and the knowledge it carries will become stagnant and cease to flow.

The most important sustaining technologies for *Managing* knowledge are communication technologies. It is much more important to attend to the flow of information than it is to archive documents formally. Today, in networked organizations, knowledge is everywhere and nowhere. It is far more effective to help everyone understand the nature and importance of the story, so they will value the shared history of their own projects. Then they will self-organize to collect what they need. Giving people leeway to capture and share in their own way frees creativity as well. For example, a consulting group in Seattle is using video technology to capture the stories of teams and workgroups.[5] Consultants like Randy Pennington also use video and theater to help teams discover insights into their culture and work norms.

Sharing Managing Knowledge

Our usual state in regard to knowledge is to be completely unaware of it. We are like fish with no concept of water because we are submerged in it. Yet, everything we create is first a product of our minds, our knowledge. Until people appreciate that knowledge itself is critically important to the creative enterprise, they cannot fully share their knowledge. They must address knowledge sharing in a deliberate and explicit way as a community. We must learn to speak the *language* of knowledge together to truly share knowledge.

A friend of mine is a rising executive in a large telecommunications company. He said to me one day that he cared little about what title or position he holds at any given moment. "I just want to be in the conversation," he said. By the conversation he means he wants to be in the middle of the story, to be an active participant. Sharing knowledge means bringing people into the conversation. First, they must learn the various *languages* of knowledge, so they can more effectively share knowledge together.

In the *Managing* mode, learning and knowledge themselves become a critical part of the conversation. Learning happens anyway, because learning is intrinsic in a social system. If we wish to learn more deliberately and effectively, however, then learning *itself* must be part of the conversation. People must understand themselves as participants in a learning community.

Vehicles for sharing *Managing* knowledge are varied. Oral and written communication is critical, because narrative often carries *Managing* knowledge. Maps, diagrams, documents, and schedules serve as illustrations for the story, but the narrative behind them needs to be shared as well.

Any communication channel can help carry the story. Computer technology supports sharing of documents, diagrams, and conceptual models that support thinking and decision making. Increasingly a shared computer work space becomes the meeting place where people generate and share knowledge. Intranet technology helps people forge working relationships with each other and pull together team members. Individuals and work teams can create Web sites to tell stories of themselves and their projects. US West Communications, for example, has launched an effort to create personal home pages for all 50,000 employees. Other powerful vehicles are meetings and action learning educational programs where people can socialize their work with each other.

Renewing *Managing* Knowledge

Managing knowledge renews when the story changes. You know the story has changed because the language changes. The self-organization of knowledge becomes very apparent in this process. First a few individuals pick up a new language. Then a few more people begin to use the same words until they reach a mysterious critical mass. At some point it becomes "the way we do things." The story has changed. Learning has taken place. A new component of organizational knowledge has appeared.

Knowledge renewal in this mode involves the development of new languages for how people can work more effectively together. Language brings shared understanding. If you would renew *Managing* knowledge, then listen for the words people use and the symbols that are emerging. Attend to the language of the emerging culture.

Managing Performance Questions

Companies with high capability in *Managing* mode appreciate collaborative problem-solving techniques and collective knowledge. They understand culture and context, while providing tools, techniques, and communication that help people understand the larger story of the work they do.

1. Are people trained in tools for tracking multiple variables and generating alternative strategies?
2. Does everyone understand the underlying logic for resource allocation and budget decisions?
3. Do people have access to resource and budget information across boundaries and functions in the organization?
4. Can roles and job functions be easily redesigned into different configurations within work groups?
5. Is there consistency in design and regular use of planning processes within functions and workgroups?
6. Do people have a way to give and receive feedback for their work across multiple levels and across functions? (360-degree feedback)
7. Are people skilled in using analytical tools, such as cause-and-effect diagrams, force-field analysis, and statistical tools that help them discover root causes of performance problems?
8. Are there varied communication media and channels, including cross-functional and bottom-up communication?
9. Are the dynamics of organizational culture widely understood and worked with in a conscious and deliberate way?

10. Do people receive coaching, training, and mentoring in their social skills and professional behavior across all roles and functions?
11. Is the social process of creating and sharing knowledge understood and supported in the culture?
12. Is there a climate of trust and sharing of information and expertise?
13. Is collaborative work supported with communication technologies, such as groupware, Intranet, and e-mail?
14. Are peopled trained, supported, and rewarded for collaboration and team work?

Reengineering the Technical Support Function

A large telecommunications company was tackling the redesign of core business processes. One of the most complex areas was technical support. Their processes involved providing technical service to a wide variety of business customers with varied technology systems. The technical support group consisted of multiple divisions and functions spread across a wide geographic area.

The improvement team approached the project systematically. They gathered a high-caliber cross-functional team and spent several months analyzing their processes, using a wide range of quality and analysis tools. They created flowcharts, organizational charts, gap analysis, statistical analysis, financial and resource analysis and demographic profiles. They pushed, probed, and prodded until they felt they knew their functional area and core process backwards and forward. Their immediate improvement and productivity gains were substantial. The team was pleased with their progress, yet still had not met their goals. They decided to try benchmarking with other companies to see if they could get one last real breakthrough.

In preparation for benchmarking, I introduced them to a systems mapping technique for depicting their technical support function in a way that would communicate to another company. There was some resistance to this at first. After all, they had just spent months analyzing their process, what more could another drawing reveal? I explained to them that the work they had been doing was focused only on the linear flow of the process and the organizational chart. They had been looking at the process and the roles people play, but they had not yet uncovered other types of patterns. They had used every *Managing* tool in the book, but no system-level tool. Systems mapping would help them explore dynamic relationships and exchanges that were working in multiple directions. It would help them see how all the pieces fit together. They agreed to give it a try.

As the mapping process unfolded, the picture of the work that began to emerge was quite different. They were suddenly able to see major communication gaps. They had overlooked key roles. Feedback loops were missing at critical points. As the system map finally took shape, the energy in the room suddenly shifted. It became very quiet. There were some whispered side conversations. I looked around the room, sensing something important.

"What is it, what's happening here?" I asked.

The team members looked at each other, shaking their heads. A team member finally stood up and walked over to the drawing. "This," he said, pointing to a heavily detailed place in the drawing. It was obvious just from the feel of the drawing that this part of the system was out of balance with the rest. "We just saw a whole group of people here that are getting in the way." He smiled a little ruefully. "Three of us on this team belong to that group. We just realized that if we do what we really need to do here, we will dismantle our own function. We never saw it before," he said, "but it seems so obvious now."

The story shows how shifting to a different language, in this case the language of systems, can help reframe a problem and reveal a solution. It is not always necessary to move to a greater level of complexity. Sometimes it is important to move in the other direction. Many times, human resource consultants or trainers are asked to do team building as a fix for other problems. Yet, analysis may reveal that they are struggling with a badly designed process. In that case, team-building work around roles and behaviors would not be very productive. It would be much more useful to use *Functional* mode engineering approaches to fix the broken process.

CHAPTER 11

Integrating:
The Quest for Elegant Solutions

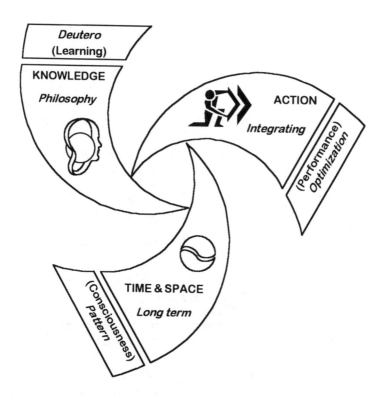

FIGURE 11.1 Relationship of Time, Knowledge, and Action—Integrating Mode.

TABLE 11.1 Integrating Mode.

KNOWLEDGE ASPECT *Philosophy* Dynamic relationships, self-organization	ACTION FOCUS *Integrating* Seeing where an activity fits the whole
LEARNING DYNAMICS *Duetero Learning* Integrative or systemic learning seeks to understand dynamic relationships and non-linear processes, discerning the patterns that connect, utilizing archetypes and metaphor. Requires recognition of the embeddedness and interdependence of systems.	**PERFORMANCE CAPABILITY** *Optimization* Understanding and managing socio-cultural system dynamics and complex processes and relationships. Focus is on long-term planning and the ability to adapt to a changing environment. Includes long-range forecasting, development of multi-level strategies, and evaluating investments and policies with regard to long-term success.
Examples: • divergent thinking • seeing dynamic patterns • questioning assumptions • developing theories • sensing archetypal patterns • systems perspective • discourse	*Business Examples*: • socio-technical systems design • multi-level strategic planning • long-range forecasting • long-term investing • establishing corporate strategy • systems integration and optimization • establishing operating principles *Tools:* • strategic planning processes • Hoshin planning • corporate storyboards • action-reflection learning • systems modeling • Dialogue • large-scale collaborative group processes • Affinity diagrams • industry benchmarking • customer surveys

TIME HORIZON: Long-term (past, present, and future)
CONSCIOUSNESS: Pattern

The *Integrating* mode is the learning edge for most of us in American business. Knowledge and action in this mode revolve around systems thinking, dynamic relationships, patterns, and the theories we develop to explain things.

Systems thinking means understanding how everything works together. We have traditionally managed, however, by breaking things down in parts, functions, or business units. We have learned to manage complexity by focusing on only one small area at a time. The ability to think, analyze, and act at the systems level requires a very different perspective.

Systems thinking requires deep self-reflection and the ability to see patterns. The domain of consciousness related to this mode is *pattern* consciousness. This particular aspect of consciousness is sometimes referred to as archetypal. Attention in this mode seeks underlying patterns.

Integrative learning is deeply self-reflective *duetero learning*. The phrase "duetero learning" means second-order learning, described by Gregory Bateson as the capacity to reflect on and inquire into previous contexts for learning.[1] This means deepening the learning process by inquiring into our own thinking processes. *Managing* mode interprets and translates context; *Integrating* calls that context itself into question.

The time horizon of this mode is very long-term, spanning years or even decades. The patterns that people can discern from this wider time horizon are dynamic patterns of relationships playing out over time. There is also a qualitative shift in time sense, a sense of many things happening at once. We become aware of the rich, dynamic interplay of events.

Along with the broader time horizon there is a corresponding spatial expansion of thought and analysis. The conceptual domain plumbs to the depths of abstract, philosophical, and theoretical concerns. The objects of analysis broaden to whole systems, societies, complex dynamics (such as knowledge!), and even complexity itself.

Integrating New Knowledge

Integrating new knowledge is critical for renewing organizational knowledge. Carl Jung suggests we really "know" something when new knowledge connects to old in such a way that both are transformed. Whenever we learn something new, we must somehow rearrange virtually everything we previously understood. We must integrate all our previous knowledge.

Transpersonal psychologist Ken Wilber describes real learning as a shift in the "deep structure" of our understanding.[2] When learning breakthroughs take place, our understanding expands. We see where the old knowledge was not wrong, but was too small. We then "translate" or reorganize all our knowledge to fit with the new and larger worldview. Learning is a constant process of reorganizing and interpreting experience. For example: a child first learns to walk. Later she learns to run, to skip, to dance. All these new ways of operating in the world do not make the old knowledge of "walking" obsolete. Rather the knowledge of walking is integrated into an expanded understanding of "dancing" or moving to rhythm and sound.

The Languages of Integration

The *Integrating* mode of knowledge addresses our fundamental understanding of how the world works. It is where we weave a cohesive worldview that helps us make sense of our world. The languages of this mode are languages of theory or philosophy, systems, patterns, archetypes, and metaphors.

Theory takes a bad rap in Western business culture. People have no patience for explorations of theory. However, we have a theory of everything whether we are aware of it or not. *Tacit* theory actually causes a lot more confusion than *explicit* theory. As Chris Argyris reminds us, there can be a huge difference between the *espoused theory* in an organization and the one actually in use.[3] It is not realistic to assume that everyone agrees on theory, or even understands which theory is in operation, just because they work in the same company. Unspoken theories are often in conflict. Yet, without a way to express them and make them explicit, there is no way to resolve the differences or create alignment.[4]

Our business theories include what motivates people, how they should work together, how the market environment operates, what "quality" is, what the future will look like, how to create profits, how to organize operations, and how the workforce should be configured. We have theories about the social contracts of the organization and the role of the enterprise in society. In addition, theory is always changing. The shelf life of a working theory can be decades (or even hundreds of years, in some societies), or it could last only moments. It is continually being tested, challenged, and revised by events. Our theories change constantly, even though we may not realize it in a conscious way.

"Without theory, experience has no meaning," says W. Edwards Deming. "Without theory, one has no questions to ask. Hence, without theory, there is no learning."[5] When people engage in duetero learning they speak directly to theory and underlying logic. They continually probe for the assumptions and mental models that lead people to particular actions. The purpose is not debate, but understanding. Since theories are always in motion and continually changing, inquiry is operational rather than seeking something absolute. Theories serve as reference points on the organizational compass. Theories help us hold steady to a chosen course.

Another language that typifies *Integrating* work is the language of systems and system dynamics. People engaged in systems work are interested in understanding the dynamic relationships between the parts of a system. They seek to understand the emergent properties of a complex system. The goal is to optimize the working of all the parts of a system while keeping the health and integrity of the whole. This is critical work for supporting transformational change.

Yet a third language is the language of patterns, archetypes, and metaphor. Metaphors are a basic structural experience through which we engage and understand our world. Aristotle calls metaphor the mark of genius. Even Howard Gardner is at a loss to explain it, leaving it outside his well-known framework of multiple intelligences.[6] Despite the strides of artificial intelligence, computers can only do concrete processing. They cannot employ the type of logic that leads poet Robert Burns to claim his love is like a red, red rose, or allows the rest of us to understand what he means.

Any situation can be viewed through many lenses. Metaphors serve as lenses that help us integrate a new area of knowledge with other ways of seeing.[7] In a very real sense the system is in the eye of the beholders. The more rigorously we test our perceptions and mental models, the more likely we are to reach insights that lead to more effective action. Metaphors are powerful tools for creating breakthrough associations and understanding complexity.

Requirements of *Integrating* Work

There are four key characteristics or requirements of *Integrating* or systems level work:

1. The use of bi-focal lenses, for understanding both the external exhibited behaviors of the system and the internal logic that sustains it.
2. A focus on dynamic relationships.
3. An emphasis on detecting the *patterns that connect.*
4. Realizing that it must be engaged in through group learning processes, since no one person can understand a system alone.

Systems thinking is very new for most of us, and still quite difficult. Our culture has powerful values, such as individual achievement, scientific specialization, and linear thinking, that seem at odds with systems values. Systems thinking requires a shift of mind.

The passage to real systems thinking can be most painful and difficult to navigate. Deep changes require letting go of old ideas, structures, and forms. Shifting into the *Integrating* mode of learning brings the sometimes painful crumbling of belief that all is ultimately "knowable" and "manageable," when in reality, it is not. This mode reveals a "quantum soup" of interconnected ideas, assumptions, and beliefs—a soup rich in self-renewing potential and creative possibilities. Thus, there is a profound shift away from the "controllable" world of objects and things and towards the realm of non-linear processes and relationships. With it comes a deeper understanding of interconnectedness and interdependence, thus reconnecting us to all of life and the flux and cycles of nature.

The Pattern That Connects

The pattern that connects is a term popularized by psychologist Gregory Bateson. It refers to both the conceptual and actual structural underpinnings of our lives. The pattern that connects could be a mathematical principle, such as those that create fractal patterns in nature. It could be conceptual, as in the underlying logic that guides the way we organize society or an organization. The pattern that connects could be a cycle of addiction or some other pattern of behavior.

What we seek today in our work life are elegant solutions. We are struggling with incredible complexity in a global, fast-moving environment. We are constantly being urged to be more flexible, more adaptable, and to be continually learning and improving performance. The old management structures and methods are simply not serving us in the way they once did. We need to find a simpler way. Seeking patterns helps us find the underlying principles and leverage points for action.

The quest to understand basic organizing principles typifies this search. This quest has led researchers and forward-thinking managers into complexity and chaos theory. Deere & Company uses insights from complexity theory to handle rapid changes on its assembly lines. Citicorp has also seen early positive results. The advance guard of explorers includes Meg Wheatley, who insists that new advances in scientific understanding will help us find a simpler way to manage complex enterprises.[8] Applying insights from complexity theory, Mike McMaster helps people ferret out the three or four key principles that drive a project.[9]

The *Integrating* mode seeks the elegant solution, the pattern that connects. Elegant solutions appear quite simple, yet they can encompass great complexity. A good principle for living is an elegant solution, a pattern of logic that guides the structure of our lives. A classic is the Golden Rule, "Do unto others as you would have them do unto you." Simple. Yet, as a living principle, it can serve as a guide to decisions in an infinite variety of daily situations.

The design of DNA uses only four chemical elements, yet as a way of organizing information it serves a myriad of organic living forms. It is a perfect example of an elegant solution.

The Elegant Solution of DNA

The story of how Watson and Crick unraveled the mystery of DNA is one of the most compelling scientific mystery stories of our era. DNA is remarkable in that a strand of just four chemical components holds all the encoded genetic information of a living being.

As Watson and Crick worked for days and months to understand DNA, they built several test models of the DNA molecule. If you have ever seen chemical models, you know they are these rather flimsy looking contraptions that bring to mind a bunch of tennis balls stuck together with sticks.

Watson and Crick built a number of these strange devices, most of them quite awkward looking. They tried various shapes and combinations, but nothing worked right. They couldn't figure out how the shape of the DNA molecule kept changing shape from one set of microscope slides to another. Then one day, they stumbled on the idea of the double helix structure. In a matter of a few short hours they put a model together and it all worked like magic. In looking back on their breakthrough they knew it was right because everyone agreed it was too pretty not to be true.[10]

Think about that for a moment. They knew it was right because it was so beautiful. What is it in us that responds to elegance, to beauty, to balance? I believe Maslow overlooked something very important in his Hierarchy of Human Needs. He missed our aesthetic needs, our sense of the beautiful. This may somehow relate to our sixth physical sense, proprioception, which is our sense of balance. Perhaps our sense of balance and our appreciation of beauty are the latent talents that will help us find simpler ways to deal with complexity.[11]

Understanding *Integrating* Performance

In an increasingly complex and turbulent environment, traditional planning processes are no longer adequate. Old ways of organizing for control are too rigid and confining. They set one part of the system against another, sub-optimizing the function of the whole. Traditional performance measures serve mostly *Functional* and *Procedural* performance. They are inadequate for understanding systems performance. We must find ways to help people think, analyze, and act with a whole systems perspective.

Expanding performance capability in the *Integrating* mode allows us to shift from managing functions or processes, to integrating a total system. As we expand our language, we expand our capacity for response in an increasingly complex economic environment. People who develop a particular vocabulary and understanding see things that are invisible to others. The traditional linear language that we inherited and use in business does not allow for emergent phenomena, polychronic events, or complex systems. The language of systems, chaos theory, and complexity does.

The linear language of the *Procedural* mode serves us well for certain purposes and is a necessary component for any well-run company. The process and engineering language of the *Functional* mode opens yet more possibilities. We expanded our *Functional* mode language with the introduction of Total Quality Management fueling a shift from organizing by function to organizing by process. The behavioral, social, and analytical language of the *Managing* mode helps us integrate multiple processes. In addition, it helped us move into a service economy, aiding our economic survival. Without a systems perspective, however, we carry some of our old problems with us. We must be careful. Instead of vertical, functional silos that don't communicate with each other, it is just as easy to create horizontal process silos (or perhaps process tube worms would be more appropriate) that don't relate to each other either.

Today, systems language and dialogue around assumptions open up still other ways of organizing and responding. *Integrating* languages and perspectives are particularly useful in the Information Economy and the networked world of the Knowledge Era. Ian Mitroff has traced the origins and structure of the inquiry systems or logical processes, drawing on the work of C. West Churchman. He contends that we need unbounded systems thinking as the logic for the Information Age. With this type of inquiry, while working on every problem we are also simultaneously working on how we organize *ourselves* to solve our problems.[12] This deeper self-questioning and inviting of diverse viewpoints and perspectives develops the capacity for true self-renewal.

Integrating Tasks

People who are *Integrating* thinkers love to explore interconnections and dynamic relationships. They pay attention to the big picture. With a long-term perspective they are intuitive strategic thinkers and enjoy doing complex planning. They also seem to be able to turn one idea into twenty at the drop of a hat. Complex mapping processes, such as system dynamics or relationship diagrams, fascinate them. They like to know the thinking behind the doing and are comfortable in the abstract realm of ideas and conceptual thinking.

Integrating tasks are mostly strategic in focus. They include conducting multi-level strategic planning, developing long-range forecasts, and evaluating long-term investments. Establishing corporate strategy and direction is of concern at the system-wide level. Another goal is assisting the system as a whole in working well. On the team or divisional level, integrating means working those same issues from the other direction. It could mean helping people understand how actions integrate with strategy, or giving feedback and input into the planning process.

There are many different processes for strategic planning. Yet, only a few take a truly integrative whole systems approach. Stuart L. Hart, of the University of Michigan, did a comparative study of strategic planning processes that identified six distinct approaches. Each is appropriate for different business situations and environments. Although he does not examine the knowledge aspect of these, they fall clearly into the modes of the archetype (see Appendix 1). This is another example of the embeddedness and holonic nature of knowledge. Even within the task of a particular mode, we still approach those tasks from the perspective of the modes that are most comfortable for us.

The most critical challenge is system integration and optimization. This is not merely the concern of a group of executives in some remote corner of corporate headquarters. The task of system optimization must involve everyone. If it doesn't, it isn't systems work—it is traditional hierarchical management. This means every work group in the organization must be able to use system analysis tools and techniques for understanding their work.

Companies that have incorporated Total Quality Management know systems analysis is the next learning edge for their people. Many of these progressive companies are actively seeking ways to introduce systems tools and thinking into the organization. Large automotive companies, such as General Motors and Ford Motor, are embracing learning organization concepts and systems thinking. Ford Motor's executive group developed guiding principles for their shift to systems and founded a Systems Learning Network to share knowledge.[13] However, systems thinking is still a new language for us. It has not yet reached critical mass for becoming "the way we do things."

Creating *Integrating* Knowledge

A number of tools and techniques are helping expand *Integrating* knowledge. When people employ such tools in their work, they are creating new theories-in-action and systems knowledge. One way to recognize new systems tools is by whether they require a group to be effective. Group tools can work for any mode, but collaboration is a necessity for systems thinking.

Some knowledge creation tools are collaborative planning processes, such as Hoshin planning. There are also large-scale collaborative group planning processes, such as the Future Search Conference technique developed by Marv Weisborg.[14] Dialogue and action-reflection learning experiments also foster *Integrating* knowledge creation. For example, General Electric Nuclear Energy uses action-learning to help new engineers learn big-picture thinking and reflect on their own learning process.[15]

Also useful are collaborative brainstorming techniques and problem-solving approaches using affinity diagrams or the facilitation technique developed by the Institute of Cultural Affairs (ICA). Benchmarking both internal and industry-wide best practices helps open up the self-inquiry process and questions underlying assumptions of how people approach their work.

The field of system dynamics, led by Jay Forrester and others at MIT, has spawned a whole generation of system-modeling softwares and approaches that help people model complex systems. Another recent addition to the systems mapping tool kit is my own HoloMapping™ technique, which shows dynamic relationships.[16] Business games and simulations can be very powerful knowledge creation devices for the *Integrating* mode. Some, referred to as Micro-Worlds, simulate the operation of a complete system or enterprise and can help uncover archetypal system behaviors.[17] Simulations, games, and other types of managerial practice fields offer excellent opportunities for learning and knowledge creation. They encourage dialogue and help reveal important assumptions and conceptual models.

In my own work with people in this mode, I find it is important to introduce tools that support the bi-focal lens requirement for systems work. Visual mapping techniques and tools help people identify and understand external behaviors. Conceptual thinking techniques, such as dialogue and the ICA collaboration technique, help people in the more abstract domain of the concepts, theory, and mental models. *Both* are needed.

Sustaining *Integrating* Knowledge

Integrating knowledge has its own particular shape and features. Tangible products may take the form of diagrams, drawings, planning documents, and working simulations that can be catalogued, indexed, and stored in some way. These all help people see and understand critical patterns. Indeed people need to access documents that depict and track the observable behaviors, components, and dynamic relationships of a system. Documentation also can help people understand the logic and thinking behind a particular design, operating principle, or strategic direction. Some companies develop internal white papers that help explain managerial thinking.

The tacit dimension of theory does not lend itself to simple documentation techniques. Documents may support theory creation, or "tell the story" of the theory. They may even describe it in exhaustive detail. However, the actual lived experience and experimentation of a theory-in-action is a creative, ongoing process. It is best to remember that theory is always operational and in process. It serves to move us forward, but if we become stuck in one theory, we might miss our future. Trying to codify or institutionalize theory can easily stifle the knowledge creation process, turning *Integrative* knowledge into just one more organizational artifact.

In this mode, we begin to appreciate the limits, not only of understanding, but even of knowledge itself. Knowledge of a system and how it operates can never be fully captured. Why would we even want to exhaust ourselves in such a task? Such a strategy would be in direct opposition to the knowledge-creation processes for this mode, where new knowledge emerges collaboratively through constant dialogue and self-questioning.

Knowledge is inexhaustible in its combinations and recombinations. Here, we must truly learn to discern what is important to pay attention to and what is not. We take in and absorb much more than we realize. We understand much more than we appreciate. We must learn to trust that when we have inquired deeply together and reached a shared understanding, that we already have what we need. We can often let the rest of it go.

Sharing *Integrating* Knowledge

In certain circles, people are very interested in what they refer to as "transfer of learning." The "problem" or question they are trying to solve is how to transfer learning or insights experienced by one group to another group or individual. I do not think we *can* transfer learning to anyone else. We can transfer knowledge or information, but *learning* itself does not seem to transfer easily.

As codified information, knowledge products that result from employing the above listed tools and techniques can be and are circulated. However, I have noticed that the learning "charge" that accompanies the creation of the knowledge curiously dissipates as it passes from individual to individual or is distributed outside the workgroup. One of the biggest frustrations in benchmarking is when major insights and performance breakthroughs do not spread in a company. One business unit achieves improvement, but nobody else picks up the new best practice, even when the team "shares" their learnings with the other group.

Collaboratively generated knowledge has a unique quality. The people who created it easily can be re-inspired by it, apply it, or pick it up and work with it again. I have noticed, however, that people who did not participate in the knowledge creation process tend to devalue the same work, or take it in a very different direction. People may not understand the documents and diagrams, or they may not agree with them and shift into criticism instead of inquiry. This quirk actually evolved into a founding principle for group processes: *people support what they help to create.* Of course, the corollary to that is people do not support what they did not help create.

Sharing and creating are intimately connected. This is true for any mode, but it is particularly true in the more abstract modes such as *Integrating, Renewing,* and *Union.* I believe this has to do with the linguistic structure of our thought world and the dynamics of the dialogue process.

Language carries meaning. In the process of knowledge creation, people perform many language "experiments." They try out ideas, they test words, they suggest metaphors and analogies, they tell stories. A participant integrates this *lived experience* of the dialogue as part of their new knowledge. Yet, it cannot effectively be captured and shared—unless, perhaps, someone was standing by with a video recorder.

If we want to share *Integrating* knowledge, we must learn to share the *learning process,* not just the codified knowledge that might result. We must give people the freedom to think deeply with each other and create together the embodied knowledge of their new understanding. Systems-level learning has a unique quality that cannot be codified and shared in traditional ways. As we all become more proficient at collaborative processes, we will increase our understanding of this type of learning. We will have a better understanding of what can and should be shared, and what cannot.

Renewing *Integrating* Knowledge

Integrating knowledge renews when there is a change in the underlying logic influencing the actions and behaviors of individuals and groups. Until the organization as a knowledge-creating society appreciates that logical discourse is valuable, neither knowledge renewal nor substantial change can take place.

Integrating **Performance Questions**

1. Is there a clear corporate theory of how your business operates?
2. Are there processes for understanding, developing, and changing focus in core knowledge competencies and core business processes?
3. Do people engage in whole system, collaborative planning processes, such as future searches and planning retreats?
4. Are people trained in systems thinking techniques?
5. Do people regularly engage in systems mapping processes where their work touches that of another work group?
6. Are there company-wide processes for openly questioning assumptions and challenging "sacred cows?"
7. Are there rewards for successful challenges to current thinking?
8. Are people encouraged to have active exchanges with the environment by participating in professional associations, conferences, and trade shows, or by obtaining continuing outside education?
9. Are corporate strategy and operating philosophies clearly defined and understood by everyone?
10. Are people within the company comfortable with contacting anyone that might be able to help solve a problem?

Harley-Davidson—The Story of a System Turnaround

Harley Davidson was in big trouble. Their market share in motorcycles had dropped from over 70 percent in the 1970s to a low of 23 percent in 1983. Quality was so poor that brand new Harleys on the showroom floor sat on cardboard to absorb the oil leaks. Today, they have almost tripled daily production, and are so inundated with orders they have a two-year backlog on some popular models. Despite demand, CEO Richard Teerlink holds firm that quality will not be sacrificed for quantity.

Harley's turnaround was not a case of better strategic planning or a deep and complex business analysis. They could not take time to do traditional planning. It was transform or die. Only a desperate, last-minute buyout by top managers prevented filing Chapter 11 bankruptcy. On the positive side of the balance sheet, Harley had one tremendous asset going for it—their extremely loyal customer base.

Harley jettisoned any business unit that was not a part of its core manufacturing business. Teerlink says, "We created a vision that was simple: survival." The company began to court and listen to its customers. They began sponsoring and holding Harley rallies as opportunities to build loyalty and listen to the customer.

With Teerlink's personal involvement and leadership, they became passionately committed to Total Quality and continuous improvement. Employees were encouraged to challenge, ask questions, and contribute their ideas. They trained like crazy in quality, and in *anything* that a critical mass of employees said they needed. A whole new culture began to emerge. A new language emerged centering around ideals such as quality, participation, productivity, flexibility, and cash flow. They began delivering new, high-quality products and services to a fiercely devoted and growing customer base. Today, they are a globally-integrated, first-class goods producer and marketer.

There are many components to this success story, as there are in any story of transformational change. However, the change grew out of one basic shift. What really changed Harley was the rediscovery of identity, purpose, and values. Their organization as a system was clearly broken and in its death throes. To survive, one thing had to change—their sense of who they were as a company.

The clarity of that rediscovered identity rings through the way they talk about themselves. "We are in the business of motorcycles by the people and for the people." They state, "We sell excitement, a way of life." They have a clear sense of their identity and a sense of community with their customers.

Core values at Harley-Davidson are simple:

1. Tell the truth.
2. Keep your promises.
3. Be fair.
4. Respect the individual.
5. Encourage intellectual curiosity.

The values were worked out at company-wide meetings in the late 1980s. As people at every level discussed what it meant to "tell the truth," norms of behavior began changing dramatically. As a result, most of the senior management team was eliminated, because they were no longer needed.

The Harley story is more than a story about large-scale change. It is a story about heart, spirit, and vision. It is a story about renewal.[18] The heart of organizational effectiveness lies even beyond systems thinking. It arises in the still more abstract domain of values, purpose, and identity.

CHAPTER 12

Renewing:
Reconnecting with Purpose

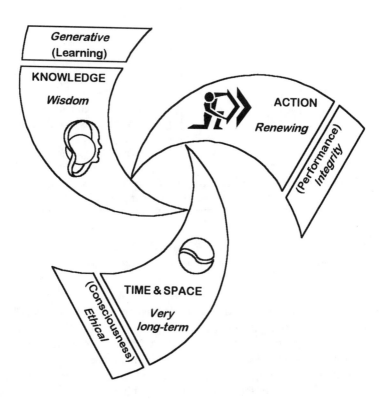

FIGURE 12.1 Relationship of Time, Knowledge, and Action—Renewing Mode.

TABLE 12.1 Renewing Mode.

KNOWLEDGE ASPECT *Wisdom* Intentionality, values, purpose	ACTION FOCUS *Renewing* Finding or reconnecting with one's purpose
LEARNING DYNAMICS *Generative Learning* Value-driven learning for the joy of learning, in open interaction with the environment. It involves creative processes, heuristic, open-ended explorations, and profound self-questioning. Allows for the discovery of one's highest capabilities, talents, and creative passion.	PERFORMANCE CAPABILITY *Integrity* Defining or reconnecting with values, vision, and corporate mission. Understanding purpose. Very long time horizon leads to deep awareness of ecology and community.
Examples: • open-ended exploration • heuristic questioning • inner explorations • spiritual practices • ceremony	*Business Examples:* • vision and values work • social activism • future trends research • environmental scanning • global travel *Tools:* • scenario building • stakeholder and customer focus groups • Quality Function Deployment • higher education • world-class benchmarking • retreats and experiential learning • sabbaticals • special assignments to academia

TIME HORIZON: Very long term (very distant past to far distant future)
CONSCIOUSNESS: Ethical or principle

Nature creates its diverse and intricate shapes by enumerating a few basic principles and then permitting great amounts of autonomy.

Margaret Wheatley

The *Renewing* mode of learning and performance touches the deepest core of values and purpose that shapes the enterprise. A company that is confident of its values and purpose has depth of character. Our character holds our uniqueness, distinguishing one person or company from another.

Generative learning characterizes this mode. For Peter Senge, the basic meaning of a "learning organization" is an organization that is continually expanding its capacity to create its future.

For such an organization, it is not enough merely to survive. "Survival learning"
or what is more often termed "adaptive learning" is important—indeed it is
necessary. But for a learning organization, "adaptive learning" must be joined
by "generative learning," learning that enhances our capacity to create.[1]

The things that deeply attract us in learning, when we do not even know why, are the very things that lead us into our future. It is our wisest selves, individually and collectively, that compel us to explore a particular direction. That creative call is generative learning.

Generative learning requires an appreciative, positive mindset. It requires a willingness to see radical possibilities beyond the boundaries of current thinking. Most of all it requires courage to go toward what is alive, compelling, and energizing. It is the call of life itself we hear and must heed.

Time Perspective

The time horizon of the *Renewing* mode is long indeed. This inter-generational perspective encompasses the very distant past to the far distant future. In one Native-American tradition, people consider their actions for the impact on the seventh generation, meaning seven generations into the future. Inter-generational perspectives emerge at Skandia's futures center by pulling together groups that include three generations: people under thirty, those between thirty and forty years in age, and people forty and older. Through the diversity of interaction, they can discover the new nurtured by the old. Americans marvel at Japanese corporations that have fifty-year plans, when our own "long-term" planning horizons average five years and seldom exceed ten.

As we move along the time continuum, our sense of time-space becomes more polychronic. Each moment is ripe with creative potential for movement in multiple directions. We sense how our every action collapses an infinity of choices to a single point of decision. We realize that in the bends and buckles of time and space, our tiniest movements cause unforeseen ripples in a complex, interwoven pattern of events.

With this polychronic inter-generational time sense we become much more aware of the creative power of our own choices. As we weigh potential courses of action and make our small daily decisions, we seek consistency and integrity in our actions. We become alert to the behavior of other people and the ramifications of small events. For example, we are able to appreciate how chaotic our world would become if, say, everybody stole what they wanted. We make choices not to steal for the sake of the whole. We do this as a conscious choice to embrace principles that lead to health and wholeness instead of destruction and chaos. This is *ethical consciousness*, the ability to discern what is right, health-enhancing, and life-giving. It is the ability to discern and understand the principles and values that shape our choices.

The Power of Purpose

Intentionality or purpose is at the heart of consciousness. Aristotle said, "What is given to the eyes (what we perceive) is the intention of the soul." Intention or purpose is the ultimate engine of creativity. Our intention and our purpose directly influence what we perceive. Values and purpose are the gatekeepers of our entire realm of knowledge, shaping and influencing our worldview.

Attention and intention, or purpose, are intimately related. In *Love and Will*, Rollo May observes, "When we analyze will with all the tools modern psychoanalysis brings us, we shall find ourselves pushed back to the level of *attention* or *intention* as the seat of will. The effort which goes into the exercise of the will is really effort of attention."[2] So, where we place our attention determines what we perceive, what we integrate into our worldview as knowledge, and ultimately, what we create.

The first *Renewing* or *Wisdom* technology is the technology of attention. It is a technology of the *human* mind. Not artificial intelligence, actual intelligence. Purpose. Intentionality. Attention. We often forget, ignore, or overlook these inner technologies. Yet we must reclaim them if we would navigate the realm of knowledge. These inner technologies affect the use of matter profoundly. The inner technologies of our mind shape products, social systems, services, and enterprises. These in turn shape our attention in a never-ending cycle.

We devalue this technology of attention and do not examine its power, because we think it is invisible. But it is not. It is the most visible technology in the world; we see the results everywhere around us. Everything humanly made we created first with this technology of attention and intention. Our creations emerge from the invisible realm of the mind.

Purpose and Vision

Deeply-rooted corporate wisdom is very powerful. Founding purpose and values persist for generations in companies. They shape corporate culture. They create a sense of identity that serves as the nucleus or attractor for the multitude of relationships forming a complex enterprise. The values of charismatic businessman J.P. Hall, the founder of Hallmark Cards, influence the company long after he has gone. The operating philosophy of Lincoln Life of Illinois even today reflects the character of its namesake, Abraham Lincoln.

Purpose, vision, and values together serve as the guiding North star of an organization. Without these, people and companies lose their way. The original vision of Apple computer was to put a personal computer in the hands of everyone, including the disadvantaged. Yet, as they grew, the vision became muddled and finally lost. Gradually Apple implemented a strategy to "lock up" the technology so tightly that it could not replicate without their complete control. As a result, the technology became more expensive. Apple began losing market share to competing PC technologies proliferating in a freer environment. What might have happened had Apple held to their original vision and sought ways to share and partner from that vision?

The Power of the Question

We were recently working with a project team to analyze their work flow using the knowledge framework.

One of the participants asked us, "Just what is a *Wisdom* question anyway?"

"*Wisdom* questions are the ones that sound stupid," we said.

He looked puzzled. "I don't understand."

"*Wisdom* questions seem stupid because they are so simple. They sound like questions a child would ask. *Wisdom* questions are questions like, 'Why are we doing this? What are we trying to do? What would make this more fun, or where is the beauty in this? This doesn't feel right, I wonder why? How does this connect to what they are doing over there?"

"Those sound like questions about goals and objectives," he said.

"No, they're bigger. *Wisdom* questions are about purpose. They push 'why' as deep as it can go."

Wisdom has a lot to do with asking the right questions. The beginning of wisdom is when we have fewer answers and more questions.

The philosopher Descartes used doubt to arrive at knowledge. You can doubt all your senses, but you cannot doubt that you are a thinking being doing this exercise of thinking. So, by doubting everything, he rethought the world from scratch, opening new creative possibilities.

When we ask difficult questions, we must grant ourselves the freedom to become the wise fool. The wise fool is the court jester who alone dares to speak the obvious truths. Or, like that famous child in the fairy tale, asks why the emperor is wearing no clothes. This is, indeed, divine ignorance—also known as wisdom.

Lived Integrity

Leadership has been a hot topic the last several years. Much of what has been published points to the importance of strong values and ethics. Integrity is a central theme in such writings as Covey's *Principle Centered Leadership*, Kouzes' *The Credibility Factor*, and Holoviak's *Golden Rule Management*.[3]

Trust demands integrity. We trust an environment that has integrity. Integrity in an organization means living by your principles and values. It means living the vision and holding firm to your identity. It means having the courage to challenge each other in a positive way to live up to those values and vision. At Harley-Davidson, Teerlink knows his people will call him on it if he fails to "walk his talk."

Lived visions, the ones that have life and energy, align every employee's actions with the company's avowed purpose and values. Visionary companies have clearly articulated core values and a mission or reason for being. Studies have shown that such vision-driven companies perform eight times better financially than their competitors.[4]

The concept of vision is an important one. In practice, however, vision often has been trivialized into a public relations gimmick. Too many corporations do not hold to the integrity of their often carefully crafted visions. When you look at strong, successful companies, you find that they live their values. At Hewlett-Packard, the founders did not make respect of the individual a core value for strategic value or good public relations. They believed it was the right way to manage and practiced it to the best of their ability.

A vision *statement* is not a vision, it is a piece of information. Unless the vision has integrity with the way people experience the culture, it is meaningless. If it does not have integrity with the assumptions and beliefs that people hold and operate by, then it is equally meaningless. The true vision is the *shared reality* of the purpose and values that really guide the organization.

Lived integrity comes when people forge a new reality *together*. People must shape their vision for the future together in order for it to happen. Without the commitment and involvement of everyone, a vision is just someone else's pretty words. Stephen Covey and his associates Roger and Rebecca Merrill talk about the compelling need within each of us to leave a legacy.[5] Visions that are alive for us are really passions. They are that "fire in the belly" that burns with our desire to make a difference, to leave an enduring legacy.

Collaborative processes around values, vision, and purpose ground high ideals and dreams in reality. People are energized by a vision that is possible; they are demoralized by one that is not. Engaging people collectively in creating the future together, brings knowledge of the whole system to the table. People together hold a collective intelligence about the future *and* about present reality. Doubts and concerns are not resistance; they are feedback from the system that more information or thinking through is needed.

Involvement at Ortho Biotech

When Ortho Biotech developed a vision for the future, it first set up a Culture Development Committee to draw up a list of new desired behaviors. They also drafted the vision statement, working on it for more than a year before they reached consensus. Then came a three-day program involving every single one of 450 employees. Every employee was given a chance to challenge the vision.

After the large-scale event, a volunteer group of employees collected the flip chart pages and revamped the statement. Then groups of employees concerned with a given issue developed an implementation strategy. The process is designed to keep the momentum going to narrow the gap between the vision and day-to-day realities.

Creating *Renewing* Knowledge

Renewing knowledge in an organization is socially constructed. It is not developed by one individual or even a group of individuals. Rather, it emerges from the collaborative intelligence of the organization in response to the environment. Leadership probably plays a much smaller part in this than we tend to think, although it is a vitally important part. When I think of a model leader I think of Disraeli, who said "Oh, there they go. I must hurry and follow for I am their leader." Leaders, too, emerge in response to their environment.

Fostering openness in the internal environment through self-questioning and appreciation of data and feedback are critical for generating *Renewing* knowledge. Equally important is openness to the external environment in the way people embrace information and new knowledge. Organizations that appreciate this deploy "scouts" to conferences, trade shows, universities, research consortiums, and even to foreign countries and other industries. They engage in world-class benchmarking projects to bring in new ideas and new ways of thinking. They use outside trainers, consultants, and educators to spark reflection and inquiry. Communication technologies are employed to scan the environment. Customers are invited into the creative process as valued resources through focus groups and participation.

Open communication and collaborative group processes support the creation of *Renewing* knowledge. For example, open-space technology is a way of creating an environment where new things are possible. It is based on the principle that life seeks order. The apparent "chaos' of open space self-organizes to accomplish its purpose. Harrison Owen first developed open-space technology more than twenty years ago, and it has been growing in use ever since.

Open space is a meeting facilitation technique where the topics and issues to be addressed emerge organically and spontaneously from the participants. An agenda is created by the group at large and people self-select discussion modules as leaders or participants. Michael Lindfield of Boeing, who has used this technology many times, holds the belief that groups of people and systems will self-organize when three vital ingredients are present:

1. A higher common purpose.
2. A willingness to work together.
3. A level of personal mastery and maturity.

Personal mastery means people must be relatively free of the gravitational pull of their own biases, agendas, and emotional turbulence. People must trust that life seeks order and the right order will emerge.[6]

Another powerful collaborative learning and knowledge-creation process is scenario building. Scenario building, as described by Peter Schwartz in *The Art of the Long View*, can help companies rethink much more than long-term strategy.[7] It can help a company reframe their identity, their operating assumptions, their values, and their vision for the future. This methodology has been employed for over twenty years by companies that include Shell Oil, Southern California Edison, Clorox, Statoil, Los Angeles Department of Water and Power, Battelle, and the U.S. Defense industry.

Sustaining *Renewing* Knowledge

Sustaining *Renewing* knowledge sounds like a contradiction in terms. What one hopes is sustained are the vision, values, and sense of identity of the organization. However, these are intangibles, abstract concepts. We can, of course, write them down. People often laminate the words of values and visions onto little cards and carry them around or use them for bookmarks. People also sometimes videotape large-scale collaborative planning processes, retreats, or interviews that become part of the corporate "story."

However, the bottom line is, *Renewing* knowledge is sustained only as those values are lived in the organization. *Renewing* knowledge is embodied knowledge. It is carried in the body, heart, and mind of the individuals. That is where it really resides. That is where it is sustained—or not.

Sharing *Renewing* Knowledge

One great paradox of knowledge is that one person's knowledge is another person's information. People share *Renewing* knowledge by creating it together. It cannot be imparted or transferred. Just as learning does not really "transfer," neither does renewal. We can, however, invite people to participate in the renewal process by supporting time and resources for reflecting together.

This is difficult. We all are caught in our day-to-day activities. We focus our attention so intensely on our own work, for such extended periods of time, that it is difficult to shift our attention away from it. And, from a corporate perspective, there is a certain risk factor. The risk is that if people take time to reflect, they may change their perspective on what is important. If a key manager takes a sabbatical, there is the risk that the manager may not want to return. If a work team charged with developing a new product begins to question the value of that product to society, then it might put the development project in jeopardy. These things do happen, but that is the nature of renewal. Old things yield so that the new might come forward.

Opportunities abound. Any time a work group moves outside its usual setting to explore, play, or learn together, they have a chance for renewal. Excellent adventure-based training is now available, ranging from ropes courses and white water rafting, to cow punching and rock climbing. These all shift people out of their usual comfort zone of thought and behavior, uncovering fresh perspectives for their work.

The language of *Renewing* knowledge resonates with symbols, metaphors, and principles. Outdoor settings are especially rich in metaphors and symbols. A mindset of inquiry and reflection in such a setting can bring powerful insights and new directions. Renewal often comes, too, in ceremony. Shared celebrations help people loosen their hold on an old reality and invite in a new one.

Renewing

True renewal means that a transformation of knowledge itself will take place. Any shift of identity and purpose redefines the nuclear core of the enterprise. Knowledge will once more self-organize around the attractor of purpose. Unneeded competencies and skills once at the core might disappear altogether. New ones will come forward. With renewal of any knowledge, something old must be unlearned.

Any serious effort to master the Knowledge Era must ask the question, *what can we unlearn?* What can we let go of? Along with developing all our strategies for acquiring, processing, and managing knowledge, why not develop strategies for losing, forgetting, and ignoring knowledge? Agnes deMille once said, "Life is a form of not being sure. The moment you know how, you begin to die a little." The moment we become smug in our knowledge, we, too, begin to die. We lose the charge, the energy, of being active learners. When we become too full of our knowledge, there is simply no room to add anything more, yet we keep pouring more and more knowledge into our overflowing cups.

Peter Vaill suggests that unlearning is not so much a matter of hitting the "delete" button as it is hitting the "reveal codes" key.[8] We must understand the genetic code of our own knowledge and worldview. Then we can reconfigure our knowledge as new information connects with the old, transforming them both. Vaill describes learning as a way of being. It is a mindset that serves us well in an age of permanent white water.

Understanding *Renewing* Performance

The measure for *Renewing* performance is simple, yet challenging. It is the quality and depth of integrity and commitment to principles, demonstrated at every level of the organization. Does the organization live according to its stated purpose, values, and vision? Performance capability is demonstrated through continuous, on-going, explicit work around these issues. People are invited into the process of co-creating the vision.

People with an aptitude for *Renewing* work in organizations are those whose own need for clarity around values and purpose also helps others get clear. They have a strong sense of the larger community and are probably passionate about issues like community involvement, justice, quality, and social responsibility. They tend to be open-minded and embrace diversity and variety, both in people and work. Such people enjoy and often lead group work around values, vision, and developing mission. Their sense of play, exploration, and commitment to learning lead the way to new thinking and innovation.

Integrating Performance Questions

1. Are there processes for continually renewing your corporate vision?
2. Does the company engage in outside research or learning, such as non-competitive, world-class benchmarking or consortium studies?
3. Are individuals and work groups encouraged to engage in reflection and renewal processes, such as retreats, sabbaticals, or special projects?
4. Is the company committed to playing a larger role in the community through social programs or learning exchanges?
5. Are people encouraged to ask really tough questions internally about ethics, purpose, vision, and "walking the talk?"
6. Is formal scenario-building built into strategic planning processes?
7. Do people engage in environmental scanning processes for important social, economic, and technological trends?
8. Does the company conduct values analysis of management practices and of both oral and written communication?
9. Does the company have a strategy for diversity and attracting a wide range of talents and specialties?
10. Does the company encourage open exploration through technologies, such as open space and appreciative inquiry?
11. Are outside thinkers, scientists, and educators regularly brought in as conduits of new thinking?
12. Does the company have a distinctive and far-sighted point of view about the future?
13. Are senior managers focused on the future and environment as well as day-to-day operations?
14. Are customers engaged in the renewal process through focus groups, research, and other types of active involvement?

Pushing "Why" as Far as it Will Go

In 1973 a young businessman in Boston sold a successful natural foods business grossing $25,000 a day and started writing a book. He had come across a community in Scotland that he thought people should hear about. He spent the next two years writing, falling in love, and forging lifetime friendships. Along with many others in that community and elsewhere, he grew in his conviction that there had to be a different way to approach the world of business.

As a young entrepreneur he had found the *Wall Street Journal* confusing. The world of big business in the popular business magazines seemed irrelevant to his small business. In search of business principles and practices that he could actually use, he even sneaked into classes at the Harvard Business School. There wasn't much help there either. He was puzzled and frustrated at the way business thinking seemed oblivious to small businesses, which are actually the lifeblood of the economy.

When he returned from Scotland, Paul Hawken once more entered the world of business. Frustrated in his own attempts to find high-quality garden tools, he founded Smith & Hawken, primarily as a mail order business. One day, Stewart Brand, publisher of Whole Earth Catalog, was nosing around the company offices when he came across a list of customer service principles. They were the work of company president, Lew Richmond. At Stewart's urging, Paul wrote them up and published them in an article. "You Are the Customer, You Are the Company," became his most widely reprinted article. Most requests came from Fortune 500 companies.

Smith & Hawken has been a working laboratory for a new approach to business. Hawken and his associates were never content to go about business as usual. They kept examining themselves and their principles. They kept pushing "why" as far as it would go. In the process, they have done much more than build a successful company. They have discovered the keys to *sustainable* business. A sustainable business is a business that takes an active ethical and co-creative stance with the world. It is a business with social and environmental responsibility as the "heart" of all its values, business theories, and day-to-day management practices.

Today, Paul Hawken and others like him are proving that there is a new way to approach the world of business. Through his books, and the lived example of his success, he is helping businesses redefine success. The high ideals at the core of such companies are quite compatible with growth and profit. Indeed, they are a requirement for sustainable success in the decades and years to come.

Personal and business renewal encompass deep processes. They take time. They take persistence. They take big ears: inner ears for listening to the heart and elephant ears scanning for the emerging whispers of the future. Most of all renewal takes the courage to listen to one's passion.

CHAPTER 13

Expanded Vision
for Union Performance

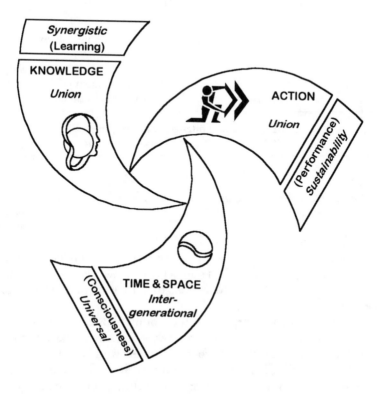

FIGURE 13.1 Relationship of Time, Knowledge, and Action—Union Mode.

TABLE 13.1 Union Mode.

KNOWLEDGE ASPECT *Union* Connection, synergy	ACTION FOCUS *Union* Understanding values in greater context
LEARNING DYNAMICS *Synergistic Learning* Learning integrates direct experience and appreciation of oneness or deep connection with the larger cosmos. Requires processes that connect purpose to the health and well-being of the larger community and the environment.	**PERFORMANCE CAPABILITY** *Sustainability* Commitment to the great good of society, the environment, and the planet. The inter-generational time perspective brings awareness of profound social, economic, and environmental responsibility. Performance is demonstrated in actions consistent with deeper values concerning the "legacy" or vision of the enterprise.
Examples: • self-questioning of self and society • communal inner explorations • spiritual practice	*Business Examples:* • environmental responsibility • global activism • high-level values work • global citizenship *Tools:* • inviting community dialogue • retreats • educational travel • special assignment global projects • environmental scanning

TIME HORIZON: Inter-generational (timeless)
CONSCIOUSNESS: Universal or Cosmic

> *Humankind did not weave the web of life; we are merely a strand in it. Whatever we do to the web we do to ourselves.*
>
> Chief Seattle, 1854

Union mode performance arises from a perspective that understands that our actions do not truly serve us unless they serve all of us. Organizations that hold this view creatively seek paths of actions that are good for business, good for people, *and* good for the planet.

Inclusion of the greater good in the world of business ethics and values seems a revolutionary concept to many. Yet, it actually marks a return to the earth-centered values of times long forgotten, when we all lived closer to nature. People who live in close harmony with nature, such as indigenous societies, live this way still. Only those of us who have been steeped in our consumer-driven culture find these ideas strange.

The learning dynamic of this mode is *synergistic*. The word synergy comes from the Greek word, *sunergos*, which means working together. In everyday experience, this is what we experience as "flow," when everything comes together in seamless harmony. In biology, this word has come to mean the way things combine to create a whole that is greater than the sum of its parts. In theology, it refers to a doctrine that regeneration is effected by a combination of human will and divine grace. In all its meanings, the word evokes a certain mystery. There is a quality of grace and revelation about synergistic learning. Abraham Maslow would describe this type of learning as a "peak experience." In such moments, truth and beauty touch our spirit, allowing us to see the world with new eyes.

The related domain of consciousness for this mode is *universal* or cosmic consciousness. It connects us to the forces of the cosmos and the eternal. Time awareness in the full expression of this mode is actually *timelessness*. Thus, we go full circle. We come once again to the timelessness that we can also experience in the immediate moment of *now*.

In this domain, we brush up against the language-bound universe of knowledge itself. The realm of knowledge is that which can be known and communicated. The world of knowledge is limited to that which we can share with another through language, symbol, gesture, or expression. The union domain nudges the edge of experiences that we can express with language. We approach the ineffable—that which cannot be explained or communicated.[1]

As we move along this continuum of time and consciousness, the questions we address expand to encompass the complexity of our entire existence. As we push the limits of knowledge, our ability to grasp complexity shifts, encompassing a very different quality of thinking. In the other modes, where time and space are more bounded, we could actually sort things out a bit. Here, we cannot. The cosmos is too big—it is too much of a muchness. As we near the freefall space beyond knowledge, however, we can also enter that clear creative space that allows us to shift our worldview.

Abraham Maslow once conducted a now classic study of peak experiences. He found that people who experience this mode of consciousness shift their sense of themselves and their place in the world. They feel a profound gratitude, perceiving the world as a beautiful place. As a result of their experience, they have an impulse to do something good for the world.[2] Kenneth Ring's studies of near-death-experiences have also shown a similar lasting impulse to give back to the world in service.[3] Such experiences and impulses are actually quite common in human experience. They can be moments of high personal drama or quiet simple moments when awareness suddenly expands.

Living from Union Values

During one of our workshops, we had a lively discussion of Union performance and values with the participants. Their company, in an energy industry, had made significant changes in the last few years attempting to become more environmentally responsible. Yet, the people in the room expressed frustration at the uneven progress—and sometimes mixed messages—they heard within the company.

During a break, one of the participants came up to me. "These different modes that you talk about make a lot of sense," she said. "I can see how most of them apply in our workgroup. I also now realize that I have very strong *Union* values. But, I think of these values as something that don't have much to do with my work. How do you bring those into the workplace?"

I looked at this intelligent and committed woman standing before me. "You already have brought them," I smiled. "You *are* the values you hold. You don't somehow leave them in the parking lot when you walk in the door. There is no *real* separation between that part of you and the work you do. The separation is only in your own mind."

She looked at me in surprise, her eyes widened. "You're right," she said. "I do act from those values. If I couldn't, then I would not be here." I watched her as she walked away. Her chin was up a little higher. She somehow seemed to stand just a little taller and walked with a firmer step. Reconnecting with our deepest values energizes us. It gives meaning to everything we do.

However, there must be language for those values and a way to express them in the workplace for them to be fully operative. The discussion of larger values was just one small part of the day's work, entailing only a few minutes, *but it was there.* I have learned it is important to spend time reflecting, even though the immediate task may be focused in another modality. It takes only a moment to remember what moves us, what has meaning for us.

Connection can be quite simple. I recall an Inuit woman who works with community saying, "I try to remember to bring the circle into everything I do." For her, the circle symbolically represents wholeness and the earth, our Mother. In this simple way, she lives her values in her daily work. Other colleagues express the same spirit. "When I begin a project I ask myself and our group, is this what the earth needs?" one says. Another tells me, "I go where the energy is, to what is most *alive* for me."

The Importance of the Word

There is a belief in many spiritual traditions that saying a particular word evokes that state of being. When we give voice to a value such as *integrity, health,* or *compassion,* we actually experience that quality in our body. What we speak of, we express. Try this for yourself. Experiment with a few different words and see how your body responds to your thought. The more we speak from a certain awareness, the more we experience that state of being.

Consider how important this is in an organization. Each day we make a thousand small decisions that altogether add up to an enormous influence. If we have no language or expression of higher values in our daily work, how can we expect people to live from their highest values? If we do not have the courage to ask tough, value-oriented questions, then how can expect another to have the courage to speak? If we punish "whistle blowers," either inadvertently or deliberately, then how can we expect people to behave ethically in the many small actions they must take every day?

People have taken a lot of pot shots at company visions, because companies so often fail to live up to them. The power of visions and values, however, lies in the power of the *word*, the new language that people begin to use. It evokes the energy of the language of the heart and spirit. This ancient language of higher values has, unfortunately, become a victim of a modern taboo, or rule, regarding workplace behavior. However, that taboo is now being overturned by a number of innovative and highly successful companies.

A courageous and growing group of people are opening up the conversation of spirit in business. Often these people work in organizational development, training, and human resources. It is no accident that spiritual matters are of interest to those most attuned to organizational health, learning, and well-being. Conferences held by the Organizational Development Network, Association for Quality and Participation, human resources associations, and leadership councils often have inspirational speakers. There you can find sessions and workshops devoted to applying universal values and principles to the workplace. Other support networks are springing up as well. As an example, Richard Barrett of the World Bank founded a Spiritual Unfoldment Society where people can support each other in living by their highest values at work.

Sustainable Enterprise

The language of this mode is also the language of sustainable business. The founders of The Body Shop, Ben and Jerry's Ice Cream, and Smith & Hawken all believed they could create a successful business that exercises a social conscience. The stories of all three of these companies have become modern-day legends of combining high values with business success.

Paul Hawken insists that, "The ultimate purpose of business is not, or should not be, simply to make money. Nor is it merely a system of making and selling things. The promise of business is to increase the general well-being of humankind through service, a creative invention and ethical philosophy."[4]

Anita Roddick, founder of The Body Shop, a world-wide retailer, agrees. Roddick has become the most outspoken activist businesswoman of the decade. Like Hawken, she has been the recipient of the United Nations Environmentalist Award. She says simply, "I believe that we, as a company, have something worthwhile to say about how to run a successful business without losing your soul."[5] Social and environmental dimensions weave the very fabric of the company. They are neither first nor last among objectives, but are an ongoing part of everything else they do. Not a single decision is taken without first considering environmental and social issues.

Ben and Jerry's Ice Cream not only holds strong environmental and social values, they have thrown humor into the pot as well. (Or, since this is ice cream, I guess they throw it into the tub.) Their original store, in a remodeled gas station, boasted its own player piano, complete with a local musician compensated with free ice cream. However, the fun and games do not mean this is not a serious business. They have steadily grown their national market share to become a premier company in their market. Their value-driven political stance for environmental and social responsibility has remained steadfast through meteoric growth.[6]

Kenny Ausubel, founder of Seeds of Change organic seed business, is a leader in innovative business practices as well. None of the seeds they grow are patented, thus allowing gardeners to save them for themselves. This practice stems from a belief that the gene pool needs to be held in as many hands as possible for the biological well-being of the planet.[7] Could this be a successful business? Absolutely. Such companies are referred to as "green" companies, due to their earth-centered business practices. They are proving that they can generate the "green energy" of profits as well.

Financial Rewards

The positive financial rewards for holding *Union* values are sometimes surprising. When actor Paul Newman started marketing spaghetti sauce, he stated he was going to give all the proceeds to charity. Much to his amazement, *Newman's Own* brand food products have turned him into one of the foremost philanthropists in the country. People do respond to genuinely expressed global values and vote their approval with their consumption dollars. These businesses are responding to an increasing global awareness that we must begin to put environmental and social concerns in the forefront of our business strategies.

These businesses are proving that a natural-resource based view of the firm can work. Stuart Hart of the University of Michigan suggests that environmental performance data, which is now available through a variety of global databases, must be factored into business analysis of competitive advantage.[8] Hazel Hendersen first wrote of these matters in 1975 in *The Politics of the Solar Age*. She predicts that development will be reconceptualized as investments in people and in the restoration and maintenance of ecosystems. More recently, Michael Rothschild has begun to model the economy itself as an ecosystem, equating business information to DNA, or the genetic code of the economy.[9]

As these new perspectives and values spread through the global consciousness, the world of business and commerce is slowly beginning to transform. We are not technology-driven creatures; we create technologies to serve our own purposes. As our values and purpose begin to change, the way we use our technologies changes as well.

Creating, Sustaining, Sharing, and *Renewing* Union Mode Knowledge

There is much we can do organizationally to advance *Union* mode knowledge. In essence, it requires living our own highest values every single day. The most powerful way we can foster this mode of awareness and knowledge is to model the behavior ourselves. We can speak the language of these values and help others express them as well.[10] This can only come about in an atmosphere and culture of trust and open inquiry. Even though a company may not have those qualities as a whole, we all have the freedom and the right to create them for ourselves and within our work groups.

We write and speak volumes expounding our philosophies and our "reasons" for holding a particular viewpoint. All that writing and conversation can, of course, be captured and shared using all the media mentioned before for other modes. *Renewing* techniques and approaches are especially useful. Conducted in an atmosphere of open and profound self-questioning, they can easily call forth *Union* knowledge and values.

But this mode of knowledge, more than any other, is one for which we must all take personal responsibility. Engaging these issues is far too important to leave to chance, or to leave to others to do. Holding to these values requires commitment and courage and we need to support each other.

Values work might call into question the very nature of many of our businesses. This is risky stuff in an organization. It brings the possibility of *real* transformation. The truth is, no matter how much we *say* we want transformational change, it also scares us. We must speak to those fears in ourselves. We must speak to those fears together.

Union Performance Questions

1. Does your company demonstrate global values, such as recycling principles, in its use of resources?
2. Do people evaluate the social and economic impact when introducing new products or entering new markets, especially in other countries?
3. Do people specifically address questions of sustainable enterprise when developing strategies, goals, and policies?
4. Are non-humans and the earth itself included in the list of stakeholders for your enterprise?
5. Is there a company strategy for fostering social well-being in the communities where your units operate?
6. Do people speak freely with each other about the global community, environmental well-being, and their own inner joy?

All Our Knowledge

In San Jose there is an interesting building called the Winchester Mystery House. It was built by the widow of the inventor of the Winchester Rifle. She was convinced that if she finished construction on the house she would die. Until she did finally die at the ripe old age of 86, she continued to add rooms, cubbyholes, niches, and ornamentation of every kind. There were odd-shaped hallways and stairs that lead nowhere. It is very interesting, but it is not beautiful.

We have made Winchester Mystery Houses of our organizations. We have created a rabbit warren of cubbyholes, isolated rooms, niches, and back hallways. These are both literal and figurative. Many office buildings actually look this way in form and function. This is how we have designed our organizational charts. Many of the reasons for creating these odd structures have long been forgotten.

I remember reading an article about IBM shortly after people realized that they had pursued a dangerously wrong strategy by insisting that PCs would never replace mainframes. The writer describes driving up to the IBM headquarters in upstate New York. He drove through a beautiful wooded setting, through rolling green lawns, and approached the impressive building nestled into these lovely surrounds. Once he was inside the building, however, he found himself walking down *narrow windowless corridors, lined with cubicles*. There was no way to see out. Is it any wonder IBM almost missed its future?

We pay much lip service to the free flow of information, to fostering an atmosphere of openness and trust, yet our steps toward these ideals are halting and uneven. In our businesses we have drawn boundaries and lines all over the place. Actual lines, psychological lines, lines of power and authority, lines of functional responsibility. We erased a few vertical lines only to draw new horizontal process lines in their place. We have fragmented our world until it makes no sense to us. Scott Adams, creator of "Dilbert," has become a popular cartoonist pointing up the fractured logic and outright nonsense that runs rampant under the guise of "managing a business."

Many barriers are barriers of language. We do not understand the dialects of different knowledge modes and often speak at cross purposes. There are also many languages of knowledge that we do not speak at all. Systems or *Integrating* language is rare, only now beginning to be understood and recognized. The language of *Renewing* is heard—occasionally—when there is time, when people are not occupied putting out fires. In some companies, *Union* values are everyday language. In other companies, they are still taboo.

Whatever name it goes by, the *Union* mode of knowledge may be *more* important than the *Procedural* and *Functional* modes that help us produce the tangible outcomes we desire. It certainly is *as* important. We do need the language of the heart in our work. We do need the language of wisdom. We need *all* the languages of knowledge to run a successful enterprise and create a sustainable future.

PART III

INTO PRACTICE

CHAPTER 14

Strategies:
Creating Practice Fields for Knowledge

In American management circles, we have a habit of jumping on the bandwagon of the latest management fad. We no sooner embrace Total Quality then up pops Reengineering. Just as we start to catch our breath, Core Competencies come along. We have barely figured out how to become a learning organization, and now we are supposed to focus on knowledge management. While all this is going on, Human Resources is trying to get us to embrace empowerment, move to cross-functional teaming, or change our culture.

People running businesses want to be on the cutting edge with new ideas. However, managers seldom have the patience or time to read the directions to put things together the right way. Then the whole thing breaks down, because they never really grasped the concept in the first place. (When the inevitable mess results, we say they are on the "bleeding edge.") Undaunted, we rush on to the next bright bauble, hoping some new "fix" will magically propel the business to profits, success, and certainty.

Individually and collectively, we have become mired in the hope that there is one right way to do something. We are chagrined if something doesn't work out and we have to start all over, especially if people are shuffled around and laid off in the process. We have become stuck in a fear-driven, Darwinian mindset of competition and survival. We are terrified that if we get it wrong, we will irrevocably fail. We have lost the bigger perspective that all this experimenting is exactly what we are supposed to do. It is the only way systems renew themselves.

There is a famous Gertrude Stein quote about the city of Oakland. "There is no there there," she said, meaning there is nothing there when you get there. There is no magical destination to get to in the way we organize and run our businesses either. When we do finally get there, or wherever we think *there* is supposed to be, what do we do? We experiment some more. Yet another form emerges in our co-creative dance with a constantly changing environment. The journey *is* the destination.

Life is in a constant process of discovery and creating. Every organism and entity reinterprets the rules, makes exceptions for itself, then rewrites the rules or creates new ones. Possibilities, like knowledge itself, unfold endlessly. The world supports incredible diversity. There is no one ideal design for an organization, any more than there is one ideal design for a butterfly or tree. Life always finds its way towards order—towards systems that are more complex and more effective. The whole process is messier than we think it should be, especially if we are caught in the mess. But it's just what it is. Living systems are learning systems.

Best Practices for Knowledge Management

What Are Best Practices?

What all this organic messiness means, of course, is that there are no best practices in knowledge management. There are no best practices anywhere. The phrase, "Best Practices for Knowledge Management," is a trick. What we actually discover when we claim to have found a best practice, is a promising experiment. Best practice companies are those companies that pay close attention to a particular type of experiment. Experiments emerge out of identity and purpose. A company may, for example, conduct particularly good experiments in customer service, in quality, in employee relations, or in product innovation. An experiment that shows the most promising results is one we call a best practice.

Best practices are observable behaviors or processes. When we find one that appears to work well, our first impulse is to try to isolate the practice so we can take a really close look at it. Then we whack it on the knee, take its temperature, have it say "ahh," and, if it has a nice gait, we pronounce it sound. What we usually overlook is that this process or behavior is only one component of a whole system. Any practice emerges within an organizational system that is unlike any other. The process enablers that make this a successful experiment in the first place are not nearly so visible. They lurk about in company culture, structure, and supporting technology. Enablers have a lot to do with the core identity and values held in the organization.

Any best practice is an expression of a system experimenting with itself. It is ridiculous to think we can successfully copy a practice in isolation. Everything is connected to everything else. For example, if a company is using a particular information technology, certain aspects of the company culture will surface as critical success factors. So, be cautious when you examine other people's experiments. They may work well for you, too, or they may not. You can bet that your results will be very different. They may be even better. Biologists Maturana and Varela caution us that you can never change a system, you can only disturb it. Some disturbances nudge a system toward health, wholeness, and creativity. Others just make it tired.

Best Practice Companies

A best practice company in the area of knowledge would be one that is beginning to pay deliberate serious attention to knowledge. The company would demonstrate a willingness to experiment by developing a knowledge strategy, reshaping their culture, implementing knowledge measurements, or appointing a high-level knowledge officer or manager of some kind. This willingness to experiment means they have created a "practice field" for knowledge. When looking for best practices companies, indication of serious interest becomes the first criteria.

In a good practice field for knowledge you would find all the navigational devices mentioned in Chapter 3.

1. *A North Star*: There must be a clear, knowledge-centered identity and purpose, as well as knowledge-sharing values around which the enterprise can self-organize. Leadership must attend to how people hold the integrity of those values. There must be continuing exploration of the company belief system regarding knowledge.
2. *A compass*: There must be an integrated, systems approach or strategy that provides a direction for knowledge experiments. There must be guiding principles for sharing knowledge. Such an approach must address all modes of knowledge.
3. *A good crew*: Company culture must support the behaviors of knowledge creation, inquiry, and sharing. People need to know how to learn together. People must be supported in linking with others to create and share knowledge.
4. *Maps and guides*: There should be flexible guides, maps, processes, and pathways for locating and sharing knowledge. People need ways to orient to knowledge so that they know where and how to access what they need.
5. *Sound vessels*: Supporting technologies, tools, and equipment must be provided to foster communication, connectivity, and the gathering of knowledge.
6. *Feedback*: Knowledge experiments need to be monitored, so people know how they are doing and can devise new experiments.

A rich practice field for knowledge building also encompasses several other key elements. Some of these have to do with the orientation of strategy. Others have to do with culture and mindset. Table 14.1 is a sample set of criteria for a best practice company in the knowledge arena.

TABLE 14.1 Criteria for Best Practices in Knowledge.

✓ Knowledge is strategically valued.
✓ Knowledge strategy is future oriented.
✓ Knowledge building and sharing includes customers and stakeholders.
✓ Measurements include innovative measures, such as knowledge-value added.
✓ Knowledge strategies are more human-centered than technology-centered.
✓ Knowledge is supported with flexible elements and technologies.
✓ The culture specifically addresses and supports knowledge creation, sharing, and learning.
✓ There are easily communicated maps or frameworks that orient people to knowledge.
✓ People are encouraged to self-organize around knowledge competencies or expertise.
✓ People have ready access to the information and knowledge they need.
✓ People are supported in their personal efforts to acquire and apply knowledge.
✓ The approach encourages expansion across *all* modes of knowledge.

The criteria in Table 14.1, like any criteria, reflect a bias. These reveal my own perspective of an organization as a self-organizing system. I view a knowledge best practice company as one where a primary design consideration is encouraging experiments in developing and sharing knowledge. This view appreciates flexibility, open communication, an orientation toward change, and a strong emphasis on people and the culture that supports them. Another perspective would result in a very different set of criteria. For example, a mechanistic view would focus more on production and control, resulting in a different list of companies.

These items all indicate that a company is providing a good practice field for knowledge creation and sharing. If needed, you could conduct a more detailed assessment of specific practices by asking all the knowledge questions in the previous chapters as well. Using the criteria in Table 14.1, some of the current best practice companies include:

Best Practice Companies in Knowledge

Arthur Andersen	Ernst & Young
Buckman Laboratories	Hewlett-Packard
Canadian Imperial Bank of Commerce	Hughes Space & Communications
Chevron Corporation	McKinsey & Company
Dow Chemical	Skandia Group Insurance

Other companies that have undertaken serious knowledge initiatives include S. A. Armstrong, Telus, VeriFone, Anglian Water Services, The Mutual

Group, Swiss Bank Corp., IBM, General Motors, Owens-Corning, Celemi, WM Data, Xerox, Monsanto, Philip Morris, Fiat, Telecom, Italia, Texas Instruments, and FASI. Also, government agencies such as the National Securities Administration, the US Army, and the US Air Force are taking a look at their knowledge practices.

Companies that are serious about knowledge demonstrate it in both strategy and operations. For example, in Hewlett-Packard's Product Processes Organization (P.P.O.), Director Bill Kay believes that information and knowledge management should be a core competence. He put his unit's Information Systems group at the center of the organization chart. In 1995 he formed a Knowledge Management Group to capture and leverage knowledge of the product-generation process in various HP divisions. They quickly developed a Web-based knowledge management system called Knowledge Links. This system will be expanded from the product-generation process to other types of knowledge. Additionally, they have developed an assessment tool for knowledge management capability, have begun mapping key knowledge domains within P.P.O., and share advice about knowledge creation and sharing.[1]

Leadership in Knowledge

Driving values for knowledge creation and sharing can actually be quite different in various companies. The way an enterprise organizes around knowledge will vary according to different belief and value systems. People in a company always organize to support the *actual* values, not the *espoused* values. The core leadership team must constantly hold the integrity of beliefs and values around knowledge. Leaders serve as role models for learning and knowledge sharing.

Robert Buckman of Buckman Laboratories takes knowledge leadership seriously, insisting that, "The climate we create as leaders has a major impact on our ability to share knowledge across time and space." He identifies trust as one of their core values. "For knowledge sharing to become a reality you have to create a climate of trust in your organization. You cannot empower someone that you do not trust and who does not trust you."[2] A code of ethics that values the individual is solidly at the core of the learning mindset. In addition, Buckman constantly reinforces that knowledge is in service to the customer. The whole point is to deploy knowledge at the point of sale—for the benefit of the customer.

Buckman Laboratories is a $270 million chemical company with operations in 80 different countries. In 1989, Buckman made a personal commitment that his company would compete on knowledge. Three years later, with the implementation of the K'Netix knowledge sharing network, Buckman and his people began to treat knowledge as their most strategic asset. At the core of the Network is a simple premise. By connecting people through a network, you replace the depth of knowledge offered in a multi-tiered hierarchy with breadth of knowledge that is the sum of the collective experience of employees. Robert Buckman says, "This is the greatest revolution in the way of doing business we have seen in our lifetime."[3]

Although the strategic intent is quite serious, knowledge sharing is fun at Buckman. The top 150 knowledge sharers have been feted at a conference. People can learn the system at home. On-line contests, such as guessing the number of messages sent in a week, keep people tuned in. Guest experts are invited to participate. People can check out a technology "survival kit" when they are traveling to other countries. Victor Baillargeon, head of Knowledge Transfer, set up the whole system through Compuserve for easy access. Mike Anstey of Buckman's Singapore office, an enthusiastic advocate, says, "It's not about definitions, numbers, or procedures, or things. It's about involvement, commitment, creativity, passion, and ultimately the freedom to do everything we can, and to use all of the knowledge we have, to make sure that we have done our utmost to satisfy our customers in all areas."

Canadian Imperial Bank of Commerce (CIBC) also has strong knowledge leadership. The driving value, however, is somewhat different from Buckman. There the key driver and value is knowledge capital, for both individuals and the organization as a whole. This stems from a philosophy and belief system centering on intellectual capital and value creation. The customer is still foremost in CIBC philosophy. However, the emphasis is on providing knowledge value-added to products and services, while at Buckman, knowledge is provided more directly to the customer. These are subtle distinctions, but they make for very different types of knowledge practices at an operational level.

CEO Ken Derr is a vocal advocate of knowledge at Chevron. The commitment to learning and knowledge is central to *The Chevron Way*, a set of strategic statements that serve as a framework for company initiatives.[4] Key elements of that strategy include facilitating a learning organization through benchmarking, sharing best practices, learning from experience, and focusing on continuous improvement. Chevron uses a benchmarking and Total Quality approach to engage in extensive internal knowledge sharing. This approach relies on informal networks, as well as regular internal conferences, for best practice exchange. Even this technology support is organized around best practice sharing.

At The World Bank global knowledge partnerships are strategically appreciated as a major driver of development. The World Bank vision of knowledge partnership includes networking, expanding the learning programs of the Economic Development Institute and connecting clients with global centers of knowledge and investment. Included in the vision is enabling even the poorest countries to realize the potential of information technology.

Knowledge Managers

Another aspect of leadership pertains to the more operational side of implementing a knowledge strategy. Among those companies that have created formal knowledge management functions are Northeast Utilities, Buckman Laboratories, Hewlett-Packard, Dow Chemical, CIBC, Hughes Space and Communications, Lincoln Life Booz-Allen & Hamilton, McKinsey, Andersen Consulting, Ernst & Young, Price Waterhouse, and A.T. Kearney.

Responsibilities generally include some or all of the following:[5]

- Mapping knowledge and information resources.
- Serving as knowledge "champions" to develop strategies and obtain funding.
- Training and guiding users in tools, techniques, and technology.
- Building knowledge networks or knowledge infrastructures.
- Monitoring outside news and information.

Tom Davenport of the University of Austin, says of the knowledge management function, "The goal should merely be to facilitate the creation, distribution, and use of knowledge by others. Furthermore, the knowledge managers themselves should not imply by their words or actions that they are more 'knowledgeable' than anyone else."[6]

This is an important point. Knowledge managers really do not manage knowledge itself. Knowledge and knowledge networks are emergent phenomena of an organizational system. As such, they cannot be "managed" anyway. However, they can certainly be attended to and cultivated. Knowledge managers can do a great deal to help people become much more self-reflective about their own knowledge processes. They can help develop and implement supporting technologies and infrastructure. They can act as guides and navigators to help people access knowledge resources and each other.

Strategies and Approaches

When it comes to knowledge, successful experiments pay deliberate attention to knowledge creation and sharing. However, people generally do not respond well to knowledge as a concept. It feels too abstract. So best practice companies provide a common vehicle for expanding knowledge across all domains. In other words, they help people develop new languages for sharing knowledge. Learning new languages to communicate about their work and thinking processes helps people make tacit knowledge explicit, so it can be shared and multiply.

Some of the best vehicles that have surfaced for knowledge creation are Total Quality, leveraging best practices, and the practice of the learning organization, which emphasizes systems thinking. These all have some similarities. First of all, they have knowledge or learning itself as a key component. They deliberately apply knowledge to knowledge. Sharing best practices is a very structured and deliberate knowledge-sharing process, at least when done the right way (see Chapter 5). Practice of learning organization principles fosters self-awareness, reflection on learning, and knowledge creation.

Total Quality also emphasizes learning and knowledge in a direct way, such as through Deming's concept of profound knowledge. He identifies several types of knowledge that contribute to profound knowledge of how an organization functions. He describes Knowledge of Variation, Knowledge of Systems, Knowledge of Psychology, and a Theory of Knowledge. All of the quality tools and techniques are designed to communicate and share knowledge around these various aspects of work and performance.

Such approaches expand several languages that help people communicate about the tasks of a particular knowledge mode. Learning organization practices, for example, help people learn the language of systems, or the *Integrating* mode in particular. In addition, organizational learning and systems thinking have also extended the vocabulary for *Managing* and *Renewing* modes.

Leveraging a best practice in one's own organization requires communicating across every domain, since understanding a practice really requires understanding the whole system. Thus, extensive best practice sharing expands communication across all modes. Total Quality first attracted people because of the way it expanded *Procedural* and *Functional* knowledge. When Total Quality is truly understood and fully implemented, however, it provides new languages and tools for working across all the modalities.

The Total Quality Approach

The language of business processes is one of the most important business languages to emerge in the last two decades. With Total Quality we have learned important new languages for sharing performance knowledge, such as the language of variation and that of empowerment. Analysis and thinking processes have become more deliberate around understanding cause and effect, weighing alternatives, and interpreting data. Advanced Total Quality companies, such as Motorola and General Motors, also avidly share best practices, both internally and with external companies. In addition, they are expanding their ability to reflect on their own learning by applying learning organization principles and systems thinking.

Motorola has consistently led the way in many new management practices. As the first winner of the prestigious Baldrige Award for Quality, their devotion to Six Sigma quality is legendary. An important MIT study identified Motorola as also being a prime example of a learning organization.[7] As Motorola's quality initiative took off in the early 1980s, support for learning skyrocketed. Motorola University, funded in 1980, expands individual knowledge, while at the same time providing a common language to spread learning across the organization. Total Quality, combined with a culture that supports learning and knowledge sharing, has led them to world leadership. Demonstrating Motorola's strategic view of knowledge, Bob Galvin says, "We have to learn more things, and learn them faster. And we have to master our knowledge, not just acquire it."

At General Motors the quality initiative has resulted in a dramatic culture change. In *United We Stand*, Tom Weekley of the United Auto Workers (UAW) and Jay Wilber of General Motors, tell the story of forging an unprecedented partnership between GM and the UAW.[8] Their charge was to adopt the tenets of Total Quality management at every level of the organization. Total Quality became the vehicle for creating the new knowledge that will carry GM into the future.

Today, the UAW-General Motors Quality Network that grew out of that partnership is a primary mechanism for sharing knowledge and developing a common language. It provides four essential elements: a value system, a structure, a process focus for analysis and understanding, and tools and techniques for continuous learning and improvement. At GM, knowledge travels the language of quality.

The Potential of Total Quality

Why is it that Total Quality proves so powerful for creating and sharing knowledge? Consider that the underlying philosophy is based on a simple but powerful idea: learning must be a part of everything you do. Total Quality provides a language for learning by spreading the use of common tools for problem solving. The quality philosophy also addresses the need for a culture that is free from fear and barriers to communication. If there is a common language for solving problems and an absence of fear in the workplace, people will provide creative solutions and deliver quality work.

Total Quality is evolving from an early emphasis on meeting customer needs to providing customer delight. It has broadened its scope from a narrow perspective on conformance to standards, to improving processes. Meeting the challenge of Total Quality brings an appreciation of cultural issues, as well as the need for employee involvement, empowerment, and cross-functional teams. When the impetus of quality thinking is fully realized, companies potentially can achieve what William Miller refers to as "Quantum Quality." Quantum Quality is the achievement of significant leaps in work processes, stakeholder benefit, and personal commitment, based on values of caring and integrity.[9] Not all companies reach the full potential of this approach. Whether they do or not depends on their commitment and where they place their attention.

Total Quality and Learning

One of my colleagues, Kathryn Alexander, is passionate about Total Quality. Together we undertook a comparative analysis of quality methods to identify tools that support different learning and performance modes (Figure 14.1). If Total Quality is the strategic vehicle for knowledge sharing, then it is important

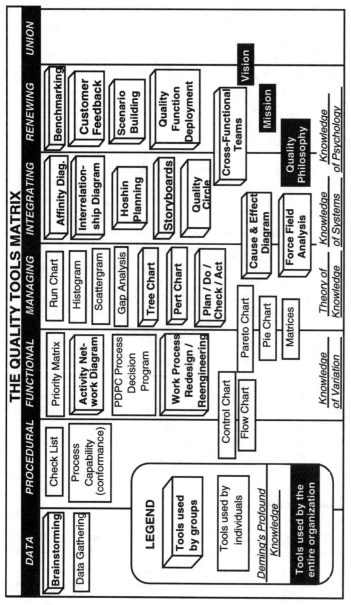

FIGURE 14.1 Quality Tools Matrix[10] (Verna Allee and Kathryn Alexander 1994)

© 1994 Verna Allee and Kathryn Alexander, Walnut Creek, CA 94596. All rights reserved.

to extend the practices across all the knowledge domains. The more types of tools and analysis techniques one embraces, the more knowledge expands across all the learning modes. Companies that employ a limited range of analysis tools also limit their capacity for knowledge sharing.

We also explored which tools could be employed by one or two people, and which require a cross-functional group or team to be used effectively. An interesting pattern emerged. As the learning modes progress to greater and greater complexity, the tools also become more collaborative. No one person can understand or analyze a complex system. System-level analysis must be conducted by a group that represents the whole system. The emphasis on "teaming" in recent years is not just because it is a good thing to do in a social sense, although it has many human benefits. More importantly, group work is necessary to meet the cognitive challenge of addressing complexity. Collaborative learning and knowledge creation are becoming ever more important.

Total Quality efforts often lead to a deeper interest in learning and sharing knowledge. Fidelity, Inc. has formed a twenty-member "Kaizen Learning Network" that grew out of the company's quality efforts. The network has produced benchmarking databases for internal and external use, and it is drafting an information architecture to support learning. The Boeing Company is a heavy user of Total Quality techniques and approaches. They also have groups of dedicated users of systems thinking tools and learning organization concepts. Aleda Roth, who has explored organizations as "knowledge factories," declares that quality is a first-order learning umbrella. Quality increases knowledge and learning by requiring people to communicate and by paving the way for flexibility and change.[11]

Benchmarking

Most companies that are advanced in Total Quality also avidly benchmark and share best practices. There is a common misconception that the purpose of benchmarking is to copy what other people are doing. This is not the purpose of serious benchmarkers. Benchmarking is a systematic learning process for identifying best practices, winning strategies, and innovative ideas that lead to superior performance—for the purpose of rethinking and improving one's own practices. This rarely means copying. Benchmarking is designed to challenge prevailing operating assumptions. It helps people discover alternative perspectives and views that could led to dramatically different ways of operating.

Benchmarking is an outward sign of an aggressive learning attitude within an organization. I once asked a person whose company was benchmarking extensively if they had competitive concerns with sharing information. The response, "If you are always learning, they can't catch you. Anything we are sharing as current practices is something we are already planning to change."

Benchmarking is a collaborative learning process. Unlike competitive intelligence, where learning is closely held as a proprietary secret, non-competitive benchmarking creates a shared learning environment. Companies engage in study and learning with each other for the purpose of mutual gain. A widely supported *Code of Conduct* provides a safe environment for sharing information. The Code was jointly developed by the Strategic Planning Institute Council on Benchmarking and the International Benchmarking Clearinghouse. This Code, or one of many slightly modified versions, is being adopted by companies all over the world.[12] Just as technical standards and protocols are easing the way to global connectivity, codes of conduct ease the way for making knowledge connections.

Benchmarking skill is a basic criteria of the Baldrige Award. Companies find that it can lead to remarkable learning breakthroughs and improvements. R.O.L. (Return on Learning) can be enormous. In a study of companies that benchmark, some report payoffs more than five times the cost of the study.[13] One project we were involved in returned a whopping $5 million in savings over 10 years on a $70,000 study. Gains from benchmarking can include finding new technologies or markets, increasing customer satisfaction and market share, reducing costs, or increasing efficiency. In some cases, benchmarking has prevented costly mistakes, such as investing in unnecessary technologies or implementing poorly designed programs.

Sharing Best Practices

One of the greatest challenges in benchmarking is effectively disseminating and sharing learning throughout the organization. Texas Instruments encourages best practice sharing by physically transferring people to different parts of the organization, providing incentives to adopt new practices through funding, and making it part of strategic goals. Developing the shared language of mapping processes is critical to knowledge transfer. Texas Instruments has established a worldwide Best Practice Sharing Facilitator Network using a custom designed knowledge base that includes best practices, company and contacts, and on-line access to a Best Practice Library. They also encourage knowledge transfer through sharing sessions.

A number of companies have created benchmarking and best practice databases, or other communication channels, to encourage knowledge sharing. Some of these benchmarking databases point to people and groups who are working in specific best practice areas, or are repositories of such knowledge. For example, Eastman Kodak, GM, Hughes Electronics, and Motorola take this approach. Alcoa and others distribute benchmarking study summaries by e-mail.

Chevron uses a Lotus Notes system, developed under the leadership of Mike Callaghan, that allows people to pose a knowledge question across the company. They can also post learnings and insights using key words and categories. Chevron also encourages interest in knowledge sharing by tracking and measuring the impact of best practices. They examine the impact on corporate performance in terms of dollars saved, customer satisfaction, public favorability, and reduced cycle time. Harder to determine, but also addressed, are the degree of integration of best practices, the number of improved processes, and usage on the database.

Other best practices databases are designed to be actual repositories of knowledge. Arthur Andersen Co., for example, under the leadership of Robert Heibeler, began creating a Global Best Practices knowledge base in 1990. They took an aggressive experimental approach that allowed their database to evolve as people were learning to use it. Calls to a hotline are sorted into business process categories as a way of determining knowledge needs. Then a support staff and researchers flesh out the information through studies and interviews. The current design is heavily dependent on a team of researchers and managers to keep knowledge updated. However, they envision a significant evolution as Web and Internet technology is incorporated into the design.

Best Practice Databases and Self-Organization

Benchmarking experts Christopher Bogan and Michael English emphasize the importance of good management for a best practices database.[14] One of the major problems is keeping such a database updated. Another problem is inflexible structures. Without some kind of management and oversight, superfluous and redundant information can be a problem. To address these issues, some companies prefer having a "librarian" act as an intermediary and enter material. Others, such as IBM, limit access. However, most of these centrally maintained repositories appear cumbersome and slow as knowledge moves increasingly faster. The challenge is to somehow create a way of sharing that is more spontaneous and self-organizing.

One effort to create a self-organizing best practices database using Web technology is underway at Golden Gate University (GGU) in San Francisco. I became involved in this effort through Americ Azevedo in the School of Science and Technology. The field of information management is moving so fast that textbooks are obsolete by the time they are published. The challenge is to create a continuously renewing current practices knowledge base that would be a core resource for graduate students in information management.

Benchmarking methodology was used as a core design concept. Self-organizing principles are incorporated in the way data would be input and accessed by GGU students. Emergent knowledge is captured by extensive use of open-ended questions. The core of the design is a coded question set organized by the *mode* of knowledge, rather than traditional subject categories (see Appendix 2). The content of the knowledge is constantly changing, but the questions do not become obsolete, because they are targeted to the type of knowledge being sought. The question set has provided both flexibility and consistency in over two hundred interviews.

The ability to share best practices is an important foundation for innovation and learning. It is so important that the U.S. government is undertaking an effort to create a sophisticated coding system to facilitate sharing across different agencies (see Chapter 8). Benchmarking and sharing best practices is an excellent way to foster the creation, sharing, and renewing of organizational knowledge. It is indispensable for helping create a learning mindset in an organization.

Learning Organizations and Systems Thinking

There is a growing awareness and conviction in senior management ranks that improving learning is an important success factor. Although the academic field of thought on this goes back over two decades, the term organizational learning came to public awareness with the popularity of Peter Senge's book, *The Fifth Discipline*, published in 1990. All organizations function as learning organizations. The purpose of learning organization strategies is to increase the speed, ability, and capacity for learning. The most successful learning organizations are those that are willing and able to uncover, test, and improve their mental models and change their behaviors.

Peter Senge first posed five skills or disciplines that organizations need to develop to become a better learning organization: team learning, personal mastery, mental models, shared vision, and, of course, systems thinking.[15] Since publication of his work, several important studies have been conducted and a number of excellent books on the subject have appeared. The Organizational Learning Center at MIT's Sloan School of Management commanded early thought leadership. Excellent articles have appeared in *Sloan Management Review* and other business publications. Interest has expanded widely, and important work is going on in many places around the country.[16]

Chapparell Steel and the Learning Organization

Companies that exemplify learning engage in systematic problem solving and experiment with new approaches. They learn from their own experience and history, as well as from the experience and best practices of others. They have devised ways to transfer knowledge quickly and efficiently throughout the organization.[17] In *Wellsprings of Knowledge*, Dorothy Leonard-Barton identifies Chapparell Steel as an example of a learning organization that does a superb job of managing its knowledge.[18]

Chaparrell's CEO, Gordon Forward, is confident in the embedded knowledge of his organization as it resides in people. He claims he can tour competitors through the plant, "show them almost everything, and we will be giving away nothing, because they can't take it home with them." If a competitor were to see anything of significance, by the time they try to imitate it, Chapparell will have moved to the next innovation.

Leonard-Barton identifies four primary activities that enhance knowledge at Chapparell Steel. Three are internally focused, one external. The four activities are: (1) Shared, creative problem solving; (2) implementing and integrating new methodologies and tools; (3) formal and informal experimentation; and (4) pulling in expertise from outside. Knowledge flows freely at Chapparell in a culture of sharing. Considerable effort has gone into removing barriers, both vertically and horizontally. There is an absence of managerial levels with all engineers and technicians having line responsibilities.

At Chapparell, employees are not tied to just one area. Production workers do 40 percent of the maintenance tasks and are free to contribute solutions in any problem area. Decisions about production are pushed down to the lowest possible level. Lead operators are selected for their ability to share and create knowledge. There is a culture of innovation and experimentation that leads to constant tinkering. Employees are continually benchmarking and scanning the world for ideas and technical knowledge.

Core Competencies

Another approach to knowledge creation and sharing is the development of a core competencies strategy. (See Chapter 2.) More and more companies are beginning to use the lens of core competencies to help focus on their identified areas of knowledge expertise and performance capabilities. Eastman Kodak uses competencies to help keep them on course through the minefields of fads, cycles, and new technologies. They have developed competencies from the direction of their technology portfolio. Other companies such as PPG Industries arrive there through an emphasis on personal core competencies. Either way, strategic alignment of organizational and individual competencies is the key to success.

Integrative Strategies

Most companies that engage in any of these approaches actually practice all of them. When knowledge itself is the strategic focus, it often serves as an umbrella for integrating Total Quality and learning organization principles. For example, the core competencies approach is also perfectly compatible with other quality and learning strategies. We do not have to throw out everything we have done before to move to a more comprehensive knowledge strategy.

CHAPTER 15

Culture, Mapping, Technology, and Measures

The real questions are how do we stay connected? How do we share knowledge? How do we function any time, anywhere, no matter what?

Robert Buckman

Now let's look at culture. Culture refers to the knowledge people hold collectively, enabling them to interpret their experience in similar ways and behave according to agreed upon norms. It is self-perpetuating, multi-layered, and resistant to change. At its deepest layer, culture is a pattern of interwoven core assumptions about how the world works. These assumptions are usually not consciously recognized by people. Yet, they are the foundation of the organization, expressed through values, behaviors, and physical aspects, such as facilities, equipment, written materials, and products.

Knowledge sharing cannot be taken for granted. Turk Enuston, of Eastman Kodak, has come smack up against the limitations of culture when it comes to sharing knowledge. Turk was one of the primary architects of the Eastman Kodak best practices database. As he tells the story, they had somewhat naively created an internal database listing all the good things being done in benchmarking: studies, conferences, and best practices. In a company already comfortable with e-mail and on-line communication, they thought all they had to do was create a file space called "benchmarking" and people would jump on board. When initial use proved disappointing, they realized they were operating on two false assumptions: (1) assuming people would use it, and (2) assuming a sharing culture exists.

What they are now beginning to realize is that sharing is *not* a strong part of the culture, despite wide use of communication technologies. People are not rewarded or recognized for helping other people. Although there is a very strong team culture, teams are mostly action-oriented. The concept and value of team learning as opposed to individual learning is quite new. "Now," Turk says, "I realize we are operating in a total system called knowledge. In order for this to work we will have to (1) change the culture, (2) create a different environment for sharing, and (3) develop a cohesive knowledge strategy."

In thinking about how to do this, they realize they have something very powerful and positive on which they can build. Under CEO George Fisher, education and learning has become much more valued and appreciated. Their current thinking is to build on that emergent value by setting targets for the sharing of knowledge and expertise with others. Ideally, this will help them identify experts and knowledge leaders within the company. Then they can begin to strengthen the natural knowledge linkages among the interest groups that already exist.

A Culture of Knowledge and Learning

A culture of learning and knowledge sharing does not happen by accident. In fact, the old practice of hoarding knowledge is so deeply ingrained in business that changing the culture is a major component of shifting into a learning mindset. *The key elements of a knowledge culture are a climate of trust and openness in an environment where constant learning and experimentation are highly valued, appreciated, and supported.*

Ooops, this is *not* what you find in the usual workplace environment, at least if cartoon character Dilbert is any indication. So what do we do? Well, we would need to start with self-inquiry. A few quick fixes in reward systems or executive proclamations won't cut it. If we truly want to change a culture it means taking time to really talk with each other. Yes, you guessed it. This means doing philosophy *together—Integrating* mode work. Together, we are going to have to dig into our own logic and thinking patterns. This is that "soft" stuff we know is really the hardest. We are going to have to grapple with our individual and group beliefs and operating assumptions.

The Underpinnings of Culture

Any culture is based on a set of assumptions and beliefs about how the world works. Edgar Schein has defined five categories of assumptions that make up our worldview: the nature of the environment, the nature of reality or truth, time and space, human activity, and human nature (Figure 15.1). If we would change a culture to support knowledge, then we must challenge our prevailing organizational assumptions and beliefs in each of these areas. We must specifically address the question of how we understand knowledge as it relates to each of these.

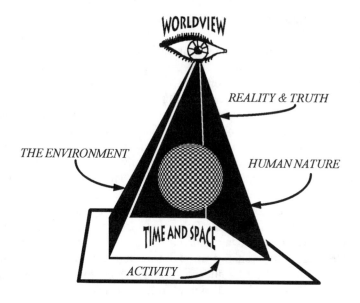

FIGURE 15.1 Edgar Schein's Five Areas of Cultural Assumptions.[1] The diagram uses the analogy of constructing a pyramid to demonstrate how our assumptions set the boundaries and determine the structure of our worldview.

Culture change must be handled with great sensitivity to both the realities of the existing culture and the hidden aspects of the new culture that is emerging. People are not naturally resistant to change. We change things all the time when we have the freedom to do so. People do resist being manipulated. They do challenge mixed messages.

People also must be collaboratively engaged in the creative process of the culture change themselves. Inquiry and experimentation around culture must involve as many people as possible. People need to find themselves in a new system. They need to understand their role. They need to understand how the rules of the game are changing and practice new behaviors. They need to understand the logic and assumptions that are operating and be free to challenge them.

Culture Change at Owens-Corning Fiberglas

When CEO Glen Hiner took the helm at Owens Corning, he set course for an ambitious future. To prepare for aggressive growth he insisted that five key influences be factored into decisions: customer focus, teaming, learning, mobility for a global workforce, and a paper-free environment. The future they have envisioned requires a more strategic focus for knowledge.

Jeff Hire, a knowledge champion at Owens Corning, works from a simple equation for building organizational knowledge: $K = (I + P)^S$. Knowledge = Information + People multiplied by Sharing. In this equation, however, internal knowledge alone is not sufficient. Owens Corning also continually scans for outside knowledge through competitive intelligence and benchmarking.

As a symbolic jettison of past ways of thinking, the entire headquarters is moving to a new building. Design of the new quarters has been undertaken with a careful eye to how people communicate and share knowledge. The building follows open design principles and incorporates the latest in communication technologies. People will be able to plug in a laptop anyplace. Another feature of the new quarters is a multi-purpose Discovery Center. This new knowledge resource will be geared both to self-improvement and business-oriented knowledge.

People know that in the future they will be expected to be more self-directed in learning and acquiring knowledge. In preparation for this culture change, people are given leeway to prepare in a variety of ways. Some are explicitly addressing culture change through training. Others are rearranging furniture in mock-ups of the new quarters to practice new ways of working. The new building represents a fundamental shift of thinking that is underway.

In any process of change, it is naive to assume that new technologies will automatically change behaviors. The presence of technologies that allow information sharing cannot in and of itself change a company culture. Yet, many people believe that appropriate information sharing behaviors will automatically follow installation of new technologies. Culture change must be part of the processes, an awareness that is at the forefront of the Owens-Corning effort. Without addressing the underlying beliefs and assumptions people hold about knowledge, learning, and sharing, the results are often disappointing.

Knowledge Focused Cultures

Genentech. In order to recruit top talent, Genentech decided to let its scientists publish their findings right away in leading journals, as if they were at a research institute instead of a for-profit company. The usual two-year delay made it impossible for the researcher to be first in their field, which is important for career recognition. Genentech's patent attorneys will scrutinize the discovery within a week, then let the researchers reveal their findings even before filing a patent application. This policy of openly sharing knowledge has yielded extraordinary results. Genentech ranks fourth among research institutions in molecular biology and genetics. The company also insists that researchers spend 25 to 35 percent of their time on their own projects. This does more than lure top minds, it also propels them to do great work. What really drives highly-educated knowledge workers is pride in accomplishment.

Minnesota Mining and Engineering (3M) is noted for product innovation. They allow engineers to spend 15 percent of their time working on innovations of their own choosing.

Federal Express is famous for its innovative pay-for-knowledge program that has been working successfully for several years. They also openly share knowledge with public Internet access to their package tracking system.

General Electric. The GE factory in Bayamon, Puerto Rico rotates workers through different work areas, boosting wages at each rotation as knowledge builds. Workers earn additional bonuses for learning new skills.

Ernst & Young makes a part of each consultant's compensation contingent on "knowledge sharing" activities.

ABB Asea Brown Boveri evaluates managers on knowledge applied, as well as results.

Lotus Development Corporation devotes 25 percent of its performance evaluation of customer support workers to knowledge sharing.

Veriphone blends a culture of sharing with extensive communication technologies in a "virtual workplace" environment.

Who or What is a Knowledge Worker?

One hears the term *knowledge worker* quite a lot these days. The term *knowledge worker* seems to be a descriptor for a particular mode of knowledge. It refers to a worker who manipulates and orchestrates symbols and concepts, one who works with knowledge and information. When Peter Drucker first coined the term, he was actually referring to an executive or manager. In usage, however, the term has expanded to mean most white-collar and professional workers.

However, the term is much too broad to be very useful. If we use it to indicate that some workers need a different type of technology and communication support, then it has some use. It may be a good way of distinguishing workers who are communication and computer dependent, rather than working with raw materials in a more physical way. However, when we work the term from the other end, we find that approach is problematic. Working from the other side of the definition, people who *don't* do knowledge work are generally defined as those who make and move things. Well, let's see. A Federal Express driver certainly moves things, but that driver might also operate an on-board terminal and telecommunications equipment, as well as navigate traffic—no knowledge required?! What about manufacturing facilities that are increasingly relying on automated equipment and sophisticated computer analysis of variation—no knowledge required?

The breadth and depth of knowledge that most people need to perform their work is much greater than it was in the past. The knowledge component of *everyone's* work has increased dramatically.

Managing Knowledge Workers

The term *knowledge worker* has a nice ring to it, though, and has sparked a flurry of articles in Human Resource, Training, and Management journals about managing the knowledge worker. What troubles me, however, is a creeping elitism lurking around the *knowledge worker* literature. It is subtly implied that those of us who do knowledge work are entitled to different treatment than a non-knowledge worker. Peter Drucker has even gone so far as to say that "Knowledge workers cannot be supervised effectively. Unless they know more about their specialty than anybody else in the organization, they are basically useless."[2]

Suggestions for "managing" knowledge workers are all very human-centered. "Knowledge workers need to participate in workplace decisions. They need greater flexibility in meeting deadlines. Knowledge workers can't be rushed or quality will suffer. Team synergy should not be disturbed." These are all great ideas, but this line of thinking makes me very uncomfortable. Who would *not* benefit from more participation, flexibility, and respect for work in progress? Why should knowledge workers be entitled to a qualitatively different type of work environment than other types of workers?

If knowledge is anywhere, it is everywhere. In a system, every part is critical for the function of the whole. It is far more useful to concentrate on the knowledge aspects of *all* the work we do. If we choose to place our attention on only certain types of knowledge, we do so at the risk of ignoring other critical modes. There are differences in knowledge modes that are important to understand. These distinctions help us make choices about how we learn and what we create. When we begin to appreciate knowledge in all its facets we realize there is no typical knowledge worker, but a whole galaxy of knowledge workers. Every worker is a knowledge worker. Everyone benefits from being treated as an intelligent, knowledgeable human being.

Mapping Organizational Knowledge

Companies that value knowledge want to know how and where to access it. With a view to knowledge as a valuable resource, many companies are undertaking "knowledge mapping" projects. Different companies take different approaches to this according to their needs and purpose. The purpose of a knowledge map is to guide people to knowledge resources inside the company.

For example, companies such as Chevron and Hughes Space & Communications are beginning to create guides to pockets of expertise inside their companies. Arian Ward of Hughes envisions a variety of maps—some computerized, some not—that would foster communication and "storytelling" between internal "experts." These would not be indexes, but "maps that show where the knowledge of the enterprise is located—in whose heads, for example." One example is an on-line "lessons learned" database in the engineering group, utilizing hypertext links to directories, abstracts, and documents.[3]

As an example of a paper-based map, Chevron has created a guide called Best Practice Resources that unfolds very much like a typical road map. It serves as a guide to groups, networks, conferences, forums, and even documents. It is designed using knowledge categories that resonate with the Malcolm Baldrige Award Criteria.[4] It was an instant hit with Chevron employees and has been widely used. The challenge in a paper-based system, of course, is keeping it updated as people move around the company and as knowledge "nodes" renew and change.

McKinsey & Co. Inc.'s first efforts, in the early 80s were paper-based. They now depend on Lotus Notes as a navigational tool. American Express's earliest map was literally a map of the United States flagged with information resources. Today, the maps are moving on-line and are utilizing key-word search capability. Virtually all of the big consulting firms have some type of knowledge map of internal experts, most using Lotus Notes. Other companies with mapping efforts are shown in the example box.

Knowledge is a constantly moving target. The big problem with all these maps and knowledge guides is, of course, maintaining them. Too many times such efforts fizzle out, because they become outdated and people simply stop using them or contributing to them. At Chemical Bank in New York, they are pushing the ability to update out to the local level. However, this still assumes a culture and environment where people are willing to contribute. Many "knowledge map" designs are too heavily dependent on a centralized group for maintenance, input, and updating.

Knowledge Cartographers

Hewlett Packard is expanding on-line knowledge maps and delivery systems. According to Robert Walker of HP, these have helped improve access and slashed costs.[5]

Hughes Space & Communications is forging a knowledge highway employing videoconferencing, Lotus Notes, employee home pages, and other technologies. It is used to spread new management practices, track patents and licenses, and gather competitive intelligence.

Teltech has an on-line thesaurus-based directory of more than 30,000 technical terms maintained by several full-time people. The old traditional tree of categories was too unwieldy, missed critical word linkages, and was difficult to navigate. This marks an important shift to mapping knowledge while it changes, rather than modeling it by categories.

U.S. West is planning to have every single one of its 50,000 employees connect to their Intranet with their own home page.

AT&T started a guide to internal experts that now includes 2,000 contact names. The initiative was driven by the strategic planning group's Martin Stark.

Continued

(Continued)

People can post queries to a bulletin board after searching name and interest lists.

IBM's Guide to Market Information includes not only the information resources, but also contact information for people responsible for the information.

Coopers & Lybrand employees can call a hotline and connect with a researcher who uses a Lotus Notes database to find the proper internal expert.

Hallmark has established an "Information Guide" in the form of a real person at each business unit to help people find information.

Next Generation Knowledge Mapping

We cannot solve our Knowledge Era questions with design approaches that came out of Information Age thinking. The current state of practice in "knowledge mapping" is cumbersome at best. In worst case situations, people are spending much time and resources in an exercise in futility. They lose sight of the self-organizing capability of knowledge. When we don't understand knowledge as a system, we often just get in the way.

Knowledge is perfectly capable of organizing itself. It does this very naturally. Efforts at knowledge mapping too often try to impose some artificial structure on knowledge, such as categories. Since these are artificial structures, the knowledge does not fit it quite right and must constantly be nudged and prodded until it does. Thus, the knowledge map must rely on an "expert" to input the knowledge in the right way, so that it fits the structure. Without constant attention, the knowledge moves on, people abandon the structure, and burned out hulks of databases sit in lonely obsolescence.

If we would understand how to "map" knowledge, then we must understand how it works. The first thing to remember is *knowledge rides language and language is always changing.* Our business vocabulary today is completely different than it was ten or twenty years ago. Despite the way people poke fun at "jargon" and "buzz words," they carry knowledge—new knowledge and new ideas.

When we create categories, we are creating a snapshot or freeze-frame of how knowledge looks at a particular point in time. Knowledge moves on, and the language of the categories no longer fits. Witness the effort of Teltech (see example box) to keep its 30,000 word thesaurus updated. If this thesaurus were not central to their core business process of providing subject matter experts, it would not be worth the trouble.

Communities of Practice

Another important thing to remember is that *knowledge wants to happen and it happens in community.* People naturally organize themselves into communities of practice. We seek people who speak the languages that reflect our interests, professional and personal.

Researchers Susan Stucky and Peter Henshel of the Institute for Research on Learning have been examining insights and learning arising from the synergy of people from different fields working together in real settings. They have concluded that learning is not about transferring knowledge. Learning is a process of building understanding in a social, physical, and temporal setting. People are attracted to those with shared interests and similar activities. Regardless of how they might be organized formally, the real organization is around community.[6]

Organizations always have both formal and informal organizations. The formal one is created by design. The informal can be thought of as an emergent organization. These communities of practice form spontaneously. They usually operate at the periphery where innovation, new ideas, and generative learning occur. Communities of practice—or communities of knowledge, if you prefer—cannot be created or designed, but they can be supported. We cannot design a seed, but we can till and water the garden in which it can grow. Companies that understand this are trying to remove barriers to the natural way people would organize to do their work. Some companies deliberately support the creation of knowledge networks and groups as the informal warp to the formal woof of the organizational fabric.

Emergent Knowledge

Trying to formalize the emergent organization is tricky business. Some people feel it is a death sentence. When Stuckey and Henshel discovered an informal community at Hewlett-Packard, they worked with the group to see if they felt the formal organization should reflect their informal practice. The group decided not to formalize the community, since they could see no advantage to doing so.

Elizabeth and Gifford Pinchot remind us that "no centrally conceived design can produce both the freedom needed to empower individual intelligence and the rapidly changing network of interconnections needed to knit free thinkers together in coordinated action with an intense focus. We cannot design intelligent organizations, we must grow them in the convergence of market and community processes."[7]

Many knowledge mapping efforts only address the more formal knowledge resources. However, formal resources may not be the ones people actually use. The best knowledge maps go after the informal knowledge as well. Informal knowledge webs reside in communities of practice.

Knowledge Networking

One way that people can self-organize around knowledge is through internal affinity groups or networks of people with common interests. An affinity group might be a group of professional peers who share experience around their work or technical knowledge.[8] These have been used as knowledge sharing vehicles at the Department of Energy, at National Grocers, Inc of Ontario, and at Virginia Polytechnic Institute and State University. Chevron provides "seed money" and funding for networks to self-organize around technology and management areas. Budgets are limited, but sufficient to allow people to establish communication links and have occasional in-person get-togethers.

In a more formal approach to knowledge networking, Corning, Inc. has created thirteen different Centers of Excellence, in areas such as materials management, competitive intelligence, manufacturing, ISO/Baldrige assessment, learning resources, and Total Quality. These are established by a process owner, a senior person who takes responsibility of an area through position, title, or desire and expertise. Members of these special interest groups are people who have related job interests. For example, The Total Quality group, as described by member Leroy Boatright, generally includes about 40-50 people. These centers put on internal conferences and provide visibility and recognition for innovation. For example, The Quality Milestones event features 10-12 teams sharing success stories.

Seeing Patterns in Knowledge

One interesting approach to mapping informal networks is network analysis. David Krackhardt and Jeffrey R. Hanson have been exploring informal networks for over a decade. They note that the influence of central figures in these networks is so strong that it can explain political conflicts and puzzling failures to achieve strategic objectives. Intriguing web-like patterns can surface by mapping responses to questions about who people talk to about work, who they trust, and who advises whom on technical matters. The resulting maps are often in stark contrast to people's mental models of the organization.[9]

Such an approach illustrates an important counter-trend in knowledge mapping. That trend focuses on knowledge relationships more than categories, exploring how knowledge moves and which clusters are in use, rather than regarding knowledge as an object that must be catalogued. Such approaches to modeling knowledge look at the ways knowledge naturally self-organizes, rather than imposing a structure.

People are experimenting with ways to see patterns in knowledge. Maps of experts are one pattern. Maps of knowledge resources reveal yet another pattern. Mapping the object-like qualities of knowledge helps us find what we need for the moment. But the system of knowledge itself moves in dynamic interrelationships. Knowledge is created and shared in community. Technologies that help people understand dynamic relationships show great promise for helping us see the patterns of knowledge in our organizations. Technologies that help us find our natural communities of practices are perhaps the most valuable of all.

As I was browsing the business section of the local bookstore one day, I came across a young man precariously balancing a huge stack of popular business books. He had all the latest books on reengineering, the current Tom Peters book, a selection on leadership. We started chatting.

"Hmmm," I said, "It looks like you are facing a major management challenge by the look of all those books. Are you a new manager?"

He nodded, surprised I could tell. "I just got promoted."

Curious, and invisibly slipping on my consultant's Sherlock Holmes hat, I asked, "What is your responsibility area? What is it you are struggling with?"

"Actually, my area is information management," he replied. "I don't know a lot about management, so I am trying to find something that will help me understand how to support managers with technology and information systems."

"Ah," I nodded knowingly. "I think I know what you are looking for." Out came my pencil. "You are probably trying to get a handle on how information technologies support the actual structure of the organization, something like this . . . " I drew a couple of overlapping circles.

"Yes, that's the idea." I had his full attention.

"Ideally," I went on, drawing another intersecting circle, "the book you are seeking would not only address those questions, but also two other questions. Those would be: 'How does the sea of knowledge and information that we could call knowledge-at-large, impact the organization?' and 'How could information technologies facilitate the building of organizational knowledge?'"

"Yes, yes, that's it!" he cried, "Where's the book?"

I suddenly felt bad about building up his hopes, only to disappoint him. "You see," I replied, "there really aren't many good books out there yet. There is a great big gap in what people are looking at. The organizational design people aren't very knowledgeable about information technology, and the information technology people aren't particularly interested in organizational design. They are just now starting to come together in the middle."

Fortunately, the conversation about knowledge is growing rapidly. More and more people are beginning to ponder this critical interface that Americ Azevedo and I describe as the Knowledge Technologies Interface (Figure 15.2).

Most big expenditures in information technologies are addressing the triangle in the very center of the diagram, the intersection between the Organization, Knowledge-at-large, and Supporting Technologies. Overspending is the result of expecting more from technology than it can reasonably deliver.

Wasting IT Resources

Our expectations of technology are unrealistic, because we have not really come to terms with the secondary overlaps in the diagram, or with selecting appropriate technologies to support them. For example, there is a secondary overlap where Supporting Technologies interface with Knowledge-At-Large. This is a very seductive overlap. Just because it is *possible* to use Information Technologies (IT) to capture huge chunks of Knowledge-At-Large, doesn't mean it should be done. The question is, "Does it really serve the organization?" How

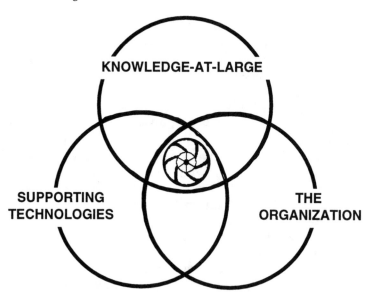

FIGURE 15.2 Knowledge Technologies Interface.

 Supporting Technologies include both computer-based and non-technical retrieval and storage systems. They include computer hardware, software for data capture, Internet and communications technology Intranets, e-mail, databases, and libraries.

 The *Organization* represents the structures, people, and processes that shape the enterprise.

 Knowledge-At-Large includes formal and informal communication, as well as learning and knowledge sharing of every kind that is accessed through the Internet, books, journals, mail, associations, partnerships, events such as conferences, and other educational experiences.

many IT dollars are wasted chasing after knowledge that is of no use to the organization?

Another area of waste is the overlap between Knowledge-At-Large and the organization. Here we find many missed opportunities, much squandered time and wasted energy, because people do not understand their own organizational learning processes. Much of the knowledge that has an impact on the organization is ineffectively deployed, because there are no appropriate sharing and communication processes for disseminating knowledge throughout the organization. Or, people are not focused on knowledge competencies, so they don't know where to place their attention.

Also misunderstood is the interface between IT and the organization, despite a great deal of attention in this area. Too many times the capability of a particular technology shapes what is created, rather than the needs of people. We have made great strides in this area, but most IT books are more focused on hardware and software design at the expense of organizational processes, structures, and culture.

The desire to support learning and knowledge building is sparking huge investments in information technology. The board of one of the world's biggest banks includes a Vice-Chairman for Information Systems. The very fact that "information systems" warrants a board of directors position indicates how important technology support has become.

Why the high-level attention? Simple dollars. Information Systems represent one of the three largest expenditures for the corporation. It ranks right up there with staffing and rent. The question is, are companies realizing the return on investment that those kinds of dollars represent? Are they realizing an ROI that includes transfer of learning and the building of knowledge capital?

We adopt new technologies because we want them to think as we think. (Or maybe we want them to do the thinking for us.) Often our technologies feel cumbersome and wasteful, or are not getting us where we want to go. When this happens, we need to look not at the technologies, but at our own thought processes. What are we trying to get the technologies to do? If our thinking is confused, our technologies will only contribute to the same confusion.

We are constantly shaping a conversation with our information environment. We ask a question, then look for the data and information that will fill in the response. Our quest is a quest for knowledge, a more complete picture. If we understand what knowledge is, and how an organization builds knowledge, then we stand a much better chance of creating real knowledge technologies. If we don't understand knowledge itself, then we haven't a clue as to how to go about creating it, building it, managing it, or supporting it with technology.

Knowledge Technologies

Most information support systems work very well to collect and organize *Data* and *Information*. A few exceptionally well-designed databases with good interfaces do a respectable job of building *Knowledge* in a few limited categories. Much newer in development are intelligent softwares that will detect patterns in bodies of data to help us make *Meaning*, or reach real understanding.

What distinguishes knowledge technology from information technology? Information technologies have generally come to mean technologies that store, organize, and transmit information. *Knowledge technologies are those that support the building, communication, and retention of knowledge.* Information technologies *serve* knowledge creation, but knowledge creation addresses a larger set of questions beyond those of information management.

In order to build a knowledge support system, you first need to understand the operations, purpose, and tasks of the organization. Different modes of work require very different types of support, as we saw in Chapters 7 to 13. Tasks must be analyzed for their knowledge or learning requirements. Only then can we identify appropriate hard and soft technologies that support knowledge creation and decision making.

Most information systems designers just briefly stick their heads up above their databases and networks, get a quick cursory sense of the organizational lay of the land, then dive back down again into building databases. Before we jump into technology investments, we need to hang out at the organizational level long enough to understand what knowledge is really needed to support high performance, and what learning and knowledging processes are needed.

Corporations individually will spend hundreds of thousands of dollars, perhaps even millions, on installing technology. Yet they seldom spend time or invest resources in questioning their design assumptions. They also rarely assess the types of learning, levels of decision making, and arenas of knowledge creation that they are trying to support.

Supporting Technologies for Knowledge Creation and Sharing

We do know enough about knowledge creation and sharing to identify a few basic technologies that are becoming "musts" for a knowledge-based organization.

Document Management

Document management is an important foundation for knowledge sharing. At Bechtel, authoring, managing, and controlling requisitions, reports, and purchase orders is so central to its business that they are now distributing this information worldwide. Engineers can access information on past projects, including plant designs. They can also use Internet links for accessing weather and earthquake data.[10]

On-line Access

Knowledge sharing is encouraged when people can readily access the information they need. Wal-Mart has gone the extra mile in this regard through their own satellite communication system, which is connected to every point of sale in the country. Databases of customer information are going on-line everywhere for company-wide access. Monsanto's agricultural group Ceregen, for example, has an on-line competitor and customer database that can be accessed by all 600 employees. It also includes reports from sales people, notes from conventions, news, and a directory of in-house experts.

E-mail Connectivity

E-mail connectivity is a must. Monsanto salespeople share news on a Lotus Notes database. Buckman Laboratories frames connectivity in the simplest of ways, through a private forum on CompuServe, open only to employees. Lotus

Notes databases, combined with e-mail, continue to grow in popularity, expanding simple communication to topic-based information resources and bulletin boards. Skandia Corp is expanding its Notes-based "knowledge bases" world-wide. Conferencing features for e-mail are expanding rapidly.

Expert Systems for Decision Making and Performance Support

Expert systems that help people make decisions have moved from executive suites out to the workers. Expert systems capture the thinking processes of experts and use that knowledge to guide people through work decisions or responding to customer questions. AT&T has a system called AAA (Access to AT&T Analysts) to disseminate expertise and competitive information to each of its employees. Financial Services Inc. (IDS) created a software program that draws on the expertise of its top account managers, reducing client loss by more than 50 percent. Other efforts are underway at California State Automobile Association (CSAA) in the development of an On-Line Guide support tool.

Technologies that See Patterns in the Data

As more and more knowledge is computerized, we are finding ways to discover patterns in the knowledge itself. Automated data mining is beginning to reveal patterns of relationships that emerge from data. An auto-discovery system, for example, will discover explicit rules, hypotheses, and knowledge hidden in large databases. It might uncover the relationship of sales on a particular cereal to another product. Another tool might display patterns such as cycles. Yet another tool might pick up anomalies that reveal data entry errors or significant variation. Others such as Netmap™ depict a variety of relationships.

Knowledge and Technology

Self-organization and the Internet

The Internet and the World Wide Web comprise an exciting experiment in self-organization of knowledge on a global scale. Technology protocols that enable one computer to link to another have granted us the capability to self-organize around knowledge and communities of practice. Note, please, that the World Wide Web is *not* a database. There is no grand designer selecting categories for people to use.

With HTTP language people *ride the language to the knowledge.* You get where you need to go by riding the words of your questions. People find their communities of practice through language. We expand our knowledge according to our interests through dynamic interaction with others. Knowledge organizes around identity and purpose; so does the Web.

Recognizing the potential of these technologies, companies are beginning to create their own Intranets. While many of these are technology companies, such as Silicon Graphics, National Semiconductor, and Sun Microsystems, others are starting to jump in. In companies that have them, the work is starting to organize according to who is on the Intranet. People are also eager to learn the technology, because it reflects what is going on in the world at large. The costs in many cases are much less than they would be in designing a database. With Web technology, people can create and retire linkages themselves. They do not need some central director to determine what is relevant and what is not.

The Web, with many of the qualities of a self-organizing system, is one of the most interesting knowledge experiments around. While its potential and future are still uncertain, early results appear promising. An independent study of the impact of the Intranet on Silicon Graphics found demonstrable positive results with improved productivity, enhanced knowledge capital, strengthened teamwork across boundaries, improved process efficiency and workflow and increased employee satisfaction.[11] This grand global experiment of the Intranet has created a wonderful practice field for knowledge.

Soft Technologies

Managers do not rely on computer-based information to make decisions anyway. Studies have shown that they receive two-thirds of their information from conversations and the remaining one-third from documents. Most of the documents managers rely on are *not* on computers. Many come from outside the organization. Informal sharing is still a primary vehicle for knowledge. A study by Xerox Corporations Palo Alto Research Center showed that service technicians learned the most about repairing copiers from sharing stories with each other, not from reading manuals.

Hard technologies and information systems can provide valuable support for learning and knowledge building. However, there are also many knowledge support technologies that rely on "soft" systems skills and group processes. Such knowledge technologies are often overlooked in the rush to buy information systems. These "soft" technologies include collaborative planning, knowledge sharing forums, and learning methods such as benchmarking. They facilitate informal exchange, fostering common problem-solving skills and language. Mentoring programs, too, are beginning to grow beyond their uses in career development to address transfer of expertise. Soft technologies can reap huge dollar and productivity returns for relatively small investments.

It is pretty obvious to most serious observers of learning and knowledge creation that formal training programs cover only a fraction of workplace learning. Training is evolving into "just-in-time" multi-media modules that can be delivered right to the workstation. Some divisions at Hewlett-Packard have eliminated 90 percent or more of classroom training. Classroom time is being devoted to skills that require group practice, such as communication and problem solving.

Measuring Knowledge

No form of measurement is neutral. What we measure in our organizations communicates our values and what we regard as important. Our measures communicate our purpose and intent, and people will self-organize to support them. Thus, any system of measurement puts attention in one area, which sometimes is to the detriment of the whole.

The challenge in any measurement system is to be sure that what we are measuring is really an indicator for what we want to observe. For example, a company may say they value learning, then boast about the number of hours their people spend in training as "proof" that people are learning. All such a measure indicates is how many hours people spend in the classroom. It does not indicate whether they actually learned anything.

Our measures indicate what we believe to be the knowledge "question." We measure the knowledge aspect that we value. If we measure knowledge by the number of patents that a company applies for in a year, then we have posed the knowledge opportunity as, "Can we generate knowledge in the form of codified knowledge that we can patent?" A very different measure is that used by Chevron and Texas Instruments to determine the number of divisions that integrate and use a the best practice. That type of measure addresses a knowledge "opportunity" of sharing and disseminating new knowledge within the organization.

How People are Measuring

As we saw in Chapter 2, companies are accounting for knowledge in a variety of ways. Measuring codified knowledge in the form of patents, copyrights, and proprietary methodologies and research is relatively easy to do. Consequently, many companies have measures for these types of knowledge "products."

Measuring knowledge efficiency is more challenging. Steven Hronec of Arthur Andersen suggests developing measures for quality, time, and cost. Looking at ways to enhance knowledge processes is as important as focusing on outputs or results.

Robert Grant and Charles-Baden Fuller suggest calculating knowledge efficiency using two factors. The first factor they suggest is the efficiency of integration mechanisms, such as converting tacit to explicit knowledge. The second knowledge success indicator they suggest is the extent of capacity utilization of knowledge. Capacity utilization describes how well the firm's product domain matches its knowledge domain.[12] While these two measures focus on sharing and competencies, they do not address sustaining or renewing knowledge.

Joseph Badaracco suggests focusing on knowledge boundaries and measuring knowledge in two primary categories. "Migratory knowledge" is knowledge that should easily flow between groups or firms. On the other hand, there is more proprietary "embedded knowledge" that is vital to a firm's success.[13] These distinctions pose only two knowledge "questions." The first has to do with transfer or sharing, while the second one has to do with ownership.

In addition to the knowledge value-added approach described in Chapter 2, people are also trying to understand how knowledge builds overall value in the company. Skandia and Dow Chemical both use the lens of knowledge or intellectual capital. In practice, however, they do things quite differently. Dow focuses on patents and codified knowledge that Dow can control and own, although this is evolving. Skandia uses a broader range of measures.

For example, one way Skandia measures effectiveness of knowledge transfer is in how long it takes them to open a new office. They have also used knowledge transfer skills to encourage cross-border sales. They view their ability to make inter-country offerings of products as an indicator of skill in knowledge transfer. Measures also include computer literacy and usage. Skandia also uses more complex measures, such as ratios that measure information technology investments as a percentage of total expenses. In addition, they factor in business development expenses and products that result from new launches.[14]

What Mode of Knowledge are You Trying to Measure?

When trying to measure overall outputs at the enterprise level, it is important to look at knowledge generation and sharing within the organization as well. Internally, I believe many of the measures people are trying to use are simply too broad to be useful. If you would understand knowledge, then it makes sense to understand which mode you are trying to support. Just as each mode has its own language, it requires different measures to understand knowledge experiments in each domain. By understanding the type of knowledge required by each performance mode, we are better able to define measures that are useful.

There is no "correct" measure. The right measure depends on the purpose of the knowledge experiment. As we refine our experiments, we will also refine our measures.

Seeing Patterns

Measures are ways to see patterns. They illuminate significant variations and help us direct our attention to a particular area. It is impossible to define and track all the measures that may be significant in a system as complex as a modern business. Even if we were somehow able to nail down all the internal measures, we would not be able to assimilate the multitude of data from the environment. Measures are invaluable feedback, but they also provide limited information. We must maintain a creative balance of sensing and scanning high-level patterns and focusing on detail. We can exhaust ourselves attempting to measure the immeasurable. Sometimes, in all those numbers, we lose the mystery.

CHAPTER 16

The Seeds of Knowledge

The meaning of my life is that life has addressed a question to me.
Carl Jung

We are in the early stages of our ability to apply our knowledge to knowledge itself. We have much yet to learn. We have many questions. The domains of knowledge we create will be a direct result of where we place our attention in the next few years. Our choices determine the way we will generate new learning. We can continue trying to jam events into traditional clocktime, or we can expand awareness to the polychronic world of space-time. How we attend to time determines where our knowledge will grow. We can focus attention narrowly in one or two domains, or we can expand all our modalities, developing new languages for our work in the process. We can treat knowledge as an object and exhaust ourselves trying to gather all the beads of knowledge in the universe. Or, we can reach an understanding of its creative flow and worry a little less about what we control.

For years, individuals have been locked into isolated knowledge universes, fretting about all they do not know as professionals or experts. Perhaps it is time to trust that together we have what we need. If we would create a healthy future together, then we must pay attention to how we learn together and reach shared understanding. We must begin to understand how we create meaning and knowledge as groups and together ask knowledge questions about knowledge itself.

Beyond Knowledge

There is a famous Zen teaching story of a student who comes to visit the master teacher. The teacher graciously offers the student tea, which she accepts.

The teacher begins pouring the tea, then keeps pouring the tea into the cup until the cup overflows and the tea spills all over the table.

"Stop, stop," the student exclaims! "Why are you doing this?"

"You are like this cup," the teacher replies. "You are already so full of what you know that I cannot add anything to it."

The Knowledge Era is like that. We are too full of information, too full of our knowledge. There is simply no room to add anything more, yet we keep pouring more and more knowledge into our overflowing cups.

We cannot see the emerging knowledge that is swimming all around us in the turbulent waters of the information ocean until we first become empty. We must learn to empty ourselves of what we think we know. When we let go of our old knowledge habits we once again can come to what in the Buddhist tradition is called "beginner's mind." Beginner's mind is a mind that is open, full of questions, and willing to learn.

Questions are the Seeds of Knowledge

Questions open the world to us. I like thinking of an egg to demonstrate the power of the question. An egg is ingeniously designed so that it is incredibly strong and resistant to outside pressure. You can pile several adult ducks on top of a duck egg and it will not break. Yet a tiny duckling need only take a few pecks from the inside to break out of the shell. Our questions have the power to break us out of the shell of our understanding into new worlds. Real knowledge always emerges in response to our questions.

Between not knowing and our urge to know is where we are most attentive and most alive. A vital question, a creative question, rivets our attention. All the creative power of our minds is focused on the question. Knowledge emerges in response to these compelling questions. They open us to new worlds and new knowledge. Questions and knowledge expand together in a creative dance. Both become deeper. Both become more diverse. This is a good thing. Systems become healthier as they become more diverse. The more we expand our questions, the healthier we become. The more diversity we express in knowledge, the healthier our society becomes.

Beyond the Knowledge Era

Our questions have led us from the Industrial Age to the Knowledge Era, and they will take us beyond into worlds we can only imagine. The quality of those new worlds depends on the quality of our questions. We may not be the only species on the planet that is able to reflect on its own actions, but we are the most important species with that capability. For we alone have the power of life and death over all the other species and of the planet herself. How often do we include as company stakeholders those societies and species that are outside our social economic system? Yet, if we do not consider what is healthy and life-sustaining for all of us, then how can we know what is healthy for ourselves? If we do not open our questions of knowledge to these considerations, then we have locked ourselves into a closed system that cannot survive.

Knowledge organizes around our sense of who we are. If we would expand knowledge, then we must look at the self that creates it. If we would master the Knowledge Era and move forward, then we must learn the art of asking self-reflective questions about our identity, our purpose, and our values. As a living system, we do not leap to a completely new identity when our consciousness of self changes. We renew and recycle the components of our knowledge, awareness, and understanding. As awareness about ourselves changes, we materialize different responses, build new knowledge, and develop new behaviors.

Self-questioning unlocks the genetic code of our own wisdom and understanding. Can we encourage this type of questioning in our organizations? Healthy systems are open systems, open to explore their self-identity, open to new information, open to different ways of thinking. Conscious self-questioning is the axis of growth. Can we encourage healthy inquiry and self-reflection? These are the real questions about knowledge "management." Given our history and culture, they are also the toughest.

Trusting Knowledge

If we would open ourselves to knowledge, then we must have the courage to ask new questions. In our organizations, how well do we support a diversity of questions and knowledge? Healthy systems constantly experiment with new connections. They are always seeking new information, continually engaging in dialogue to create meaning. Do we know how to ask questions of ourselves? Do we know how to explore our questions together?

Real knowledge management is much more than managing the flow of information. It means nothing less than setting knowledge free to find its own paths. It means fueling the creative fire of self-questioning in organizations. This means thinking less about knowledge management and more about knowledge partnering. We must give people freedom to express their knowledge and wisdom by inviting openness and exchange, both internally and externally. With that invitation knowledge will find its way. People will self-organize to knowledge together, selecting appropriate technologies for their purposes as they go.

Can we learn to really trust ourselves and the power of our own knowledge? It seems to me that most of the messes we make are not because of what we know, but because of what we do not allow ourselves to know. We pull back from the full power of our knowledge. We do not see that we already have the emergent knowledge that will guide us into the future. The knowledge that guides us to healthy enterprise is not the knowledge of our minds, it is the knowledge of our hearts. When we allow ourselves to experience the full power of the questions of our hearts, we will move beyond the Knowledge Era to a world that is healthier and more diverse, more cooperative and, yes, a little wiser, too.

APPENDIX 1

The Knowledge Archetype in Theoretical Constructs

NOTES

1. Verna Allee, Performance Modes as described in Chapter 4.

2. Peter Senge, *The Fifth Discipline.* Senge suggests five disciplines for a learning organization: *personal mastery, mental models, shared vision, team learning,* and *systems thinking.* Systems thinking and explicit dialogue around concepts, assumptions, and beliefs is the focus of *Integrating* performance. Senge suggests supporting this work with a culture of team learning, which would address *Managing* issues. The wisdom aspects of his approach include personal mastery and shared vision, demonstrating a *Renewing* performance focus.

3. Ikujiro Nonaka and Hirotaka Takeuchi, *The Knowledge-Creating Company.* In Chapter 3, "Theory of Knowledge Creation" (pp. 56–94), Nonaka and Takeuchi describe the modes of knowledge as four quadrants that are passed through in stages during the "knowledge spiral" process of knowledge creation. In their view, knowledge creation usually begins with socializing *Sympathized knowledge,* progressing next through externalized *Conceptual knowledge.* The cycle completes with the combination stage of *Systemic knowledge,* then knowledge is finally internalized once again as *Operational knowledge.*

4. Dorothy Leonard-Barton, *Wellsprings of Knowledge: Building and Sustaining the Sources of Innovation.* See Chapter 1, "Core Capabilities," pp. 3–28. In her book, Leonard-Barton depicts a systemic approach to core technology competencies, drawn as a series of concentric circles with Physical Systems at the center and Values in the outermost circle. In dynamic, clockwise, circular movment around this knowledge "universe," she shows four key knowledge processes of *problem solving, implementing and integrating, experimenting,* and *importing knowledge.* This model depicts the more tangible "physical" aspects at the center, with the abstract components of knowledge, such as values, in the outer circles.

KNOWLEDGE ASPECTS

THEORETICAL CONSTRUCT (See notes)	Data	Information	Knowledge	Meaning	Philosophy	Wisdom	Union
1. Performance Modes [Allee]	*Data*	*Procedural*	*Functional*	*Managing*	*Integrating*	*Renewing*	*Union*
2. Five Disciplines [Peter Senge]				team learning	systems thinking & mental models	shared vision & personal mastery	
3. Knowledge Conversion Modes [Nonaka/Takeuchi]		operational knowledge	systemic knowledge	sympathized knowledge	conceptual knowledge		
4. Dimensions of Core Capabilities [Leonard-Barton]		physical systems		managerial systems	employee knowledge & skills (interfaces)	values & norms	
5. Managerial Focus [Erich Jantsch]		resources	tactical targets: products/services	social functions: roles/relationships	policy & systems dynamics	values	
6. Viable Systems [Stafford Beer]		system 1	system 2		system 3	system 4 / system 5	environment
7. Stratified Systems [Elliott Jacques]	1st order: linear stringing	2nd order: diagnostic accumulation	3rd order: alternate paths	4th order: multiple paths	5th order: unified whole systems	6th order: worldwide diagnostics	7th order: constructing whole systems
8. Russell Ackoff	data	information (description)	knowledge (instruction)		understanding (explanation)	wisdom (evaluation)	
9. Quality Philosophy [Edward Deming]	data	action		knowledge (theory)	prediction		
10. Strategy Processes [S. Hart]		command	rational	transactional	generative	symbolic	
11. Hierarchy of Needs [Abraham Maslow]	physiological needs	safety needs (order)	belongingness needs		self-esteem needs	self-actualization needs	transcendence
12. Moral Development [Lawrence Kohlberg]		obedience / instrumental relativist	conformity	law & order	social contract	universal ethics	cosmic
13. Cognitive Development [Jean Piaget]	sensory motor	pre-conceptual / intuitive pre-operational	concrete operational		formal operational		
14. Theory of Process [Young]	potential	substance	form	combine/separation	self organization	mobility	dominion
15. Yogic Philosophy [Chakra System]	1st - root material, food	2nd - sexual combination	3rd - hara power	4th - heart love, belonging	5th - throat expression	6th - third eye higher knowledge	7th - crown transcendence
16. Levels of Consciousness [Ken Wilbur]	physical - non-living matter/energy	biological - living, sentient matter/energy	psychological mind, ego	psychological logic, thinking	subtle - archetypal, intuitive	causal formless radiance, transcendence	ultimate - consciousness as such
17. Intuition Inspiral [Franquemont]	instinctual intuition	psychic intuition	creative intuition	archetypal intuition	visionary intuition	identification intuition	universal intuition
18. Symbols [Allee]	Dot •	Cross ✚	Square □	Circle ○	Spiral	Triangle ▽	Mobius ∞

The Knowledge Archetype in Theoretical Constructs. (© Verna Allee 1994)

5. Erich Jantsch, *The Self-Organizing Universe: Scientific and Human Implications of the Emerging Paradigm of Evolution*, especially Chapter 16, "Ethics, Morality and System Management," pp. 263–274. In his classic work on self-organizing systems, Eric Jantz introduces the managerial focus framework in the context of strategic planning, demonstrating the different time horizons pertinent for each level of logic. This time-horizon aspect moves on a continuum from long-range for values and policy (system dynamics), to short-term for tactical targets. He also suggests that the management tasks are very different at each of these levels, since different types of logic are operative.

6. Stafford Beer, *Diagnosing the System for Organizations*. The viable system model includes five kinds of organizational context: System 1—Production and delivery processes; System 2—coordination of independent business units; System 3—allocation of resources; System 4—preparing and planning for the future; System 5—identity of the whole (by ultimate decision makers). The viable systems model is also recursive, meaning that each of the parts is itself organized in the same way as the whole. Also defining the system is the *environment* in which it operates. Beer's model emphasizes communication and the flow of information according to the laws of cybernetics. He compares the organization of an enterprise system with an observation that the human nervous system is organized into five levels or neural structures, which process different types of information.

7. Elliot Jacques, *Requisite Organization: The CEO's Guide to Creative Structure and Leadership*. Jacques' description of the levels of complexity in organizations follows the archetype quite closely. In application, however, he suggests that "ownership" of a particular level should reside in a particular function. This way of organizing is typical in traditional bureaucracies. However, with the move to network organizations and self-managed teams, there is a trend toward shared responsibilities and cross-functional management. All tasks must be attended to, but not necessarily by confining responsiblity to one person. He also explores the levels in relation to an expanding time dimension.

8. Russell Ackoff, in opening remarks at the GOAL/QPC annual conference in November of 1994 and in *The Democratic Corporation*. Ackoff proposes a continuum of knowledge where *data* are symbols that represent properties of objects or events, *information* is description, *knowledge* is the level of instruction, *understanding* is the explanation or "why" of certain events, and *wisdom* is the level of evaluation or judgement.

9. W. Edward Deming, in *Deming's Road to Continual Improvement* by William W. Scherkenback (pp. 196–198), and as summarized by John H. Little in "Administrative Man Faces the Quality Transformation: Comparing the Ideas of Herbert A. Simon and W. Edward Deming," *American Review of Public Administration* (pp. 67–85). Deming defined fourteen points or practices to develop "profound knowledge," which comprise four interrelated parts: (1) appreciation for a system; (2) knowledge about variation; (3) theory of knoweldge; (4) psychology of individuals, society, and change.

   By *systems* Deming means the configuration of people, materials, methods, and equipment working in support of each other. Understanding *variation* is key to quality and consistency in output. A theory of *psychology* is for the purpose of understanding change. A theory of *knowledge* means understanding the operating principles or theory underlying the action. Deming's theory of knowledge is often described as the Plan, Do, Check, Act cycle.

A synthesis and integration of Deming's theory of knowledge and the Allee Learning and Performance framework is further explored and developed by Kathryn Alexander, *Holistic Knowing*, an unpublished manuscript.

10. Stuart L. Hart, "An Integrative Framework for Strategy-Making Processes," *Academy of Management Review*, pp. 327–351. Hart's analysis suggests that different modalities are appropriate in different environmental contexts. He views strategy making as an organization-wide phenomenon, emphasising the complementary roles between top managers and organizational members.

11. Abraham Maslow, *Toward A Psychology of Being, 2nd Edition*. The usual depiction of Maslow's hierarchy of needs is in pyramid form, with physio-biological needs forming the base and self-actualization serving as the top. Maslow's later work, however, emphasizes "peak experiences" and defines health as transcendence of the environment. With these distinctions, the pyramid is sometimes depicted with a "capstone" of transcendence as the highest need of the human psyche. Given the overall unitary consciousness of his work, I believe this is an appropriate enhancement.

12. Lawrence Kohlberg's stages of moral development have been verified in many international and cross-cultural studies. In his later work, "Stages and Aging in Moral Development: Some Speculations," *Gerontologist*, pp. 497–502, Kohlberg proposes a seventh adult stage that apparently unfolds in some, but not all, individuals later in life and involves adoption of a religious and cosmic perspective. Kohlberg's stages are "hierarchical integrations," where thinking at a higher stage includes or comprehends within it lower-stage thinking. His model is also developmental, in that movement is always to the next stage up, except in conditions of extreme trauma.

13. Jean Piaget, as described by Ruth M. Beard in *An Outline of Piaget's Developmental Psychology*. Piaget's developmental psychology has been foundational in Western cognitive science. One of the limitations of his groundbreaking work is that most of his developmental studies were conducted on male children. As Carol Gilligan has pointed out in *A Different Voice*, this has led to a "blind spot" in developmental psychology regarding the higher relationship identification skills of female children. This may be why Piaget did not go further in identifying more abstract thinking skills, such as the ability to discern dynamic relationships, which is vital for systems thinking.

14. Arthur Young, *The Reflexive Universe: Evolution of Consciousness*. Aside from his early work on the development of the helicoptor, one of Arthur Young's enduring contributions to thought is a theory of process that integrates data from a variety of disciplines. The underlying process that most intrigues him is how form comes in and out of being, and how we might understand different life forms from an evolutionary perspective. His approach is recursive, suggesting that each stage is itself a microcosm of all the stages of process.

15. There are many sources available on the chakras and their correlating domains of intelligence. I especially recommend Rolf von Eckartsberg's "Maps of the Mind: The Cartography of Consciousness," in *The Metaphors of Consciousness*, Ronald S. Valle and Rolf von Eckartsberg, eds. Von Eckartsberg's synthesis of Eastern and Western psychology is exceptionally clear and straightforward. His integrative model of the human "psychocosm" is remarkable for its integration of depth psychology and modalities of thought and consciousness. The chakra system has been in use for over 2,000 years and has a rich heritage. Each of the energy centers and domains of consciousness is also associated with a particular color of the spectrum. Out of respect

for this ancient system, I use the traditional chakra colors when depicting the modes of knowing. Corresponding colors would be Data—Red, Information—Orange, Knowledge—Yellow, Meaning—Green, Philosophy—Light Blue, Wisdom—Dark Blue or Indigo, Union—Violet or Purple.

16. Ken Wilber, *The Atman Project*. Wilber is a distinguished scholar in the field of transpersonal psychology. His analysis of Eastern and Western psychological approaches is unique in the breadth of his scholarship and the clarity and depth of his thinking. He is also interested in the evolutionary process of human development and has published many books on personal and social development. *The Atman Project* most clearly articulates his thinking in psychological development.

17. Sharon Franquemont, *You Already Know What to Do*. Franquemont's work on intuition spans more than twenty years of research and practice. Her work is cross-cultural, drawing from a variety of disciplines and world philosophies. The first two intuitive modes, the *instinctual* and *psychic*, deal with data and information at the physical and emotional levels respectively. *Creative* intuition is a more cognitive intuitive level involving independent action. *Archetypal* intuition is the realm of metaphor, story, and context. *Visionary* intuition incorporates the integrative aspect of seeing the pathways to accomplish the vision, as well as defining the vision itself. *Identification* intuition describes value-related intuitive experiences involving communal connections, while *Universal* intuition is the experience of connectedness with the ultimate. A frequent response to the knowledge archetype is to ask, "Where is intuition?" Franquemont's work demonstrates that if intuition is anywhere, it is everywhere. Each of the modes of knowledge embraces both analytical and intuitive aspects of knowing.

18. Symbolic systems that relate to intelligence or consciousness are not as common as word-based systems, yet there are a few that would be interesting to explore further. The symbols described here are based on the work of Angeles Arrien, a cross-cultural anthropologist who has researched symbolic systems from a variety of world cultures. She is the author of several books on symbolic systems. In *Signs of Life* she describes the orientation and application of five universal symbols: the square, cross, circle, triangle, and spiral. The dot and the mobius are suggested here as an extension of this symbolic system.

19. A special note regarding multiple intelligences theory. The above comparison does not include the multiple intelligences typology of Howard Gardner described in *Frames of Mind: The Theory of Multiple Intelligences*, and in *Multiple Intelligences: The Theory in Practice*. The cognitive aspects addressed by Howard Gardner are quite different from those authors I have selected for comparison. Gardner's studies of intelligences explore underlying cognitive processes that support reason and understanding at every level of complexity. His work has contributed enormously to an understanding of adult learning modes, and fostered appreciation for previously ignored cognitive skills.

For example, one of the intelligences that Gardner identifies is musical intelligence. This is a very large category of processes that include appreciation of rhythm, melody, structure, harmony, interval or relationships, and a host of other aspects of sound and rhythm. These sensitivities are critical for any thought process, even though individuals may vary in degree of mastery. The other intelligences he identifies are bodily-kinesthetic, logical-mathematical, linguistic, spatial, interpersonal, and intrapersonal. Each of these "intelligences" is actually a form of cognitive processing that helps us deal with complexity at multiple task levels. All are relevant to business performance. For Example, Charles Savage, in *5th Generation Management: Co-creating Through Virtual Enterprising, Dynamic Teaming, and Knowledge Networking* (pp. 219–229), describes the use of musical intelligence in business planning and decision-making.

Peter Koestenbaum, in *The Heart of Business: Ethics, Power and Philosophy*, takes a similar approach to that of Gardner in exploring multiple organizational intelligences. He identifies logical, somatic, aesthetic, transcendental, marketing, motivational, wisdom, and team intelligences that are operative in organizations. Although his approach to organizational intelligence is different from the archetype presented here, his thoughtful and insightful exploration of organizational intelligence is a landmark work. He addresses difficult questions of ethics, morals, and spirit in a work environment. Neither Gardner nor Koestenbaum define their intelligences on a continuum of increasing complexity. Since they themselves did not undertake to order intelligence in this way, I have not included them in my comparative analysis.

Also quite interesting and relevant to the exploration of this archetype is the work of Gareth Morgan in *Images of the Organization*. Morgan's study of organizational theory describes several discrete metaphors. These metaphors appear to correspond to the knowledge archetypes, but the relationships are not as clear cut as others in the table. The metaphors and models he describes are machine, organism, brain, political system or culture, and organizations as flux and change.

APPENDIX 2

Sample Question Set for Knowledge Building in Information Management

This is a sample set of questions for a comparative study of current practices in the management of information systems. These questions were developed from approximately 200 interview questions from the first case studies interviews conducted by graduate students at Golden Gate University.

The purpose of the basic question set serves several purposes:

- It determines the boundaries of the inquiry—what is included, what is excluded.
- It provides a standard set of questions, so that captured responses can be easily compared.
- It assures that all of the domains of knowledge have been covered with minimum redundancy.
- It provides a common language that facilitates inquiry and comparison.

QUESTION SET

Legend for Coding

C	=	Context questions (company background)
D	=	Data mode questions
P	=	Procedural mode questions
F	=	Functional mode questions
M	=	Managing mode questions
I	=	Integrating mode questions
R	=	Renewing mode questions
U	=	Union mode questions

Context Questions (background and company information)

C1   Can you give me some background information about this company?

    C1a   Address and phone number
    C1b   Chief Executive Officer
    C1c   Type of Industry
    C1d   Net Worth
    C1e   Annual Revenue
    C1f   Number of employees
    C1g   Description of products or services
    C1h   Who are your customers?

C2   What is special about your requirements for information systems?

C3   How has IS technology affected your industry?

C4   What is your area of responsibility in the company? (also function, job title)

C5   How are you involved in information management? (internal customer or user, system administrator, designer, external consultant?)

C6   Please give us an overview of the institution's information systems(s).

C7   How do you define IS and what is included in that?

Data/Data (measurements and numbers)

D1   In relation to annual revenues, what percentage is spent annually on information systems?

    D1a   What percentage is allocated for hardware?
    D1b   What percentage is allocated for software?

D2   Do you track technology-based IS separately from non-computer-based IS? If so, how do you break down those expenditures?

D3   How many IS employees do you have?

    D3a   How many users does IS support?
    D3b   What is the ratio of IS staff to users?

D4   What is the average wait time for assistance?

D5   What percentage of employees actively use the Internet?

    D5a   What do they use it for?

D6   Does your business have a "Home Page" on the Internet?

D7   What percentage of employees have a computer workstation?

D8   How do you measure customer satisfaction?

D9   How do you measure performance?

D10   Do you conduct cost/benefit analysis?

D11   What are your primary data sources?

D12   What types of electronic communication are accessed in your system? What percentage of people in your organization use each type?

    D12a   Internet
    D12b   World Wide Web
    D12c   Dial Up services
    D12d   Video conference and downlinks

D12e   ISSN

D12f   Other _____

Procedural/Information (step-by-step procedures and conformance to standards)

P1   Do you have a disaster recovery plan for IS?

    P1a   What are some of the features (back up system recovery procedures for documentation, alternate power supplies, obtaining vendor source codes, etc.)

P2   Do you have a backup system?

    P2a   Where is it located?

    P2b   What are its features?

P3   Do you test your contingency plan? If so, how often?

P4   How rigorous is your selection process for picking software?

P5   How are requests for IS needs by various users articulated to the IS department?

P6   What is the process for responding to IS requests?

P7   Does your system produce audit trails?

    P7a   What is included in the audit trail? (that is, transaction updates; security events, such as changes in user authorizations, changes in resource protection, attempted security violations, and system utilization)

P8   What type of security system do you have?

    P8a   What are some of the features?

P9   Do you have an internal or external control on security?

P10   What is your level of concern with security? Why?

P11   Do outside personnel or vendors have access to the system?

P12   Are there screens and filters for who has access to particular information?

P13   Do you have a help desk?

    P13a   Do you use help-desk software?

P14   What are the main features of your data processing function? (that is, batch files, on-line processing)

P15   How do you ensure consistency of messages?

P16   How do you ensure alignment across technical platforms?

Functional/Knowledge (key processes, technology, structure)

F1   How do you approach the organization of the *content* of the IS system? In other words, what categories of systems applications do you use? Please give examples of what is included in these categories, if you use this type of organization.

    F1a   Human Resources

    F1b   Operations

    F1c   Financial

    F1d   Marketing

    F1e   Inventory

    F1f   Project Management

    F1g   Process Management

F1h   Planning
F1i   Executive Information Systems
F1j   Other _____

F2   Is there critical company information, data, and statistics that are not included or catalogued in the IS system?

    F2a   How are these compiled and maintained?

F3   Would you regard the flexibility of your system as poor, average, or excellent?

F4   How are major changes evaluated and implemented?

F5   Does your company follow a formal methodology for the development of systems projects?

F6   Is your system energy efficient?

F7   How do you maintain connectivity with other internal systems?

F8   What type of architecture are you using, and do you plan to change it soon? (i.e., LAN, WAN, H/W)

F9   Have you reduced the actual number of documents and files that are in hard copy or physical storage? By how much, and over what time period?

F10   How do you use customer feedback to evaluate and change the system?

F11   Do you have a clearly defined process for identifying problems and developing solutions? Please describe it.

F12   Do you have a clearly defined testing and modification process during implementation?

F13   What kind of training do you do, and how often is it offered?

F14   Do you feel that you have enough time to do a thorough and personally satisfying completion of each assignment?

Managing/Meaning (goals, systems administration, technology planning, user requirements, roles)

M1   Generally speaking, what do you view as the single biggest problem in IS? (Past, present, or future.) What do you feel can be done about this problem?

M2   In your particular situation, what do you feel is your biggest problem with your current system? What do you see as the solution?

M3   How did the Information System(s) come to be as they are? How did they evolve?

    M3a   Who originally designed the system? When?

M4   What changes to your Information System(s) are already planned? Over what time period will these changes be implemented?

M5   How do you gather user requirements for content and output?

M6   What kind of review do you do to make sure the system keeps up with changing technology and the needs of the industry?

M7   How are IS requests prioritized? By what criteria? (i.e., time, costs, political factors?)

    M7a   Who makes decisions about priorities?

M8   How do you get money allocated for maintaining or enhancing your communication package?

M9   What are the current goals for IS?

M10   If your organization is multi-location, is IS decentralized or centralized?

M10a   How much autonomy do decentralized units have?

M10b   Where is MIS headquartered?

M11   What does this enterprise contribute, if anything, to the IS systems of its customers, supplier, etc.?

M12   To what extent do executives depend on specific information developed periodically by IS systems?

M12a   How is the information accessed?

M12b   How is the information presented?

M12c   Who maintains it?

M13   Do you have an Executive Information System? If so, what are its features?

M14   What level of support do you get from vendors or companies from whom you buy equipment or software?

M15   Does IS take the initiative to introduce to management new technologies or information systems (hardware or software) to solve perceived problems?

M16   Does the IS group install systems that they do not maintain?

M17   Who makes the decisions for IS investments?

M18   Does the programming staff share data-processing operations responsibilities?

M19   Is the responsibility for security administration clearly identified?

M20   What do you feel are the key success factors in systems design?

M21   How would you describe the management style in IS?

Integrating/Philosophy (overall business integration and IS strategy)

I1   What are the main internal and external drivers having an impact on the company?

I2   How does IS support the overall strategic goals of the company?

I3   Where do you see information technology leading the company? (within 5 years)

I4   How do you discriminate between what is and is not important information to manage?

I5   Are there plans for changes to improve IS to help the organization achieve its goals?

I6   Is it important to have uniformity in the IS environment throughout the company?

I6a   How is this accomplished?

I7   How do institutional politics influence the IS department?

I8   Does your institution use multi-level and cross-functional strategic management teams?

I8a   How does IT help these teams accomplish their goals?

I9   Are there plans to extend your business through the Internet?

Renewing/Wisdom (purpose, values, and vision)

R1   What is your wish list? Why?

R2   How does the organization value MIS?

R3   How does information management relate to and support the purpose, vision, and mission of the organization?

R4   As someone deeply involved with IS, where do you see all this taking us in the future?

R5   Where do you think people in your organization need to be paying more attention?

Union/Union (alignment with the greater good)

U1   Do you feel information technology is making a contribution to the greater good?

U2   What are your concerns and reservations about IS in society?

U3   What do you think we all need to be paying more attention to?

Chapter Notes

Preface

1. Lewis Thomas, "Natural Science," in *The Lives of a Cell*.
2. Russell Ackoff, *The Democratic Organization*, pp. 210–212.

Chapter 1. Introduction: The Knowledge Era

1. Rosabeth Moss Kantor, "Mastering Change," pp. 71–83, in *Learning Organizations: Developing Cultures for Tomorrow's Workplace*.
2. George Land and Beth Jarman, *Breakpoint and Beyond*.
3. See Fritjof Capra, *The Turning Point: Science, Society and the Rising Culture*, Willis Harman, *Global Mind Change: The Promise of the Last Years of the 20th Century*, and Michael Ray and Alan Rinzler, eds., *The New Paradigm in Business: Emerging Strategies for Leadership and Organizational Change*.
4. Peter Drucker, *Post-Capitalist Society*, p. 8.
5. Ibid., pp.19–47.
6. Ibid., p. 42.
7. Marvin R. Weisbord, *Productive Workplaces*, pp. 70–105.
8. Chris Argyris and Donald A. Schon, *Organizational Learning: A Theory of Action Perspective*.
9. Hubert Saint-Onge, in remarks made at the *Knowledge Imperative Symposium*, Houston, September 1995.
10. Valery Kanavsky, as quoted in *Knowledge Report: Report from the Knowledge Imperative Symposium*, Arthur Andersen Worldwide, SC, 1996.
11. Laurence Prusak, "The Knowledge Advantage," *Strategy & Leadership*, p. 6.
12. Tom Peters, "Six Big Ideas," *Incentive*.
13. Robert J. Hiebeler, "Benchmarking Knowledge Management," *Strategy & Leadership*, pp. 22–29.
14. Barbara Townley, "Foucault, Power/Knowledge, and its Relevance for Human Resource Management," *Academy of Management Review*, pp. 518–545.

15. AlvinToffler, *Powershift: Knowledge, Wealth and Violence at the Edge of the 21st Century*, p. 20.

16. Taichi Sakaiya. *The Knowledge-Value Revolution*, pp. 274–275.

17. Leif Edvinsson and Michael Malone, *Intellectual Capital: Realizing Your Company's True Value by Finding Its Hidden Brainpower*.

18. Peter Senge, *The Fifth Discipline*.

19. Chris Argyris and Donald Schon, *Organizational Learning: A Theory of Action Perspective*.

20. Westin Agor, *Intuition in Organizations: Leading and Managing Productively*.

21. Sharon Franquemont, *You Already Know What to Do*.

22. Ikujiro Nonaka and Hirotaka Takeuchi, *The Knowledge Creating Company*.

23. In *The Ken Awakening: Management Strategies for Knowledge Innovation*, Debra Amidon traces the historic path of the emerging knowledge management perspective.

24. James Champy, *Reengineering Management*.

25. Tom Peters, "Six Big Ideas," *Incentive*, p. 18.

26. Henry Mintzberg, "The Fall and Rise of Strategic Planning," *Harvard Business Review*, pp. 107–114.

Chapter 2. Knowledge Competencies for Adaptive Enterprises

1. C.K. Prahalad and Gary Hamel, "The Core Competence of the Corporation," *Harvard Business Review*, pp. 79–81.

2. Gary Hamel and C.K. Prahalad, *Competing for the Future*, pp. 202–211.

3. George Stalk Jr., "Time-Based Competition and Beyond: Competing on Capabilities, *Planning Review*, pp. 27–29. Also see George Stalk Jr., Philip Evans, and Lawrence E. Shulman, "Competing on Capabilities: The New Rules of the Game," *Harvard Business Review*, pp. 57–69.

4. Hamel and Prahalad, pp. 52–59.

5. James Brian Quinn, "The Intelligent Enterprise: A New Paradigm," *Academy of Management Executive*, pp. 48–63.

6. Paul J. Shoemaker, "How to Link Strategic Vision to Core Capabilities," *Sloan Management Review*.

7. See Edward P. Przybylowicz and Terrence W. Faulkner, "Kodak Applies Strategic Intent to the Management of Technology," *Research-Technology Management*, pp. 31–38.

8. Dorothy Leonard-Barton, *Wellsprings of Knowledge: Building and Sustaining the Sources of Innovation*, pp. 18–28.

9. These distinctions are proposed by James Brian Quinn, Philip Andersen, and Sydney Findelstein, in "Managing Professional Intellect: Making the Most of the Best," *Harvard Business Review*, pp. 71–80. They suggest four levels presented in order of increasing importance:

    1. Cognitive Knowledge (know-what)—the basic mastery of a discipline.
    2. Advanced skills (know-how)—the ability to apply a discipline to real-world problems.

3. Systems understanding (know-why)—deep knowledge of cause-and-effect relationships.

4. Self-motivated creativity (care-why)—will, motivation, and adaptability for success.

10. Stephen Martin, "A Futures Market for Competencies," *People Management*, pp. 20–24.

11. Ibid.

12. Thomas A. Stewart, "Your Company's Most Valuable Asset: Intellectual Capital," *Fortune*, pp. 68–74.

13. Anonymous, "How to Get Ahead at Xerox," *Datamation*, pp. 44–47.

14. Calhoun W. Wick and Lu Stanton Leon, "Individual Learning Nurtures J.P. Morgan," *Personnel Journal*, pp. 50–54.

15. Hubert Saint-Onge, remarks at *The Knowledge Imperative Symposium*, co-sponsored by the American Productivity and Quality Center and Arthur Andersen, Houston, Texas, September 11, 1995.

16. Alan M. Kantrow interview with James Brian Quinn, "Intelligent Enterprise and Public Markets," *McKinsey Quarterly*, n2, pp. 83–89, 1994.

17. Tom Housel and Valery Kanavsky, "A New Methodology for Business Process Auditing," *Planning Review*, v23n3, pp. 31–36, May/June 1995.

18. Vincent Alonzo and Daniel McQuillen, "Best Corporate Asset: Brain Power," *Incentive*, 170n1, January 1996, pp. 7.

19. The term "balanced scorecard," in regard to corporate performance measures was introduced by Robert S. Kaplan in "The Balanced Scorecard—Measures That Drive Performance," *Harvard Business Review*, v70n, Sept–Oct. 1995.

20. Hubert Saint-Onge, "Tacit Knowledge: The Key to the Strategic Alignment of Intellectual Capital," *Strategy & Leadership*, pp. 10–14.

21. Ibid.

22. Leif Edvinsson and Michael Malone, *Intellectual Capital: Realizing Your Company's True Value by Finding Its Hidden Brainpower*.

23. Karl-Erik Sveiby, *The New Organizational Wealth: Managing and Measuring Knowledge-Based Assets*.

24. Craig Marine, "All the Copyrighted Moves," *San Francisco Examiner*, Sunday June 23, 1996, pp. D1–D4.

25. Thomas A. Stewart, "Your Company's Most Valuable Asset: Intellectual Capital," *Fortune*, pp. 68–74.

Chapter 3. The Knowledge Navigators

1. Dava Sobel, *Longitude: The True Story of a Lone Genius Who Solved the Greatest Scientific Problem of His Time*. Latitude is fairly easy to determine, since the sun is the device for knowing where you are in relation to the fixed line of the equator. Longitude, the North-South axis, is much more challenging to calculate, due to the spin of the earth. To determine longitude you need an accurate clock. The pendulum clock, the most advanced timepiece in the Age of Exploration, would not work on the rolling deck of a ship. The moons of Jupiter, which work very nicely as a clock, are so small they can only be seen from a stable platform, such as dry ground. Still

no good for the pitching, rolling deck of a ship. It was two centuries before the chronometer was developed in the 1700s. Only then did navigation really move from art to science.

2. William Morris, ed., *The American Heritage Dictionary of the English Language*.

3. Robert J. Sternberg, "Wisdom and its Relation to Intelligence and Creativity," *Wisdom: Its Nature, Origins and Development*.

4. Robert W. Galvin, "Knowledge Makes the Difference at Motorola."

5. Michael Polanyi, *The Tacit Dimension*.

6. Ikujiro Nonaka and Hirotaka Takeuchi, *The Knowledge Creating Company*, pp. 59–64.

7. Ibid.

8. David Bohm, *Wholeness and the Implicit Order*, pp. 49–50 (Arck Paperback edition, 1983, pp. 48–64).

9. Michael Polanyi, *The Tacit Dimension*.

10. One of my favorite books on quantum physics is *The Dancing Wu Li Masters: An Overview of the New Physics*, by Gary Zukav. It is a delightful introduction to physics for those of us who are fascinated with the concepts, but flee in terror from mathematics.

11. The diagram was presented in a talk given by Robert J. Hiebeler at the *Knowledge Imperative Symposium*, co-sponsored by Arthur Andersen and the American Productivity and Quality Center, September, 1995, Houston, Texas.

12. See *Knowledge Report: Report from the Knowledge Imperative Symposium*, Arthur Andersen Worldwide, SC, 1996. A discussion of the findings of the first round of benchmarking using this assessment is in Robert J. Hiebeler, "Benchmarking Knowledge Management," *Strategy & Leadership*, pp. 22–29.

13. Ikujiro Nonaka and Hirotaka Takeuchi, pp. 70–73.

14. For an excellent discussion of intentionality see Rollo May, *Love and Will*, pp. 223–245.

15. See Charles M. Savage, *Fifth Generation Management*, pp. 215–220.

16. Gary Zukav, *The Dancing Wu Li Masters*.

Chapter 4. Seeing Patterns of Knowledge, Learning, and Performance

1. Erich Jantsch, *The Self-Organizing Universe: Scientific and Human Implications of the Emerging Paradigm of Evolution*, Oxford: Pergamon Press, 1980, Chapter 16, "Ethics, Morality and System Management," pp. 263–274.

2. Elliot Jacques, *Requisite Organization: The CEO's Guide to Creative Structure and Leadership*.

3. Ken Wilber, *The Atman Project*.

4. Lawrence Kohlberg, "Stages and Aging in Moral Development: Some Speculations," *Gerontologist*, pp. 497–502.

5. Aldous Huxley, *The Perennial Philosophy*.

6. Paul D. MacLean, *A Triune Concept of Brain and Behavior*. Other theorists of interest are discussed in Appendix 1. Also of interest is J.P. Guilford's cubic factors; see Charles Hampden-Turner, *Maps of the Mind*, pp. 114–115.

7. An excellent discussion of these reasoning processes is provided by Chris Argyris in *Overcoming Organizational Defenses*. In this book he introduces a Ladder of Inference that is also described in Peter Senge, Charlotte Roberts, Richard Ross, Bryan Smith, and Art Kleiner, *The Fifth Discipline Fieldbook*, pp. 242–261. Brian Hall is doing groundbreaking work on the power and influence of values in organizational life described in his book, *Values Shift*.

Chapter 5. Knowledge Archetypes in Action

1. From a presentation by Verna Allee and Mary Ann Whitney of Chevron, "From Information to Knowledge: The Next Evolution," at the 12th Annual Conference of *GOAL/QPC*, Boston, September 1995.

2. Verna Allee, *Learning Links: Enhancing Individual and Team Performance*, San Francisco: Pfeiffer, Inc., 1996.

3. For in-depth discussion, suggestions, and techniques for dialogue, see *The Fifth Discipline Fieldbook* by Peter Senge, et al., especially "Team Learning," pp. 351–445 and pp. 253–264.

4. For a complete case study of a benchmarking project using this methodology, see the articles by Verna Allee, "Breakthrough Benchmarking: An Organizational Learning Approach for Comparative Analysis," *Competitive Intelligence Review*, and by Derek Ransley, "Benchmarking the External Technology Watching Process: Chevron's Experience," *Competitive Intelligence Review*.

5. Categories and award criteria in the table are as described and numbered in *Malcolm Baldrige National Quality Award*, 1997 Award Criteria, Gaithersburg, MD: National Institute of Standards and Technology, 1996. Phone: 301-975-2036.

Chapter 6. Knowledge, Learning, and Organizations

1. A nod of thanks for helping spark the thinking on these principles goes to the work of Meg Wheatley, "The Unplanned Organization," *Noetic Sciences Review*, pp. 17–23 and Draper L. Kauffman, Jr., *Systems 1: An Introduction to Systems Thinking*.

2. David Kolb, *Experiential Learning: Experience as the Source of Learning and Development*.

3. John C. Redding and Ralph F. Catalanello, *Strategic Readiness: The Making of the Learning Organization*. Some interesting work has also been done by Tom Leal on a cybernetic model, "The Cybernetic Learning Cycle," unpublished article, *The Synergy Group*, 1996.

4. Nonaka and Takeuchi, *The Knowledge–Creating Company*.

5. Edwin C. Nevis, Anthony J. DiBella, and Janet M. Gould, "Understanding Organizations as Learning Systems, *Sloan Management Review*, pp. 73–85.

6. Michael Marquardt and Angus Reynolds, *The Global Learning Organization*.

7. Edwin C. Nevis, Anthony J. DiBella, and Janet M. Gould, "Understanding Organizations as Learning Systems," *Sloan Management Review*, pp. 73–85.

8. Duane Elgin, "The Living Cosmos: A Theory of Continuous Creation," *Revision*, pp. 3–22. Elgin is also author of *Voluntary Simplicity*, a classic in simplified living.

9. Raymond E. Miles and Charles C. Snow, "Causes of Failure in Network Organizations," *California Management Review*, pp. 53–72.

10. Elizabeth and Gifford Pinchot, *The End of Bureaucracy and the Rise of the Intelligent Organization.*

11. Steven Kerr and David Ulrich, "Creating the Boundaryless Organization: The Radical Reconstruction of Organization Capabilities," *Planning Review*, pp. 41–45.

12. Simon Caulkin, "Chaos, Inc.," *Across the Board*, pp. 33–36.

13. Tom Brown, "The Rise of the Intelligent Organization," *Industry Week*, pp. 16–21.

14. William H. Davidow and Michael S. Malone, *The Virtual Corporation.*

15. Charles Savage, *5th Generation Management: Co-Creating Through Virtual Enterprising, Dynamic Teaming, and Knowledge Networking*, pp. 193–238.

16. Gianni Lorenzoni and Charles Baden-Fuller, "Creating a Strategic Center to Manage a Web of Partners," *California Management Review*, pp. 146–163. The NovaCare example is described by James Brian Quinn in "Managing Professional Intellect, Making the Most of the Best," *Harvard Business Review*, pp. 71–80.

17. Larry Hirschorn and Thomas Gilmore, "The New Boundaries of the Boundaryless Company," *Harvard Business Review*, pp. 104–115.

18. Jessica Lipnack and Jeffrey Stamps, *The Age of the Network.*

19. Sally Helgesen, *The Web of Inclusion: A New Architecture for Building Great Organizations.*

20. James Gleick, *Chaos: Making a New Science.*

21. Arthur Koestler, *The Ghost in the Machine.*

22. Karl Pribram, the renowned Stanford researcher, suggests that the human brain also works holographically. His groundbreaking book, *Languages of the Brain*, is now a classic. Another important theorist in the holographic model is David Bohm, *Wholeness and the Implicate Order.*

23. Nonaka and Takeuchi, pp. 75–83. Nonaka and Takeuchi refer to the knowledge-networked organization as the *hypertext organization*. I prefer to attempt to describe its characteristics, rather than to pin a name on it. Our tendency is to describe things in terms of our latest sciences, since the metaphors are so inviting. A term such as hypertext comes from computer technology. Yet, even at their best, the operations of computers pale in comparison to either the workings of the mind or the complexities of social systems.

Chapter 7. Doing the Data Two-Step

1. Donald J. Wheeler, *Understanding Variation: The Key to Managing Chaos.*

2. Peter Senge, *The Fifth Discipline: The Art and Practice of the Learning Organization.*

3. Bill Moyers, *The Language of Life: A Festival of Poets.*

Chapter 8. Gigamonsters and Other Dragons

1. Chris Argyris and Donald A. Schon, *Organizational Learning: A Theory of Action Perspective.*

2. Charles D. Winslow and William L. Bramer, *FutureWork: Putting Knowledge to Work in the Knowledge Economy*, pp. 168–173.

3. Diane Filipowski, "How Federal Express Makes Your Package Its Most Important," *Personnel Journal*, v71n2, February 1992, pp. 40–46.

4. Chris Marshall, Larry Prusak, and David Shpilberg, "Financial Risk and the Need for Superior Knowledge Management," *California Management Review*, pp. 77–101.

5. This story was reported by Associated Press reporter, Jane E. Allen and published in my local paper, *The Contra Costa Times*, as "DNA as Math Problem Solver? It Computes," May 7, 1996, p. 5C.

Chapter 9. Building Functional Knowledge

1. Marc Meyer and Kathleen Foley Curley, "An Applied Framework for Classifying the Complexity of Knowledge–Based Systems," *MIS Quarterly*, pp. 454–472.

2. Wendi Bukowitz, "In the Know," *CIO*.

3. Vannevar Bush, "As We May Think," *The Atlantic Monthly*, pp. 101–108.

Chapter 10. The Making of Meaning

1. Alfonso Montuori and Isabella Conti, *The Power of Partnership*.

2. Bill Moyers, *The Language of Life: A Festival of Poets*.

3. Robert Shank, remarks in a keynote address at *American Society for Training and Development, International Conference*, June 1995.

4. Graphic Guides and Whole Systems Associates are in the San Francisco Bay Area. See also Sharin Bennett and Juanita Brown, "Mindshift: Strategic Dialogue for Breakthrough Thinking."

5. Justin Harris, Peggy Holman, and Anne Stadler, "Engaging the Essence: Discovering our Story Through Video."

Chapter 11. Integrating

1. Gregory Bateson, *Steps to An Ecology of Mind*, pp. 166–176.

2. Ken Wilber, *The Atman Project*.

3. Chris Argyris, "Good Communication that Blocks Learning," *Harvard Business Review*, pp. 77–85.

4. A delightful discussion on resolving dilemmas can be found in Charles Hampden-Turner, *Charting the Corporate Mind*.

5. W. Edwards Deming, *The New Economics for Industry, Government, Education*, p. 105.

6. Howard Gardner, *Frames of Mind: The Theory of Multiple Intelligences*, p. 287.

7. Gareth Morgan has explored powerful organizational metaphors that influence organizational structures in *Images of Organizations*.

8. Margaret J. Wheatley, *Leadership and the New Science* and Margaret J. Wheatley and Myron Kellner-Rogers, *A Simpler Way*.

9. Michael D. McMaster, *The Intelligence Advantage: Organizing for Complexity*.

10. James Watson, *The Double Helix*, New York: Dutton, 1969.

11. See Antonio Strati, "Aesthetic Understanding of Organizational Life," *Academy of Management Review*, pp. 568–581.

12. Ian I. Mitroff and Harold A. Linstone, *The Unbounded Mind*.

13. Remarks made by Victor Leo, Director of Organizational Learning at Ford Motor Company's Executive Development Center, in "Lessons Learned on the Knowledge Highways and Byways," *Strategy & Leadership*, pp. 19–20.

14. Marvin R. Weisbord, *Productive Workplaces*. An excellent case study of a large-scale future search conference at Motorola is recounted by Steven Cabana and Janet Fiero, in "Motorola, Strategic Planning and the Search Conference," *Journal for Quality and Participation*, pp. 22–31.

15. Arlene Scott, "Action Learning: Creating a Learning Organization at General Electric," *Vision Action*, pp. 19–23.

16. Verna Allee, "Systems Tools for Understanding Complexity."

17. For an excellent overview of a number of these, as well as further resources, see J. Bernard Keys, Robert R. Fulcrum, and Stephen A. Stump, "Microworlds and Simuworlds: Practice Fields for the Learning Organization," *Organizational Dynamics*, pp. 36–49.

18. See Brian S. Moskai, "Born to Be Real," *Industry Week*, pp. 14–18, and Martha H. Peak, "Harley-Davidson: Going Whole Hog to Provide Stakeholder Satisfaction," *Management Review*, pp. 53–55.

Chapter 12. Renewing

1. Peter Senge, *The Fifth Discipline: The Art and Practice of the Learning Organization*.

2. Rollo May, *Love and Will*, p. 220.

3. Stephen Covey, *Principle Centered Leadership*; James Kouzes, *The Credibility Factor*; Stephen J. Holoviak, *Golden Rule Management: Give Respect, Get Results*.

4. Chris Lee, "The Vision Thing," *Training*, pp. 25–34.

5. Stephen R. Covey, A Roger Merill, and Rebecca R. Merrill, *First Things First*.

6. Michael Lindfield, "Open Space Technology," unpublished paper.

7. Peter Schwartz, *The Art of the Long View*.

8. Peter Vaill, *Learning As a Way of Being*.

Chapter 13. Expanded Vision for Union Performance

1. Psychologist Ken Wilber, writing in *Eye to Eye: the Quest for the New Paradigm*, suggests that there are three modes of attaining knowledge: 1. The eye of *flesh*, by which we perceive the external world of space, time, and objects; 2. The eye of reason, by which we attain a knowledge of philosophy, logic, and the mind itself; 3. The eye of contemplation, by which we rise to knowledge of transcendent realities. The burden of "proof" for each of these in turn is analytical reasoning, phenomenological experience, and shared experience.

2. Abraham H. Maslow, *Toward a Psychology of Being*.

3. Kenneth Ring, *Heading Toward Omega*.

4. Paul Hawken, *The Ecology of Commerce*.

5. Anita Roddick, *Body and Soul*.

6. Lager, Fred "Chico," *Ben & Jerry's: The Inside Scoop*.

7. Kenny Ausubel, *Seeds of Change: The Living Treasure*.

8. Stuart L. Hart, "A Natural Resource-Based View of the Firm," *Academy of Management Review*, pp. 996–1014.

9. Michael Rothschild, *Bionomics: Economy as Ecosystem*.

10. Brian Hall, *Values Shift*.

Chapter 14. Strategies

1. Thomas H. Davenport, "Some Principles of Knowledge Management," *Strategy & Business*, pp. 34–40.

2. Robert H. Buckman, "Knowledge Transfer," presentation, *The Knowledge Imperative Symposium*, Houston, September 11–13, 1995.

3. David C. Kaufman, "Getting Real About Brain Power," *Fortune*, pp. 201–203.

4. *The Chevron Way*, The Chevron Corporation, 1995.

5. Joseph Maglitta, "Smarten Up," *Computerworld*, pp. 84–86.

6. Thomas H. Davenport, "Some Principles of Knowledge Management," *Strategy & Business*, pp. 34–40.

7. Edwin C. Nevis, Anthony J. DiBella, and Janet M. Gould, "Understanding Organizations as Learning Systems," *Sloan Managment Review*, pp. 73–84.

8. Thomas L. Weekley and Jay C. Wilber, *United We Stand: The Unprecedented Story of the GM-UAW Quality Partnership*.

9. William Miller, *Quantum Quality: Quality Improvement Through Innovation, Learning & Creativity*.

10. Verna Allee and Kathryn Alexander, *The Quality Tools Matrix*.

11. See Aleda V. Roth, "Achieving Strategic Agility Through Economies of Knowledge," *Strategy and Leadership*, pp. 30–37; and Aleda V. Roth, Ann S. Marucheck, Alex Kemp, and D. Trimble, "The Knowledge Factory for Accelerated Learning Practices," *Planning Review*, pp. 26–33, 46.

12. Available from the Strategic Planning Institute Council on Benchmarking, Cambridge, MA, or the International Benchmarking Clearinghouse, Houston, TX.

13. Study conducted by the International Benchmarking Clearinghouse, 1993

14. Christopher E. Bogen and Michael E. English, *Benchmarking for Best Practices; Winning Through Innovative Adaptation*.

15. Peter Senge, *The Fifth Discipline*.

16. Many other contributors to this field of thought are mentioned throughout this book. In addition, some very fine work has been done by Karen E. Watkins and Victoria J. Marsick, *Sculpting the Learning Organization: Lessons in the Art and Science of Systemic Change*. See also Michael J. O'Brien, *Learning Organization Practices Profile*.

17. See David A. Garvin, "Building a Learning Organization," *Harvard Business Review*, pp. 78–91.

18. Dorothy Leonard-Barton, *Wellsprings of Knowledge: Building and Sustaining the Sources of Innovation*.

Chapter 15. Culture, Mapping, Technology, and Measures

1. Edgar H. Schein, *Organizational Culture and Leadership*.

2. Peter Drucker, "The New Society of Organizations," *Harvard Business Review*, pp. 95–104.

3. Thomas A. Stewart, "Your Company's Most Valuable Asset: Intellectual Capital," *Fortune*, pp. 68–74.

4. *Best Practice Resource Map*, Chevron Corporation.

5. Joseph Maglitta, "Smarten up," *Computerworld*, pp. 84–86.

6. See Patricia A. Galagan, "The Search for the Poetry of Work," *Training & Development*, pp. 33–37.

7. Gifford Pinchot and Elizabeth Pinchot, "Unleashing Intelligence," *Executive Excellence*, pp. 7–8.

8. Eileen M. Van Aken, Dominic J. Monetta, and Scott D. Sink, "Affinity Groups: The Missing Link in Employee Involvement," *Organizational Dynamics*, pp. 38–54.

9. David Krackhardt and Jeffrey R. Hanson, "Informal Networks: The Company Behind the Chart," *Harvard Business Review*, pp. 105–111.

10. Joseph Maglitta, "Know How, Inc," *Computerworld*, pp. 73–75.

11. Claremont Technology Group, *Claremont Intranet Study: Impact on Silicon Graphics*.

12. Robert M. Grant and Charles Baden-Fuller, "A Knowledge-Based Theory of Inter-Firm Collaboration," *Academy of Management Journal Best Paper Proceedings*, pp. 17–21.

13. Joseph L. Badaracco, Jr., *The Knowledge Link*.

14. Thomas A. Stewart, "Your Company's Most Valuable Asset: Intellectual Capital," *Fortune*, pp. 68–74.

Bibliography and References

Ackoff, Russell. *The Democratic Organization*. Oxford: Oxford University Press, 1994.

Agor, Weston. *Intuition in Organizations: Leading and Managing Productively*. Newbury Park: Sage Publications, 1989.

Allee, Verna. "Breakthrough Benchmarking: An Organizational Learning Approach for Comparative Analysis." *Competitive Intelligence Review*, v6n4, Winter 1995.

——. *Learning Links: Enhancing Individual and Team Performance*. San Francisco: Pfeiffer, 1996.

——. *Systems Tools for Understanding Complexity*. (White Paper). Walnut Creek, CA: Integral Performance Group, 1996.

—— and Alexander, Kathryn. *The Quality Tools Matrix*. Walnut Creek, CA: Integral Performance Group, 1994.

—— and Whitney, Mary Ann. "From Information to Knowledge: The Next Evolution." Presentation at the 12th Annual Conference of *GOAL/QPC*, Boston, September 1995.

Allen, Jane E. "DNA as Math Problem Solver? It Computes." *The Contra Costa Times*. May 7, 1996.

Alexander, Kathryn. "Holistic Knowing." Unpublished manuscript. Walnut Creek, CA: K.A. Consulting.

Alonzo, Vincent and McQuillen, Daniel. "Best Corporate Asset: Brain Power." *Incentive*, 170n1, January 1996.

Amidon, Debra M. *Innovation Strategy for the Knowledge Economy: The Ken Awakening*. Boston: Butterworth-Heinemann, 1997.

Anonymous. "How to Get Ahead at Xerox." *Datamation*, v41n1, January 15, 1995.

Argyris, Chris. "Good Communication that Blocks Learning." *Harvard Business Review*, v72n4, July–August, 1994.

——. *Overcoming Organizational Defenses: Facilitating Organizational Learning*. Boston: Allyn and Bacon, 1990.

—— and Schon, Donald. *Organizational Learning: A Theory of Action Perspective*. Reading, MA: Addison Wesley, 1978.

Arrien, Angeles. *Signs of Life*. Sonoma, CA: Arcus, 1992.

Arthur Andersen Worldwide, SC. *Knowledge Report: Report from the Knowledge Imperative Symposium*, 1996.

Ausubel, Kenny. *Seeds of Change: The Living Treasure*. San Francisco: Harper Collins, 1994.

Badaracco, Joseph L. *The Knowledge Link*. Boston: Harvard Business School Press, 1991.

Bateson, Gregory. *Steps to An Ecology of Mind*. New York: Ballantine, 1972.

255

Beard, Ruth M. *An Outline of Piaget's Developmental Psychology*. London: Routledge & Kegan Paul, 1969.

Beer, Stafford. *Diagnosing the System for Organizations*. Chichester: John Wiley, 1985.

Bennett, Sharin and Brown, Juanita. "Mindshift: Strategic Dialogue for Breakthrough Thinking." *Learning Organizations: Developing Cultures for Tomorrow's Workplace*. Ed. by Sarita Chawla and John Renesch. Portland, OR: Productivity Press, 1995.

Bogen, Christopher E. and English, Michael E. *Benchmarking for Best Practices: Winning Through Innovative Adaptation*. New York: McGraw-Hill, 1994.

Bohm, David. *Wholeness and the Implicate Order*. London: Routledge & Kegan Paul, 1980.

Brown, Tom. "The Rise of the Intelligent Organization." *Industry Week*, v24n5, March 7, 1994.

Buckman, Robert H. "Knowledge Transfer." Presentation at, *The Knowledge Imperative Symposium*, Houston, September 11–13, 1995.

Bukowitz, Wendi. "In the Know." *CIO*, v9n13, April 15, 1996.

Bush, Vannevar. "As We May Think." *The Atlantic Monthly*, July 1945.

Cabana, Steven and Fiero, Janet. "Motorola, Strategic Planning and the Search Conference." *Journal for Quality and Participation*, v18n4, July–August 1995.

Capra, Fritjof. *The Turning Point: Science, Society and the Rising Culture*. New York: Simon & Schuster, 1982.

Caulkin, Simon. "Chaos, Inc." *Across the Board*, v32n7, July–August, 1995.

Champy, James. *Reengineering Management*. New York: Harper Collins, 1995.

Chevron Corporation. *Best Practice Resource Map*. September, 1995.

———. *The Chevron Way*. 1995.

Claremont Technology Group. *Claremont Intranet Study: Impact on Silicon Graphics*. Beaverton, OR: Claremont Technology Group, 1996.

Covey, Stephen R., Merrill, A. Roger and Merrill, Rebecca R. *First Things First*. New York: Simon and Schuster, 1994.

Covey, Stephen. *Principle Centered Leadership*. New York: Simon & Shuster, 1995.

Davenport, Thomas H. "Some Principles of Knowledge Management." *Strategy & Business*, v1n2, Winter 1996.

Davenport, Thomas H. "Saving IT's Soul: Human Centered Information Management." *Harvard Business Review*, v72n2, Mar/April, 1994.

Davidow, William H., and Malone, Michael S. *The Virtual Corporation*. New York: Harper Collins, 1992.

Deming, W. Edwards. *The New Economics for Industry, Government, Education*. Cambridge, MA: MIT Center for Advanced Engineering Study, 1993.

Drucker, Peter. *Post-Capitalist Society*. New York: Harper Collins, 1993.

———. "The New Society of Organizations." *Harvard Business Review*, v70n5, Sept–Oct 1992.

Edvinsson, Leif and Malone, Michael. *Intellectual Capital: Realizing Your Company's True Value by Finding Its Hidden Brainpower*. New York: Harper Business, 1997.

Elgin, Duane. "The Living Cosmos: A Theory of Continuous Creation." *Revision*, Summer 1988: 3–22.

———. *Voluntary Simplicity*. Fairfield, N.J.: William Morrow, 1981.

Filipowski, Diane. "How Federal Express Makes Your Package Its Most Important." *Personnel Journal*, v71n2, February 1992:40–46.

Franquemont, Sharon. *You Already Know What to Do*. Los Angeles: Tarcher, 1997.

Galagan, Patricia A. "The Search for the Poetry of Work." *Training & Development,* v47n10: 33–37.

Galvin, Robert W. "Knowledge Makes the Difference at Motorola." Keynote speech at *Strategic Leadership Forum Knowledge Advantage II Conference,* November 16–17, 1995.

Gardner, Howard. *Frames of Mind: The Theory of Multiple Intelligences.* New York: Harper Collins, Basic, 1983.

——. *Multiple Intelligences: The Theory in Practice.* New York: Harper Collins, Basic, 1983.

Garvin, David A. "Building a Learning Organization." *Harvard Business Review,* v71n4, July–Aug, 1993.

Gleick, James. *Chaos: Making a New Science.* New York: Viking Penguin, 1987.

Gilligan, Carol. *In a Different Voice.* Cambridge: Harvard University Press, 1982.

Grant, Robert M. and Baden-Fuller, Charles. "A Knowledge-Based Theory of Inter-Firm Collaboration." *Academy of Management Journal Best Paper Proceedings,* 1995.

Hall, Brian. *Values Shift.* Rockport, MA: Twin Lights Publishers, 1995.

Hamel, Gary and Prahalad, C.K. *Competing for the Future.* Boston: Harvard Business School Press, 1994.

Hampden-Turner, Charles. *Maps of the Mind: Graphic Solutions to Business Conflicts.* New York: MacMillan Collier, 1981.

——. *Charting the Corporate Mind.* New York: MacMillan, Free Press, 1990.

—— and Trompenaars, Alfons. *The Seven Cultures of Capitalism.* New York: Currency, Doubleday, 1993.

Harman, Willis. *Global Mind Change: The Promise of the Last Years of the Twentieth Century.* Indianapolis: Knowledge Systems, 1988.

Harris, Justin; Holman, Peggy; and Stadler, Anne. "Engaging the Essence: Discovering our Story Through Video." Unpublished article. *Grey Dawn Productions,* Seattle.

Hart, Stuart L. "A Natural Resource-Based View of the Firm." *Academy of Management Review,* v20n4, October 1995.

——. "An Integrative Framework for Strategy-Making Processes." *Academy of Management Review,* v17n2, 1992.

Hawken, Paul. *The Ecology of Commerce.* San Francisco: Harper Collins, 1993.

Helgesen, Sally. *The Web of Inclusion: A New Architecture for Building Great Organizations.* New York: Currency, Doubleday, 1995.

Heibeler, Robert J. "Benchmarking Knowledge Management." *Strategy & Leadership,* v24n2, March/April 1996.

Hirschhorn, Larry and Gilmore, Thomas. "The New Boundaries of the Boundaryless Company." *Harvard Business Review,* v70n3, May–June 1992.

Holoviak, Stephen J. *Golden Rule Management: Give Respect, Get Results.* Reading, MA: Addison-Wesley, 1993.

Housel, Tom and Kanevsky, Valery. "A New Methodology for Business Process Auditing." *Planning Review,* v23n3, May/June 1995.

Huxley, Aldous. *The Perennial Philosophy.* New York: Harper & Row, 1944.

International Benchmarking Clearinghouse. *Best Practices Study.* 1993.

Jacques, Elliot. *Requisite Organization: The CEO's Guide to Creative Structure and Leadership.* Federalsburg, MD: Cason Hall, 1989.

Jantsch, Erich. *The Self-Organizing Universe: Scientific and Human Implications of the Emerging Paradigm of Evolution.* Oxford: Pergamon, 1980.

Kantor, Rosabeth Moss. "Mastering Change." *Learning Organizations: Developing Cultures for Tomorrow's Workplace.* Ed. by Sarita Chawla and John Renesh. Portland: Productivity Press, 1995.

Kantrow, Alan M. Interview with James Brian Quinn. "Intelligent Enterprise and Public Markets." *McKinsey Quarterly*, n2, 1994.

Kaplan, Robert S. "The Balanced Scorecard—Measures That Drive Performance." *Harvard Business Review*, v70n, Sept–Oct 1995.

Kauffman. Draper L. Jr. *Systems 1: An Introduction to Systems Thinking,* Minneapolis, MN: Carlton, 1980.

Kaufman, David C. "Getting Real About Brain Power." *Fortune,* v132n11, November 27, 1995: 201–203.

Kerr, Steven and Ulrich, David. "Creating the Boundaryless Organization: The Radical Reconstruction of Organization Capabilities." *Planning Review*, v23n5, Sept–Oct 1995.

Keys, J. Bernard; Fulcrum, Robert R.; and Stump, Stephen A. "Microworlds and Simuworlds: Practice Fields for the Learning Organization." *Organizational Dynamics*, v24n4, Spring 1996: 36–49.

Koestenbaum, Peter. *The Heart of Business: Ethics, Power and Philosophy.* San Francisco: Saybrook, 1987.

Koestler, Arthur. *The Ghost in the Machine.* London: Hutchinson, 1967.

Kohlberg, Lawrence. "Stages and Aging in Moral Development: Some Speculations." *Gerontologist*, v13n4, Winter 1973.

Kolb, David. *Experiential Learning: Experience as the Source of Learning and Development.* Englewood Cliffs, NJ: Prentice-Hall, 1984.

Kouzes, James. *The Credibility Factor.* San Francisco: Jossey-Bass, 1993.

Krackhardt, David and Hanson, Jeffrey R. "Informal Networks: The Company Behind the Chart." *Harvard Business Review*, v71n4, July–Aug 1993: 105–111.

Lager, Fred "Chico." *Ben & Jerry's: The Inside Scooop.* New York: Crown, 1994.

Land, George, and Jarman, Beth. *Breakpoint and Beyond.* New York: Harper Collins, 1992.

Leal, Tom. "The Cybernetic Learning Cycle." Unpublished article. The Synergy Group, 1996.

Lee, Chris. "The Vision Thing." *Training*, v30n2, Feb 1993, pp: 25–34.

Leo, Victor. "Lessons Learned on the Knowledge Highways and Byways." *Strategy & Leadership*, v24n2, March–April, 1995: 19–20.

Leonard-Barton, Dorothy. *Wellsprings of Knowledge: Building and Sustaining the Sources of Innovation.* Boston: Harvard Business School Press, 1995.

Lindfield, Michael. "Open Space Technology." Unpublished paper.

Lipnack, Jessica and Stamps, Jeffrey. *The Age of the Network.* Esses Junction, NY: Omeno, 1994.

Little, John H. "Administrative Man Faces the Quality Transformation: Comparing the Ideas of Herbert A. Simon and W. Edwards Deming." *American Review of Public Administation*, v24n1, March 1994.

Lorenzoni, Gianni, and Baden-Fuller, Charles. "Creating a Strategic Center to Manage a Web of Partners." *California Management Review*, v37n3, Spring 1995.

MacLean, Paul D. *A Triune Concept of Brain and Behavior.* Toronto: University of Toronto Press, 1973.

McMaster, Michael D. *The Intelligence Advantage: Organizing for Complexity.* Boston: Butterworth-Heinemann, 1996.

Maglitta, Joseph. "Know How, Inc." *Computerworld*, v30n3: 73–75.

——. "Smarten Up." *Computerworld*, v29n23, June 5, 1995.

Malcolm Baldrige National Quality Award, 1997 Award Criteria. Gaithersburg, MD: National Institute of Standards and Technology, 1996.

Marine, Craig. "All the Copyrighted Moves." *San Francisco Examiner,* Sunday June 23, 1996.

Marquardt, Michael and Reynolds, Angus. *The Global Learning Organization.* New York: Irwin, 1994.

Marshall, Chris; Prusak, Larry; and Shpilberg, David. "Financial Risk and the Need for Superior Knowledge Management." *California Management Review,* v28n3, Spring 1996: 77–101.

Martin, Stephen. "A Futures Market for Competencies." *People Management,* v1n6, Mar 23, 1995.

Maslow, Abraham H. *Toward a Psychology of Being.* New York: D. Van Nostrand, 1968.

May, Rollo. *Love and Will.* New York: Dell, 1969.

Meyer, Marc and Curley, Kathleen Foley. "An Applied Framework for Classifying the Complexity of Knowledge-Based Systems." *MIS Quarterly,* v15n4, December 1991.

Miles, Raymond E. and Snow, Charles C. "Causes of Failure in Network Organizations." *California Management Review,* v34n4, Summer 1992.

Miller, William. *Quantum Quality: Quality Improvement Through Innovation, Learning and Creativity.* White Plains, NY: Quality Resources, 1993.

Mintzberg, Henry. "The Fall and Rise of Strategic Planning." *Harvard Business Review,* v72n1, Jan–Feb 1994.

Mitroff, Ian I. and Linstone, Harold A. *The Unbounded Mind.* Oxford: Oxford University Press, 1993.

Montuori, Alfonso and Conti, Isabella. *The Power of Partnership.* San Francisco: Harper Collins, 1993.

Morgan, Gareth. *Images of the Organization.* Newbury Park, CA: Sage, 1986.

Morris, William, ed. *The American Heritage College Dictionary of the English Language.* Boston: Houghton Mifflin, 1993.

Moskai, Brian S. "Born to Be Real." *Industry Week,* v242n15 Aug 2 1993: 14–18.

Moyers, Bill. *The Language of Life: A Festival of Poets.* New York: Doubleday, 1995.

Nevis, Edwin C.; DiBella, Anthony J.; and Gould, Janet M. "Understanding Organizations as Learning Systems." *Sloan Management Review,* v36n2, Winter 1995.

Nonaka, Ikujiro and Takeuchi, Hirotaka. *The Knowledge-Creating Company.* Oxford: Oxford University Press, 1995.

O'Brien. Michael J. *Learning Organization Practices Profile.* San Diego: Pfeiffer, 1994.

Peak, Martha H. "Harley-Davidson: Going Whole Hog to Provide Stakeholder Satisfaction." *Management Review,* v82n6, June 1993.

Peters, Tom. "Six Big Ideas." *Incentive,* v169n1, Jan 1995.

Pinchot, Elizabeth and Pinchot, Gifford. *The End of Bureaucracy and the Rise of the Intelligent Organization.* San Francisco: Berrett-Koehler, 1994.

——. "Unleashing Intelligence." *Executive Excellence,* v10n9, Sept 1993.

Polanyi, Michael. *The Tacit Dimension.* London: Routledge & Kegan Paul, 1966.

Prahalad, C.K. and Hamel, Gary. "The Core Competence of the Corporation." *Harvard Business Review,* v68n3, May–June 1990.

Pribram, Karl. *Languages of the Brain.* Englewood Cliffs, NJ: Prentice Hall, 1971.

Prusak, Laurence. "The Knowledge Advantage." *Strategy & Leadership,* v24n2, March/April, 1996.

Przybylowicz, Edward P. and Faulkner, Terrence W. "Kodak Applies Strategic Intent to the Management of Technology." *Research-Technology Management,* v26n1, Jan/Feb 1993.

Quinn, James Brian; Andersen, Philip; and Findelstein, Sydney. "Managing Professional Intellect: Making the Most of the Best." *Harvard Business Review*, v74n2, March–April 1996.

——. "The Intelligent Enterprise: A New Paradigm." *Academy of Management Executive*, v6n4, Nov 1992.

Ransley, Derek. "Benchmarking the External Technology Watching Process: Chevron's Experience." *Competitive Intelligence Review*, v7n3, Fall 1996.

Ray, Michael and Rinzler, Alan, eds. *The New Paradigm in Business: Emerging Strategies for Leadership and Organizational Change*. New York: Putnam, Tarcher/Preigee, 1993.

Redding, John C., and Catalanello, Ralph F. *Strategic Readiness: The Making of the Learning Organization*. San Francisco: Jossey-Bass, 1994.

Ring, Kenneth. *Heading Toward Omega*. New York: William Morrow, 1985.

Roddick, Anita. *Body and Soul*. New York: Crown, 1991.

Roth, Aleda V. "Achieving Strategic Agility Through Economics of Knowledge." *Strategy & Leadership*, v24n2, March/April 1995.

——.; Marucheck, Ann S.; Kema, Alex; and Trimble, D. "The Knowledge Factory for Accelerated Learning Practices." *Planning Review*, v22n3, May/June, 1994.

Rothschild, Michael. *Bionomics: Economy as Ecosystem*. New York: Holt, 1990.

Saint-Onge, Hubert. "Tacit Knowledge: The Key to the Strategic Alignment of Intellectual Capital." *Strategy & Leadership*, v24n2, March/April 1996.

——. Presentation at *Knowledge Imperative Symposium*, Houston, September 1995.

Sakaiya, Taichi. *The Knowledge-Value Revolution*. New York: Kodansha, 1991.

Savage, Charles M. *5th Generation Management: Co-Creating Through Virtual Enterprising, Dynamic Teaming, and Knowledge Networking*. Boston: Butterworth-Heinemann, 1996.

Schein, Edgar H. *Organizational Culture and Leadership*. San Francisco: Jossey-Bass, 1991.

Schwartz, Peter. *The Art of the Long View*. New York: Doubleday, Currency, 1991.

Scott, Arlene. "Action Learning: Creating a Learning Organization at General Electric. *Vision Action*, Spring 1995: 19–23.

Senge, Peter. *The Fifth Discipline: The Art and Practice of the Learning Organization*. New York: Doubleday, Currency, 1990.

——; Roberts, Charlotte; Ross, Richard B.; Smith, Bryan J.; and Kleiner, Art. *The Fifth Discipline Fieldbook*. New York: Doubleday, Currency, 1994.

Shank, Robert. Keynote address at *American Society for Training and Development, International Conference*, June 1995.

Sherkenback, William. *Deming's Road to Continual Improvement*. Knoxville: SPC Press, 1991.

Shoemaker, Paul J. "How to Link Strategic Vision to Core Capabilities." *Sloan Management Review*, v34n1, 1992.

Sobel, Dava. *Longitude: The True Story of a Lone Genius Who Solved the Greatest Scientific Problem of His Time*. New York: Walker, 1995.

Stalk, George Jr. "Time-Based Competition and Beyond: Competing on Capabilities." *Planning Review*, v20n5, Sep/Oct 1992: 27–29.

——.; Evans, Philip; and Shulman, Lawrence E. "Competing on Capabilities: The New Rules of the Game." *Harvard Business Review*, v70n2, Mar/Apr 1992.

Sternberg, Robert J. *Wisdom: It's Nature, Origins and Development*. Cambridge: Cambridge University Press, 1990.

Stewart, Thomas A. "Your Company's Most Valuable Asset: Intellectual Capital." *Fortune*, v130n7, October 3, 1994.

Strati, Antonio. "Aesthetic Understanding of Organizational Life." *Academy of Management Review*, v17n3, July 1992: 568–581.

Sveiby, Karl-Erik. *The New Organizational Wealth: Managing and Measuring Knowledge-Based Assets*. San Francisco: Berrett-Koehler, 1997.

Thomas, Lewis. *The Lives of a Cell*. Toronto: Bantam, 1974.

Toffler, Alvin. *Powershift: Knowledge, Wealth and Violence at the Edge of the 21st Century*. New York: Bantam, 1990.

Townley, Barbara. "Foucault, Power/Knowledge, and its Relevance for Human Resource Management." *Academy of Management Review*, v18n3, July 1993.

Vaill, Peter B. *Learning as a Way of Being*. San Francisco: Jossey-Bass, 1996.

Valle, Ronald S. and Von Eckartsberg, Rolf, eds. *The Metaphors of Consciousness*. New York: Plenum, 1981.

Van Aken, Eileen M; Monetta, Dominic J.; and Sink, Scott D. "Affinity Groups: The Missing Link in Employee Involvement." *Organizational Dynamics* v22n4.

Von Eckartsberg, Rolf. "Maps of the Mind: The Cartography of Consciousness." *The Metaphors of Consciousness*. Ed. by Ronald S. Valle and Rolf von Eckartsberg. New York: Plenum, 1981.

Watkins, Karen E. and Marsick, Victoria J. *Sculpting the Learning Organization: Lessons in the Art and Science of Systemic Change*. San Francisco: Jossey-Bass, 1993.

Watson, James. *The Double Helix*. New York: Dutton, 1969.

Weekley, Thomas L. and Wilber, Jay C. *United We Stand: The Unprecedented Story of the GM-UAW Quality Partnership*. New York: McGraw-Hill, 1996.

Weisbord, Marvin R. *Productive Workplaces*. San Francisco: Jossey-Bass, 1991.

——. *Discovering Common Ground*. San Francisco: Berrett-Koehler, 1992.

Wheatley, Margaret J. *Leadership and the New Science: Learning About Organization from an Orderly Universe*, San Francisco: Berrett-Koehler, 1992.

——. "The Unplanned Organization." *Noetic Sciences Review*, Spring 1996.

—— and Kellner-Rogers, Myron. *A Simpler Way*. San Francisco: Berrett-Koehler, 1996.

Wheeler, Donald J. *Understanding Variation: The Key to Managing Chaos*. Knoxville, TN: SPC Press, 1993.

Wick, Calhoun W. and Leon, Lu Stanton. "Individual Learning Nurtures J.P. Morgan." *Personnel Journal*, Nov 1993.

Wilber, Ken. *Eye to Eye: the Quest for the New Paradigm*. New York: Doubleday, Anchor Press, 1983.

——. *The Atman Project*. Wheaton, Ill: Theosophical Publishing, 1980.

Winslow, Charles D. and Bramer, William L. *FutureWork: Putting Knowledge to Work in the Knowledge Economy*. New York: MacMillan, The Free Press, 1994.

Young, Arthur. *The Reflexive Universe: Evolution of Consciousness*. Lake Oswego, OR: Delacorte, 1976.

Zukav, Gary. *The Dancing Wu Li Masters: An Overview of the New Physics*. Toronto: Bantam, 1979.

Index

Butterworth-Heinemann Business Books . . .

for Transforming Business

Beyond Strategic Vision: Effective Corporate Action with Hoshin Planning
Michael Cowley and Ellen Domb, 0-7506-9843-8

Beyond Time Management: Business with Purpose
Robert A. Wright, 0-7506-9799-7

Breakdown of Hierarchy: Communicating in the Evolving Workplace, The
Eugene Marlow and Patricia O'Connor Wilson, 0-7056-9746-6

Business and the Feminine Principle: The Untapped Resource
Carol R. Frenier, 0-7506-9829-2

Cultivating Common Ground: Releasing the Power of Relationships at Work
Daniel S. Hanson, 0-7506-9832-2

Fifth Generation Management: Co-creating Through Virtual Enterprising, Dynamic Teaming, and Knowledge Networking, Revised Edition
Charles M. Savage, 0-7506-9701-6

Flight of the Phoenix: Soaring to Success in the 21st Century
John Whiteside and Sandra Egli, 0-7506-9798-9

Getting a Grip on Tomorrow: Your Guide to Survival and Success in the Changed World of Work
Mike Johnson, 0-7506-9758-X

Innovation Strategy for the Knowledge Economy: The Ken *Awakening*
Debra M. Amidon, 0-7506-9841-1

Intelligence Advantage: Organizing for Complexity, The
Michael D. McMaster, 0-7506-9792-X

Knowledge Evolution: Expanding Organizational Intelligence, The
Verna Allee, 0-7506-9842-X

Leadership in a Challenging World: A Sacred Journey
Barbara Shipka, 0-7506-9750-4

To purchase a copy of any Butterworth–Heinemann title, please visit your local bookstore or call 1-800-366-2665.

Verna Allee is Founder and President of Integral Performance Group, whose customers include AT&T, Chevron, Sun Microsystems, General Public Utilities, Kennecott Energy, the U.S. Forest Service, Pacific Bell, and others. In addition to knowledge management and the learning organization, Verna consults in systems thinking, benchmarking support, best practices research, and strategic development. She has served on the Executive Committee for the Special Interest Group for the Learning Organization of ASTD and is a frequent conference presenter.

Verna's insights into knowledge-based enterprises and collaborative learning have led to innovative performance-focused approaches. She is the developer of the HoloMapping™ process for understanding complex systems, co-editor of *Elegant Solutions: The Power of Systems Thinking*, co-author of a quality tools guide, the *Quality Tools Matrix*, and has published articles in the United States and abroad. She can be reached at:

Integral Performance Group
500 Ygnacio Valley Road, Suite 250
Walnut Creek, CA 94596
510-825-2663
510-825-1515 fax
73042.2210@compuserve.com